Career Paths in Psychology

Where your degree can take you

EDITED BY ROBERT J. STERNBERG

American Psychological Association
Washington, DC

First printing March 1997
Second printing August 1997
Third printing March 1998

Published by
American Psychological Association
750 First Street, NE
Washington, DC 20002

Copies may be ordered from
APA Order Department
P.O. Box 92984
Washington, DC 20090-2984

In the United Kingdom and Europe, copies may be ordered from
American Psychological Association
3 Henrietta Street
Covent Garden
London WC2E 8LU
England

Typeset in Meridien by Harlowe Typography, Inc., Cottage City, MD

Printer: Wickersham Printing Company, Inc., Westminster, MD
Cover designer: Design Concepts, San Diego, CA
Technical/production editors: Sarah J. Trembath and Olin J. Nettles

Library of Congress Cataloging-in-Publication Data
Career paths in psychology :   where your degree can take you   /   edited
   by Robert J. Sternberg.
      p.   cm.
   Includes bibliographical references and index.
   ISBN 1-55798-411-5 (pbk.) (acid-free paper)
   1. Psychological—Vocational guidance.   I. Sternberg, Robert J.
BF76.C38   1997
150'.23'73—dc21   96-39943
                                                                   CIP

British Library Cataloguing-in-Publication Data
A CIP record is available from the British Library.

Printed in the United States of America

Contents

Contributors

Ted W. Allen, Ted Allen ET AL., Bethesda, MD

Anne E. Beall, National Analysts, Philadelphia, PA

Kelly D. Brownell, Department of Psychology, Yale University, New Haven, CT

Robert Calfee, School of Education, Stanford University, Stanford, CA

Kathleen L. Davis, Department of Educational and Counseling Psychology, University of Tennessee, Knoxville, TN

Douglas Herrmann, Department of Psychology, Indiana State University, Terre Haute, IN

Ira Iscoe, Department of Psychology, University of Texas at Austin

Raymond S. Nickerson, Department of Psychology, Tufts University, Medford, MA

Stephen F. Poland, private practice, Albuquerque, NM

Henry L. Roediger, III, Department of Psychology, Washington University, St. Louis, MO

Peter Salovey, Department of Psychology, Yale University, New Haven, CT

Robert J. Sternberg, Department of Psychology, Yale University, New Haven, CT

Billie S. Strauss, Michael Reese Hospital, Chicago, IL

Mary L. Tenopyr, AT&T, Morristown, NJ

Victor H. Vroom, School of Management, Yale University, New Haven, CT

Marjorie E. Weishaar, Brown University School of Medicine, Providence, RI

Martin F. Wiskoff, BDM International, Inc., Monterey, CA

Jeffrey Young, Columbia University College of Physicians and Surgeons, New York, NY

Acknowledgments

I am grateful to Division 1 of the American Psychological Association, the Division of General Psychology, for sponsoring this book. All royalties from the book will go to the Division. I would also like to thank the many very busy psychologists who took the time to write chapters for the book. Finally, I would like to thank the various editors at APA who have made such valuable contributions to the shaping of the book. My own efforts toward the fulfillment of this book were supported in part by Grant R206R50001 from the U.S. Office of Educational Research and Improvement and by a contract from the U.S. Army Research Institute.

Robert J. Sternberg

Introduction

F ew fields of study offer more career opportunities than does psychology. This book is about those career opportunities. They are diverse. They are challenging. They are fun. And, for the most part, they pay well. They are also flexible: People can switch, often fairly easily and with a minimum of adjustment, from one career within psychology to another. Moreover, even within a single career, the variety of challenges and activities will interest even the most easily bored individuals.

In a randomly chosen week, I may fly across country to give a departmental colloquium, teach courses to both undergraduate and graduate students, work on an article for a professional journal, work on an article for a popular magazine, work on a chapter of a textbook for undergraduates, consult with an educational or business organization, write part of a grant proposal, meet one-on-one with students I supervise, review an article for a journal, answer several calls from parents whose children are having problems in school, correspond with collaborators on other continents about how our joint research enterprises are going, attend a faculty meeting, meet with a job candidate and attend the candidate's talk, have an informal dinner meeting with members of my research group in which we informally discuss research, and also see my wife and children. I love the amazing variety of activities I do in my job, and I represent only one of many possible careers in psychology—that of an academic psychologist! Other psychologists combine clinical practice, research, teaching, and administration. How could anyone ever be bored?

Psychology is not only one of the most interesting fields of study; it is also one of the most diverse: Few fields offer a greater number and variety of career opportunities. College students who decide to major in psychology, therefore, open up a world of possibilities for themselves. Graduate students can be confident of diverse kinds of careers, and practicing psychologists often can change the kind of work they do or the setting they work in while remaining within the field of psychology.

Psychology is one of the most rewarding fields a person can enter. Psychology is fun. It helps people, advances scientific and clinical understanding, and pays relatively well. Most psychologists earn well above the median salary in the United States. Few earn stratospheric wages, but some do—generally highly successful psychologists in private practice, organizational psychologists, or writers of either textbooks or books for the popular press. Realistically, chances are you will neither go broke nor live in a palatial mansion if you choose a career in psychology! What you will do is help people improve their lives, help students learn to understand themselves and others, perhaps advance the state of our knowledge, and have a great time while you are doing it.

This book will help you start on a career path in psychology, or perhaps continue on one or even change the path you are on. The chapters in this book will tell you about 14 different graduate-level careers in psychology (that is, those achieved with a PhD, EdD, or PsyD). Each chapter will discuss (a) what the career is, (b) how to prepare for the career, (c) typical activities people pursue while they engage in the career, (d) the approximate range of financial compensation for the career,[1] (e) the advantages and disadvantages people typically find in the career, (f) personal and professional attributes desirable for success in the career, and (g) opportunities for employment and advancement in the career.

The authors of the chapters were chosen for their distinction in their chosen careers. They all have achieved a level of prominence and a depth of experience that any budding graduate student would do well to emulate. They were asked to speak on their careers not only because of their stature in their respective fields, but also for their ability to convey the excitement of their careers to readers of this book.

Of course, one could not cover in a book of this length every possible career, but the careers that are covered are fairly representative

---

[1] The level of information provided on financial compensation varies from chapter to chapter according to the availability of data in each subfield.

of the range of work psychologists can do, and also represent the range of careers that have been chosen by a substantial proportion of psychologists.

The book is divided into four main parts. Each of the parts considers a different facet of career paths in psychology: careers in academic organizations; careers in clinical, counseling, and community psychology, usually through private practice; careers in nonacademic organizations; and careers that cut across these various kinds of settings. Of course, this organization of the chapters is only one of many possible, but it does seem to capture a way in which many people organize the field.

I hope readers find in this volume a series of examples that will both inspire and enthuse. Psychology is a field that offers many possibilities, and I wish you well on your journey of discovery.

ACADEMIC CAREERS

Henry L. Roediger, III

Teaching, Research, and More: Psychologists in an Academic Career

1

W riters of this book make one fact abundantly clear: Psychologists work in many different settings at many different occupations. However, virtually all were trained in colleges and universities, and therefore almost everyone in the field is familiar to some degree with psychology in an academic setting. Most students reading this book are also in an academic setting and so have some appreciation for what their professors do. However, my experience from talking to students over the past 25 years is that, whereas they understand some of the prominent aspects of a career in academic settings, they do not know about parts of the profession that are less apparent from their own vantage point. Some of these more hidden features are discussed in this chapter.

Writing about the academic career in psychology is difficult because academia affords a number of different types of careers. The psychologist teaching in a community college, for example, may be a part-time professor who has another job outside academia. Professors in liberal arts colleges may devote much of their time to teaching, often teaching three or four courses a semester. Whereas the

Henry L. Roediger, III, is professor and chair of the Psychology Department at Washington University in St. Louis. He received a BA in psychology from Washington and Lee University in 1969 and a PhD from Yale University in 1973. His research has primarily been concerned with human memory.

This chapter benefited from the comments of Lyn Goff, Kathleen McDermott, Kerry Robinson, and Dave Schneider.

teaching loads in community colleges and other liberal arts colleges may leave little time for research or other activities, faculty at larger universities with graduate programs (often called *research universities*) are expected to conduct research and publish it in scholarly journals. Typically, faculty at these institutions teach one or two courses a semester, which may be divided between graduate and undergraduate courses.

Although the careers in academic psychology are different in these various academic settings, all share certain features, such as teaching and counseling students. In this chapter, I try to cover the common features while touching on aspects of the job that vary among different academic settings. I draw on my own academic experiences in teaching at Yale University, Purdue University, the University of Toronto, and Rice University, and being educated at Washington and Lee. All of the schools at which I have taught are research universities, but two (Purdue and Toronto) are *public* (i.e., supported by government) and two (Yale and Rice) are *private* (i.e., supported largely by privately raised monies). Enrollments at these schools vary widely, from around 33,000 students at Purdue to about 4,000 at Rice and about 1,200 students (and 6 psychology majors!) at Washington and Lee when I was there. In writing this chapter, I include examples from my own diverse experiences to illustrate some points being made.

The Nature of the Career

The nature of careers in academia depends, as noted previously, partly on the kind of academic institution in which a psychologist works. The most obvious characteristic of a career in academia is teaching. That is the common thread at all institutions of higher learning. Anyone devoting his or her life to an academic career should have a love of learning and of teaching, and a desire to instill that love of learning in others. Teaching, in its broadest sense, occurs on many levels and may take place in several settings. Besides teaching formal courses, professors interact with students in small seminars, private consultations, research meetings, and sometimes (depending on the school) settings outside the classroom such as dining halls. And one of the most delightful benefits for faculty members of being in an academic setting is the opportunity to learn from students as well as to teach them. Students new to psychology often have different and interesting viewpoints. Also, faculty learn about new topics when students pick novel topics for term papers or research papers, or when they do an outstanding job reviewing what is known.

It is wrong (or, at best, only partly right) to think of a college professor as someone who learned about his or her field in graduate school and who then went out to teach the knowledge gained in graduate school. Rather, graduate school only begins the process of learning that continues throughout the career of teaching in academia. Professors must continually keep up with their fast-changing fields in order to keep their courses current. Of course, no one can master all aspects of every field he or she teaches, but being a professor causes one to keep up with at least the broad sweep—the main ideas and major new developments—in the topics they teach.

In sum, the primary features of devoting oneself to an academic career are the love of learning and the desire to instill that love in others. But what does one do in academic settings besides teach? I turn to this issue next.

Activities of College Professors

What do professors do besides teach? Lots of things! They conduct research, write, and serve on committees, to mention a few activities. College professors are often criticized because, the way some outsiders see it, they teach so little. What people mean by that is that the number of hours actually spent in the classroom is relatively small, say, when compared with high school teachers' hours. However, this does not mean that college professors are not in a demanding profession or that they do not work hard. They do. But most people outside the profession are unaware of the range of demands faced by professors. The illustrations in the following sections are somewhat personal because I do all these things, but most of the same activities are performed by professors at some point in their careers.

COURSE PREPARATION

Before a professor actually walks into a classroom, a huge amount of preparation is required. Preparing for a lecture that lasts an hour may take several hours of background reading, note-taking, preparation of overheads, or other activities such as arranging a classroom demonstration. The professor must know what is in the assigned text, but must also consult other books, book chapters, and research articles in preparing the lecture because the lecture usually goes far beyond the text material. Students sometimes complain about the workload or amount of reading in a course, but typically the professor is doing much more. College professors who are just beginning teaching often spend much of their time in course preparation. Beginning professors often teach large lecture courses, and preparing material for 40 or so lectures for each course over the period of a semester takes huge amounts of time. Even experienced professors, who have been teaching for years, must continually update their material. And if they decide to teach a course on a new topic, they must begin preparation from scratch. For professors who teach three or four courses a semester, course preparation may take virtually all their time in their early years in the profession.

Recent advances in technology have changed course preparation somewhat. Many publishers of college textbooks offer various packages to help professors prepare. These might include traditional aids (e.g., books of adjunct readings for the course, or acetate transparencies) or the latest in technology (e.g., videodisks, CD-ROM programs, hypertext). These aids can be wonderfully helpful in making large lecture courses more interesting, but in a way they increase demands placed on the professor to learn more about these new technologies, to preview the materials, and to integrate them into the course.

TEACHING

Professors may teach in lecture courses, in small seminars that combine lecture with discussion, or in reading groups in which everyone has read the material and the purpose is to discuss it. Although the lecture method of teaching has been under attack for years, it is probably still the most common form of teaching. However, much has been written to instruct professors on converting standard (i.e., noninteractive) lectures into experiences in which the students participate more fully (e.g., small break-out discussions among groups, class exercises or experiments, and demonstrations, among other means). Everyone reading this book knows that there are huge individual differences in teaching: Some people are gifted teachers by some combination of personality, knowledge, eloquence, humor, and showmanship. But probably everyone can be a more effective teacher by working at it. (See, for example, W. J. McKeachie's [1987] chapter, "Tips on Teaching".)

As noted previously, the actual time professors spend in the classroom is often not great. Currently, I am teaching two undergraduate courses at Rice University and so spend about 6 hours a week in the classroom. But I probably work 60 to 70 hours in a typical week because my time is occupied by all the other activities listed in this section.

MAKING AND GRADING TESTS AND ESSAYS

Composing and grading tests and essays is part of teaching, but is separate from course preparation and spending time in class. Depending on the number of courses taught, the number of students in the course, and the type of tests and assignments given, this activity can take great amounts of time. Multiple-choice tests (and other *objective tests*, such as true/false or matching tests) are easy to grade, but they often require considerable time to compose. Designing essay and short answer tests is often quicker, but then these tests take much longer to grade.

In my own case, I dislike giving only objective types of questions. Evidence indicates that these sorts of tests cause students to focus on learning isolated facts rather than drawing material together to see the larger picture and the overarching themes. So I prefer tests that require students to write some essays, to encourage them to look for interrelated themes when studying. Currently I am teaching a course in introductory psychology in which the four tests are composed of a mixture of essay and objective questions. In addition, all students write an essay on a book and take a cumulative final examination. In my other undergraduate course, which is on human memory, students take two 2-hour essay tests, write two essay papers, and take a cumulative (essay) final examination. The test construction and grading for these two courses, which have enrollments of 85 and 35, is not trivial; luckily, although I do some grading myself, I have teaching assistants in both courses who help with this chore. When I teach graduate courses, students are usually required to write a few shorter essays on various topics during the course of the semester and then write a long paper reviewing a body of research pertaining to any topic of the course that they find of interest. At the end of the paper, they are required to write a proposal for future research that would add to knowledge in the field.

CONSULTING WITH STUDENTS

Most professors enjoy meeting with students outside of class. Depending on the type of institution, students feel varying degrees of freedom to visit with faculty and either talk about problems in a course, ask for advice about courses or careers, learn more about the material, or discuss ideas. For universities with graduate programs, a considerable amount of faculty time is devoted to advising graduate students on their research and discussing research with them.

RESEARCH

Many faculty members conduct psychological research. This is especially true in research universities, but psychologists in all types of schools can have programs of interesting and important research. Planning this research takes time, although it usually occurs in the natural course of other activities, such as consulting with students, reading articles, and writing proposals for research. Research may seem a mysterious process at first, but it is the lifeblood of every academic discipline because the discoveries and advances in every field all come from new research. Scientists know the state of knowledge in their fields, and their curiosity about the unexplained leads them to push back the frontiers of knowledge. The motivations for future research are many—exploring unexplained past findings, testing implications of theories to see if they hold true, seeing if findings obtained in one setting generalize to another, and many others. The researcher usually works from a theory to generate hypotheses and then collects data to evaluate the hypotheses. When students first come into a field, they often wonder about the source of all the ideas that generate the research they are reading about and whether they will be able to generate their own ideas. Later, after being immersed in the field, most researchers lament the lack of time and resources to conduct all the research they would like to do.

When students first enter graduate school, a professor often guides them in their initial research projects. No one expects students just beginning in a field to design and conduct cutting-edge research, because the process of becoming a researcher is a gradual one. Collaboration is critical as the student learns to conduct research. Typically, students who are beginning to work with me will begin part of a project, which might already be ongoing, to get their feet wet and to get immersed in the problems and procedures of the field with me directing the project. However, throughout the 4 or 5 years that I work with the student, he or she gradually becomes more independent and begins designing, conducting, and writing about research, needing less consultation with me.

Students often learn about conducting research in one-on-one meetings with their major professors. Students who work with me meet once a week for our lab meeting. Sometimes a student will present his or her research, or plans for future research, but often I select a recent article or chapter for all of us to read and to discuss. Often ideas for future research come out of these meetings. Other aspects of research are covered in other activities discussed in other sections of this chapter.

WRITING LETTERS OF REFERENCE

Surely, you say, this activity does not deserve a separate listing. Yes, it does. During certain times of the year, writing letters of reference takes a great deal of time. Undergraduate students need letters of reference for applications for graduate school and for jobs. Graduate students need employment letters of reference, each of which could go to the

20 or more places to which each student may apply. Former students and colleagues in the field need letters for different jobs to which they apply. Also, as one becomes more senior in the field, requests are made from other universities for letters about candidates who are being considered for promotion and *tenure*. (Tenure is the award of lifetime job security to faculty so that they may investigate any topic freely, without fear of reprisal for investigating taboo topics.) Often these requests are accompanied by a selection of relevant writings of the candidate, a statement of his or her research accomplishments and plans, and a curriculum vitae. Processing all this information before writing the letter can take several hours. I estimate that in a given year I write 10 or so letters of reference for students and colleagues, and that I am asked to write letters for 7 to 10 candidates for promotion at other universities. All these letters take time, especially during the fall and winter. Writing letters of reference is seasonal labor.

FACULTY MEETINGS AND COMMITTEE MEETINGS

A university is, among other things, a large organization with a hierarchical structure. Organizations need to have various groups that deal with particular matters to run smoothly. Within the typical psychology department there may be (a) a space committee to assign research space to people, (b) a committee for subject use to oversee proposals for testing human and animal subjects, (c) an animal-care committee to oversee care and housing of animals, (d) a promotion and tenure committee composed of senior professors, (e) a graduate committee to oversee the graduate program, and (f) an undergraduate committee to perform the same service for the undergraduate program. Of course, an individual professor might only be assigned to one or two of these committees, but the assignments do take time. In addition, there are general faculty meetings of the department and of the university faculty as a whole.

There are also committee meetings for students. In undergraduate programs with honors degrees, a professor may be part of a two- or three-member committee that advises and examines the research of an honors student. In universities with graduate programs, each student typically has both a committee for the master's degree and one for the PhD. Professors may meet with students to discuss the proposal that deals with the research the student is planning and how it is to be carried out. Then, eventually, faculty must read the thesis and dissertation that the student has written and is to defend at another meeting. Some universities also require preliminary examinations or qualifying examinations of students prior to their embarking on the PhD, which necessitates faculty attendance at other committee meetings.

There are still other committee meetings in addition to those just listed. Professors may need to staff search committees when their department is hiring a new faculty member; these take a large amount of time, first to go through the hundreds of applications, then to interview three or four candidates, and then to decide whom to recommend for the position. Professors may also be involved with any of the other committees that exist for the entire university, such as search committees for new deans, a provost, or a president. Most universities have still other committees to advise on such matters as athletics and admissions. At certain times during the academic year, committee work can require large amounts of time. Sometimes it is not fascinating work, but it is critical to the overall good of the department and the university.

COMMUNICATION WITH OTHER SCHOLARS WITH SIMILAR INTERESTS

One curious fact about universities is that individual faculty members may be intensely interested in one topic, whether it be the history of ancient Rome, the poetry of Wordsworth, the stars of the Orion nebula, or some specific topic in psychology. Often no one with your particular scholarly interest exists at your university, and yet you want to maintain contact with others in your specific field to share ideas and to learn of late-breaking developments. A century ago, scholarly communication was largely confined to reading others' books and articles, when they appeared, or writing letters. Communication is much faster now, and the advent of electronic mail permits people to stay in constant contact and to learn of new developments almost instantaneously, either through informal contact or through formal bulletin boards. Many professors are now finding themselves glued to their computer terminals, communicating with others with like interests. Many research collaborations blossom by e-mail; this mode of communication can especially aid professors at smaller colleges and universities by allowing them to communicate with almost anyone in the field. Although fascinating, this activity takes time and it seems likely to become increasingly important.

ATTENDING PROFESSIONAL MEETINGS

This is another activity that permits academics to keep pace with their fields. People go to professional meetings to present their own research findings by giving papers or displaying posters. In addition, they hear and see the work of many others. In psychology there are national meetings of large organizations like the American Psychological

Association and the American Psychological Society, of regional groups (e.g., the Midwestern Psychological Association), and of more specialized groups interested in particular topics (e.g., the Society for Research in Child Development). Years ago, the big national meetings dominated the scene, but now many professors choose to go to more specialized meetings concerned with their area of interest instead of or in addition to the large conventions . The meetings usually last 2 to 3 days. Attendance at such meetings is optional; some professors go to many and others go to practically none. Attending at least some meetings is a good idea, because it would allow you to become acquainted with people with interests similar to yours. Networking is important in academia as in other spheres of life.

WRITING

For psychologists active in research, technical writing is a critical skill. The greatest research ever conducted would never have been known if it had not been effectively communicated. Psychologists in research universities must be skilled in writing research articles in order to communicate their findings clearly. There are also opportunities to write chapters for scholarly books (like this one), and some will write *monographs* (treatises written by one author, usually on specialized areas of learning) to communicate their research to interested scholars. Technical and scholarly writing can be difficult skills to learn, but several useful guides exist (see Bem, 1987; Sternberg, 1993). In addition, researchers seeking support for their research usually write grant proposals to federal agencies and to foundations. Psychologists in academia are also sometimes asked to write book reviews of recent publications by others. Writing is a critical skill for the academic psychologist, one that must be continually honed.

Some professors choose to write textbooks in their areas of interest (e.g., developmental or social psychology) or general textbooks (on research methods or introductory psychology, for example). Writing textbooks can be lucrative, and is also a critical part of the educational process. An outstanding teacher at one university, no matter how brilliant, has a limited impact: He or she will affect only the students attending those classes at that campus. But a professor who writes an outstanding textbook can literally help teach an entire generation of students about a given topic and entice those students further into this field of study. Curiously, textbook writing is often not professionally rewarded within university settings; colleagues and administrators do not see this kind of publication as the scholarly equal of other kinds of works. However, with the great emphasis on the importance of teaching now reinvigorating universities, perhaps this attitude will be relaxed. After all, a textbook writer is a teacher of thousands of students and the text is the main course contact for many students. In my own case, I have been coauthor of a text on experimental psychology (in its sixth edition), one on research methods (fifth edition), and one on introductory psychology (fourth edition)[1]. In addition to the satisfaction I have obtained from having these books used widely over the past 15 to 20 years and from educating many students, I have learned much about psychology while researching material for the books.

REVIEWING AND EDITING

Another task in academia that can take significant amounts of time is the evaluation of scholarly publications. Publishing in scholarly journals occurs by a process of *peer review*. If I submit a paper for publication to a journal, the editor will send it to several experts in the field of inquiry (the peers), who will be asked to read the paper and to write evaluations of the research, answering such questions as, Does the paper deserve to be published? and Does it make a significant contribution to knowledge?

Serving as a referee on a paper entails considerable work. The manuscript deserves a careful and thoughtful reading and a fair and unbiased review. Reviewing a manuscript properly can take hours of time, and some researchers who may be called upon by many journals get many manuscripts to review. This can place a large burden on already overworked scholars, but there are rewards. A person learns about the latest findings in his or her field by reviewing manuscripts. In some cases (usually after a trial period during which the editor of the journal finds the person's reviewing especially good and insightful) reviewers will become consulting editors for a journal. Scholars who serve as editors or associate editors of journals are the ones who make the final decisions about the publishability of papers in that journal. Some journals receive hundreds of manuscripts a year, which means that editors must find time to read the papers, read the reviews of consultants, and then write letters of acceptance or rejection to the authors. The editorial process is critical in every field, but requires great amounts of time from editors and reviewers.

Other types of reviewing may be required of the academic psychologist. For instance, textbooks are reviewed by many teachers

---

[1] These three textbooks are listed in the references as Elmes, Kantowitz, & Roediger, 1995; Kantowitz, Roediger, & Elmes, 1997; and Roediger, Capaldi, Paris, Polivy & Herman, 1996.

before they are published and during the revision process. In addition, many scholars evaluate books in book reviews published in scholarly journals or in the popular press.

CONSULTING

Some psychology professors consult with organizations in industry or the legal profession about their areas of interest. This is not an activity in which I partake very often, but many others do. Human factors psychologists may consult on the design of equipment to take the "human factor" into account to make the product more easily usable. Industrial–organizational psychologists may consult with industries on personnel selection or on how to improve the morale of the organization. Indeed, virtually every area of psychology has something to offer some industry or occupation. Psychologists in academia often step outside the academy to offer advice on more practical matters of the world.

COMMUNITY SERVICE

Psychologists may also be called on for various kinds of community service. For example, they may be asked to educate the general public through lectures to civic and religious groups. In addition, they may work with community groups, such as Alcoholics Anonymous or a local crisis center, on various social or personal problems. Some psychologists appear on radio and television programs to explain psychological issues to wider audiences. Academics differ widely in how much time they spend in community service, but it can be rewarding because the teaching involved extends the traditional forums.

SUMMARY

The dozen or so activities just listed include most of the activities in which psychologists in a psychology department might be involved. Of course, the list is not exhaustive. Professors can and do participate in other activities, but this sample provides a reasonable range of the usual activities. After reading the foregoing account, your opinion might have swung from "college professors don't do much; they only teach a few hours a week" to "how can anyone do all these things?" Keep in mind that the list above includes activities that occur over the course of a year; not all are done every day. One important feature of being a professor is that there is considerable time (namely, summers and holidays) when teaching requirements are reduced or absent altogether. These are not times of relaxation for professors. Most professors work as hard or harder during the summer months and vacations, but they work on different activities than those that occupy them during the academic year when classes are in session.

Academic Settings

Psychology departments appear in all kinds of institutions of higher education, as already noted. Almost every city or town of any size has a community college to, as the name implies, serve the members of the community. Professors in these settings usually devote most of their time to teaching (rather than research). There are also hundreds of relatively small private and public colleges and universities in the United States that offer undergraduate education in psychology culminating in a BA or BS degree. Each of these colleges and universities has a psychology department. Larger public and private schools provide both graduate and undergraduate education in psychology, so usually they have larger departments with faculty who specialize in various fields in psychology.

Students aspiring to an academic career in psychology may seek a position in any of these types of schools or others, such as the independent schools in clinical psychology that give graduate degrees. Each type of school has its benefits and can be a very attractive place to work. For example, community colleges often have adult students who have worked and experienced more of life before they decided to return and further their education. Often these students are very eager to learn and appreciative of their opportunity for learning in a way that the 18- to 21-year-old undergraduate may not be. Other professors love teaching in small liberal arts colleges. The student–faculty ratio is often low, which promotes good interactions with students. Similarly, faculty at larger schools or research universities may enjoy interacting with graduate students, conducting research, and publishing in scholarly journals. The demands and rewards of the various academic settings are different, and some may appeal more to one type of person than to another. If you are considering a career in academia, you should carefully consider which type of setting might suit you best.

Preparation for the Academic Career

The standard preparation for a career in a psychology department is usually fairly straightforward. Typically, a person should have an undergraduate degree in psychology, or a degree in some related field such as biology, anthropology, or neuroscience and a considerable amount of psychology coursework. Next, a student interested in an academic career in psychology should apply to graduate school. Students do not apply to graduate school in the general area of psychology, but rather to a specialized field in which they are interested (e.g., cognitive psychology, social psychology, clinical psychology). If you intend to apply to graduate school in psychology, you should find out from your advisors and from other sources which schools have good programs in your area of interest and then apply only to those schools. (Every year at Rice University, we get a significant number of applications for our clinical psychology program. However, Rice does not have a clinical psychology program.)

Graduate school training usually takes from 4 to 6 years, although longer periods are not unheard of, depending on what other duties a student may have (e.g., heavy teaching requirements, a part-time job for financial support). Typically, students receive a master's degree in 2 or 3 years and then begin working on the PhD. Students receiving a PhD in clinical psychology need to complete an internship if they want to be licensed to practice, which most do. Students receiving PhDs in other areas may take a postdoctoral fellowship following completion of their degree to further their research training.

While in graduate school, the student learns about the subject matter of psychology in general, and his or her field in particular. Coursework, reading, attending talks and colloquia, and discussions with advisors and other faculty are the usual means of learning. Students usually receive their research training through an apprentice system in which they work closely with one or more faculty members to learn how to conduct research. Many other professional aspects of psychology are learned almost by osmosis (or observational learning), from watching how successful people in the profession operate. However, as discussed previously, graduate education in a field should be considered only the beginning. Psychologists continue learning their entire lifetimes, and in academia they do so from continual course preparation, students, research, reading, and professional meetings.

My Interest in Psychology: How Did I Choose This Career?

The story of how one comes to choose a career in academic psychology is different for everyone. But since you (or at least the editor of this volume) asked, my story starts in high school. I attended Riverside Military Academy, which had two campuses at that time. In the fall and spring we were in Gainesville, Georgia, but from January to March we were in Hollywood, Florida, which is located between Miami and Fort Lauderdale. I suspect everyone is interested to some degree in human behavior, in what makes people tick. Being in a military school for my tender high school years increased my curiosity, due to experiences that I need not relate here. (Strange things happen in military schools, and the conditions, which are often harder than those in public high schools, can make life interesting. Some of these conditions can be glimpsed in Pat Conroy's(1980) *The Lords of Discipline*, although my experiences were not as severe as those recounted in this novel.)

To get on with the story, during the winter of 1964 my guidance counselor, a man named Jerry Sullivan, approached me with a letter and packet of material from Stetson University in DeLand, Florida. That university offered a special program for selected high school juniors from Florida: They could enroll at Stetson in summer school between their junior and senior years in high school, and if they did well in three regular college courses, they could skip their senior years in high school and go right on to college at Stetson or go back to high school. Stetson apparently wanted to capture some of Florida's bright high school students before they headed North to attend college, so they tried to attract them with this program. I liked the idea of spending the summer at college, my parents agreed to foot the bill, and off I went.

I had to take English and mathematics and was given one elective. I chose psychology, knowing nothing about it except that it sounded vaguely interesting and different. I loved it. I had a fine professor (a Dr. Jones) and we used a good book, which I still have: *Scientific Principles of Psychology* by Donald J. Lewis (1993). Although we covered only half the book, I thought all the material was fascinating. I recall being especially struck and enlightened by material on classical and operant conditioning—here was how to control behavior!—and about the measurement of intelligence. Wonderful knowledge was available in this field, and I had known nothing about it before this course. In addition, even though the book was in its second printing, it was filled with small errors. When students bought the book, they were given three pages of "errata" and had to piece together correct information from the misprints in the book. Through this experience, I learned that the printed word in books was not immutable truth. Someone actually wrote these books and he or she, and the publisher, made errors. (Yes, I should have known that, but I didn't.) I got A's in English and psychology that summer and a B in mathematics—the story of my life. I was admitted to Stetson, but (after long thought) went back to Riverside because, I figured, you only get to be cadet colonel and battalion commander once in your life.

The next year I faced the question of where to go to college. Again, psychology intervened in an important way. I had received an appointment to the United States Military Academy at West Point, passed the physical and mental examinations, and was admitted. Did I really want to go? The Vietnam War was just heating up in 1965, but this did not much permeate my thinking. Instead, I looked at the psychology offerings in the various college catalogs I had because I thought I wanted to study psychology. At West Point the offerings were slim; as I recall it now, the closest courses to psychology were those such as military science and hygiene. I decided against West Point and went to Washington and Lee (W & L) University. My freshman year I was required to take many courses and could not work psychology in, but I did take a course in my sophomore year (from Joseph Thompson) and continued on that path by taking almost all the courses available in psychology (from David Elmes and William Hinton, as well as Thompson). I was also near to completing a major in sociology and anthropology. There was no course in social psychology at W & L during my era, but one of my professors told me that the best textbook in this area was *Social Psychology* by Roger Brown (1965). I read it and decided to go to graduate school in this area, despite my relative ignorance of the topic. (Although I also was admitted to graduate school in two anthropology departments, social psychology seemed a good blend of my interests in sociology, anthropology, and psychology.) Surprisingly, my lack of credentials or research experience in social psychology did not prevent me from being admitted to the social psychology graduate program at Yale, and off I went. However, I switched into the cognitive psychology program during my first year there.

So, that is how I wound up in psychology. It is more than you wanted to know, perhaps, but I imagine that every psychologist has a story like it: What we wind up doing is determined in large part by various accidents of life.

The Range of Financial Compensation

I write in February, 1996. My guess is that the range of salaries for full-time university professors in psychology is anywhere from $30,000 per year to upwards of $175,000 for an academic year appointment. The salaries in this upper range are very rare, so the distribution would be quite skewed in the positive direction. For those interested in looking into the salary ranges of psychologists, the American Psychological Association publishes figures based on surveys of its membership. Salary differences in my field occur between types of schools, geographic regions, universities in small towns and those in large cities, and the various specialty areas within psychology. The 1995–1996 figures are shown in Table 1 and are from a report by the Research Office of the American Psychological Association (Wicherski & Kohout, 1996). The mean salary for all ranks at those universities with doctoral programs was $56,492 for 1995–1996.

Psychology professors will never be accused of entering their profession in order to become rich. Professors can usually live comfortably, if not opulently. However, professors can augment their academic salaries by consulting, writing textbooks, reviewing textbooks for publishers, obtaining research grants (which pay summer salaries), and doing extra teaching (during summer sessions or at night). In addition, most colleges and universities offer good fringe benefit packages in the form of health care and the like, as well as good retirement programs. So, although no one is likely to become another instant mil-

TABLE 1

1995–96 Salaries for Full-time Faculty in U.S. Doctoral Psychology Departments in Public Institutions for all U.S. Regions (113 Departments), Rank, and Years in Rank

	Median	10%	25%	75%	90%	Mean	SD	n
Full professor								
12 or more years	69,800	51,078	59,579	82,525	96,300	72,067	17,343	772
6–11 years	65,060	50,996	57,713	75,000	84,610	67,305	13,809	362
3–5 years	61,105	47,000	52,789	70,300	78,554	62,141	12,939	172
Less than 3 years	56,042	46,719	51,550	65,000	72,100	58,975	11,861	186
All years	65,495	50,000	56,442	77,140	90,300	68,149	16,154	1,494
Associate professor								
6 or more years	47,523	37,008	42,515	53,200	59,536	48,102	8,576	347
3–5 years	48,034	41,034	44,072	52,786	59,463	49,114	7,299	176
Less than 3 years	45,02	38,745	41,500	48,902	53,016	45,851	6,336	242
All years	46,600	38,586	42,603	51,700	57,652	47,623	7,732	765
Assistant professor								
3 or more years	40,019	35,181	37,369	42,904	47,005	40,509	4,765	310
Less than 3 years	38,700	34,000	36,000	41,500	44,183	39,068	4,532	301
All years	39,550	34,795	36,838	42,120	45,900	39,799	4,704	611
All ranks	52,490	37,800	42,700	66,645	80,234	56,492	17,572	2,891

Note: Adapted from Wicherski & Kohout, 1996.

lionaire like Bill Gates by teaching in a college or university, professors are usually able to afford a comfortable lifestyle.

Advantages and Disadvantages of the Career

Some people contemplating a career in academia consider the range of salaries the major drawback. Probably a person could make more money over his or her lifetime by becoming a doctor, lawyer, or engineer, or by obtaining an MBA and going into business. If you definitely have personal wealth as the major goal in your life, then an academic career may not be appropriate for you. But most professors have other goals in mind. The benefits of an academic career are many, but they have more to do with the quality and style of life and less to do with money. First, there is considerable freedom and flexibility in arranging one's time. Besides being in one's classes and attending some mandatory meetings, one is often free to manage time as needed, so long as the work gets done. I write this section of this chapter after 11 PM. However, I spent a good part of the afternoon on this particular day attending parent–teacher conferences for my children. I sometimes play squash during my lunch hour, which is stretched to more like an hour and a half. Unlike the working conditions in other large organizations, no one is paying much attention to my comings and goings, as long as I get my work done. I do much of my writing at home, in fact. Academic positions offer great freedom in arranging what one does and when one chooses to do it. In addition, no one tells me what research I should be doing, what books and articles I should be reading, and (within some limits) what courses I have to teach. It is rare in the world of work to be permitted to decide what you want to do and then have someone pay you to do it.

Another advantage of a university atmosphere is continued education. Professors in psychology will often know professors in other disciplines and can discuss interesting topics in, say, anthropology or astronomy or history. Universities are abuzz with activities, like colloquia, concerts, plays, sporting events, public addresses, and debates. There is always something interesting happening, and the difficulty is usually being able to go to events and still get one's work done. Professors usually love to interact and to work with students. (If they don't, they are in the wrong field.) The best students are lively, probing, challenging, and fun. They keep the faculty informed and teach the faculty new things, as they are being taught by the faculty. The faculty member ages, but the student body stays at about the same age, so students help keep the faculty young, to some degree.

The detriments of being a professor are, in my opinion, not great. Some faculty complain about bureaucracy, but every large organization has a bureaucracy. Faculty politics and political bickering can sometimes break out and, in some cases, can achieve legendary proportions. (A famous academic law is Sayre's "Third Law of Politics: Academic politics are so bitter, because the stakes are so small.")

The life of a college professor is, in my opinion, a wonderful one. I have never for a moment regretted my career choice. I never want to retire, although of course I may change my mind in 25 more years.

Attributes Needed for Success in the Career

Some of the required attributes are obvious. A certain level of verbal and mathematical intelligence is required. However, beyond some required level of intelligence, sheer IQ probably does not account for too much in academia (or in other demanding jobs). Graduate schools have already selected for intelligence because a person must have good grades in college and reasonably good scores on standardized tests to be admitted to graduate school. And several factors in the 4 to 7 years in a graduate school program further eliminate people along the way, for better or worse. More than half the people who enter doctoral programs drop out before obtaining the PhD, for one reason or another. Anyone who receives a PhD has the intelligence to be a psychologist in academia or elsewhere.

Besides intelligence, what else matters? As one editor of this volume maintains (Sternberg, 1988), there are other types of intelligence, too. Practical intelligence (i.e., "street smarts"), social intelligence, and what is informally called "common sense" can all make an important difference. So can the desire to learn, creativity, and communication skills. All of these help, and the stereotype of the brilliant but absent-minded professor did not arise from nothing. Universities do seem to acquire more than their fair share of eccentrics, who excel in their fields but seem barely able to cope with life outside. That helps make universities interesting places, even if the presence of a few unusual people does sometimes strain university administrations that try to manage faculty who, at the best of times, are an independent, sometimes fractious, lot. Faculty are often resistant to change within the university—try changing the required curriculum for students to see this quality come out—even while they profess to like change as a general principle.

If I had to put my finger on two characteristics that predict academic success, the two would be *achievement motivation* (how much you really want to do this and how hard you are willing to work) and *persistence* (whether you will keep coming back even if you have suffered setbacks and rejection). Most of the really successful academics have these qualities, in my opinion, although I cannot point to empirical studies to show this.

Range of Opportunities for Employment

It is no secret that the academic job market is relatively poor today. Although there are about 4,000 junior colleges, colleges, and universities in the United States, the 150 to 200 research universities that produce most of the PhD students still produce them in greater numbers than the academic job market requires. The reasons for this state of affairs are complex. On the supply side, graduate departments have not much reduced the number of graduate students they admit, even though everyone recognizes that the job market in academia is weak. This may be because faculty at research universities enjoy working with graduate students and simply seek those students interested in conducting research with them. In addition, many universities (especially large state universities) need graduate students to help teach undergraduates, either in the capacities of graders and teaching assistants or as undergraduate instructors. So, the fact that there are fewer jobs for doctoral-level graduates does not necessarily serve as a disincentive to the admission of new graduate students at most universities.

Why isn't there a greater opportunity for positions? Again, the causes are complex. Just 15 years ago predictions were made that there would be an undersupply of candidates for professor positions in the 1990s! However, the federal government has banned compulsory retirement at age 70 (as age discrimination) in universities, so some professors are staying on, which prevents openings for younger people just out of graduate school. The federal government has also cut back research support to universities, which reduces funding and also inhibits more hiring of professors. State governments, feeling the same pressures as the federal government, have frequently reduced aid to higher education. Many private colleges and universities feel similar financial pressures. Consequently, given that few universities are growing significantly—many are not even replacing people who leave—and that fewer professors are retiring, the result is that the many students receiving PhDs are chasing too few jobs in academia.

That is the bad news. The good news is that there are still many jobs available in higher education. These differ across the specialty areas in psychology and change from year to year. But, for those students who establish outstanding records in graduate school, there are still job opportunities. In addition, in many fields in psychology it is possible and even desirable to seek an appointment as a postdoctoral fellow after receiving a PhD, in order to continue conducting research before going onto the job market and embarking on a career. Taking a 2- to 3-year postdoctoral fellowship permits a young psychologist to gain additional valuable research experience (usually in a new environment from that in which he or she received the PhD), to build a stronger publication record, and therefore to be in a much more favorable position when he or she enters the job market later.

The other bit of good news about receiving a PhD in psychology (rather than, say, English or history) is that a wide range of job opportunities exist outside academia. Indeed, the other chapters in this volume attest to the wide range of possibilities for a career in psychology outside of an academic setting. Good advice for graduate students in this day and age is to take a wide variety of courses in graduate school and to keep a broad perspective for career opportunities. Many exciting possibilities exist outside university teaching and research.

A Day in the Life

Contributors to this volume were asked to write about a typical day in their lives. One problem with this requirement for me is that no day is really typical. Given the range of activities in which a college professor is engaged, activities differ dramatically from day to day, so I will use yesterday as typical.

I am up at 6:30 this Wednesday morning and, with no more than the usual commotion and bother, leave with my children for their school at 7:35. I get them deposited and make it to my office by 8 a.m.. I have a lecture at 9 a.m. for my introductory psychology course, so first I prepare that. Luckily, the lecture is on visual illusions and the constructive nature of perception. I like to think it is one of my best lectures, but I review my notes, because it has been 2 years since I gave this version of the lecture, and go over some 20 overhead transparencies that I will use. I add 2 new ones that I have collected. I finish preparing for class in half an hour and decide to see what new messages have come overnight by electronic mail. (Telephoning and correspondence by regular mail is becoming obsolete for me and others in academia; most important news is delivered via e-mail.) I read and respond to most of the 13 new messages that have appeared before I leave for class.

The lecture seems to go successfully, and several students ask questions during and after class. On the way back from class, I pick up my mail. I receive considerable mail from a journal that I edit— *Psychonomic Bulletin & Review*, published by the Psychonomic Society— as well as other kinds of mail. I sort the journal mail and discover several reviews of manuscripts and one new manuscript that has been submitted. I go to the journal office and talk about various matters with the secretary for the journal and examine the new submission, which looks quite promising. I assign the manuscript reviewers who will evaluate it for the journal and provide advice that will help me decide on its acceptability. I get back to my office at 10:45 and finish my e-mail correspondence.

It is now shortly after 11 a.m., and I realize the meeting of my lab group is looming at noon. We are to discuss the draft of a paper by Endel Tulving entitled "Episodic Memory: From Mind to Brain," which will be published in the *Quarterly Journal of Experimental Psychology* as an invited submission. I had wanted to read it and thought it would be good for my graduate students to read, too. Now the meeting is less than an hour away and I have not finished the paper. So off I go to a hiding place in the basement (it has no telephone), which I use when I need to read in a quiet environment. (There are too many interruptions in my office.) I get the paper finished, wolf down some lunch, and go off to my noon meeting. The session is quite lively, with some students suggesting items for further research. We spend some time analyzing statements or passages that seem ambiguous or unclear. One student, in particular, picks up what seems to be a weak point in the logic. I raise some points of my own, which the group discusses. I am jotting down notes, because I promised Dr. Tulving I would write with comments based on the group's discussion.

After the lab meeting, I have an appointment with one student to discuss her master's thesis. That lasts about 20 minutes, so it is now 1:20, and I begin to prepare the afternoon lecture for my course on human memory. We are discussing the issues of the malleability of memory and of eyewitness testimony, and the possibility of false memories occurring in therapy. The students are reading *The Myth of Repressed Memory* by Elizabeth Loftus and Katherine Ketcham at this point in the course, and they seem to be enjoying it. I am discussing evidence for various memory illusions in class. However, I need to prepare some overhead transparencies to display some recent results, so this chore occupies me until my class begins. After the lecture, two students come by to ask (rather nervously) about the nature of the test to be given the following week. They ask questions about material in one of the textbooks in paralyzing depth, much more than I would ever expect on the test, and we cover the intricate topics they have asked about. I suspect that they have little to worry about if they know the material in such detail, but I keep my suspicions to myself.

When the afternoon mail, which includes two journals, arrives, I scan the journals' contents and zip through one article that is of particular interest to me. Then it is 4 p.m. and time for me to meet with a PhD student about his dissertation. He has some of the first results of a test of nearly 700 subjects in a large-scale project. He lays out the preliminary findings and the news is exceedingly good: The part of the research that had to work out a certain way for the rest to make an interesting contribution did come out as expected. He is very encouraged and so am I. He leaves to embark on the additional analyses.

Now it is 4:30 and I deal with half a dozen e-mail messages that arrived during the day. Finally, I turn to a manuscript that I need to evaluate for my journal. The reviews of the paper are mixed, so it looks as if a difficult decision will be required. I read until 5:20 and head for home. That night, after the children are safely asleep, I finish the manuscript and dictate a letter.

This is a reasonably typical weekday, which includes about 10 to 11 hours of work. However, most of my teaching is confined to Mondays, Wednesdays, and Fridays, so on Tuesday and Thursday I work more at my own research, writing, and editing. The activities those days would be quite different.

Conclusion

The life of a college professor may not be rich and glamorous, but it has its own rewards: being a part of the continual search for knowledge; being surrounded by young, inquisitive minds; being in an academic setting with people interested in every imaginable topic; and having a great degree of personal freedom and autonomy, among others. Most professors I know would not trade their occupations for any other. Indeed, most do not think of themselves as having a "job" in the traditional sense. They are doing what they most want to do and getting paid for it, which is a happy bargain.

References

Bem, D. J. (1987). Writing the empirical journal article. In M. P. Zanna & J. M. Darley (Eds.), *The compleat academic: A practical guide for the beginning social scientist*. New York: Random House.

Brown, R. (1965). *Social psychology*. New York: Free Press.

Conroy, P. (1980). *The lords of discipline*. Boston: Houghton-Mifflin.

Elmes, D. G., Kantowitz, B. H., & Roediger, H. L. (1995). *Research methods in psychology* (5th ed.). St. Paul, MN: West.

Kantowitz, B. H., Roediger, H. L., & Elmes, D. G. (1997). *Experimental psychology: Understanding psychological research* (6th ed.). St. Paul, MN: West.

Lewis, D. J. (1963). *Scientific principles of psychology*. Englewood Cliffs, NJ: Prentice-Hall.

McKeachie, W. J. (1987). Tips for college teachers. In M. P. Zanna & J. M. Darley (Eds.), *The compleat academic: A practical guide for the beginning social scientist*. New York: McGraw-Hill.

Roediger, H. L., Capaldi, E. D., Paris, S. G., Polivy, J., & Herman, C. P. (1996). *Psychology* (4th ed). St. Paul, MN: West.

Sternberg, R. J. (1988). *The triarchic mind: A new theory of human intelligence*. New York: Viking.

Sternberg, R. J. (1993). *The psychologist's companion: A guide to scientific writing for students and psychologists* (2nd ed.). Cambridge, England: Cambridge University Press.

Wicherski, M., & Kohout, J. (1996). *1995–1996 Faculty salaries in graduate departments of psychology*. Washington, DC: American Psychological Association Research Office.

Robert Calfee

Learning About Learning: Psychologists in Schools of Education

2

Educational Psychology: Theory, Research, and Practice

P sychology is the study of the individual in context; education is the social institution by which a society transmits its cultural heritage to children and young adults. Educational psychology stands at the intersection of these two domains. Educational psychologists study how people think, behave, and learn, as individuals and in learning communities. A century ago, psychologists' work ranged from armchairs to laboratories to real-world situations; today their work is not much different. In the United States, practical applications were important from the early days, and the improvement of school learning was often at the top of this list (Glover & Ronning, 1987; James, 1899/1983). Schools are complex organizations, and today psychologists deal with a broad range of issues, including special education,

Robert Calfee is a cognitive psychologist with research interests in the effect of schooling on the intellectual potential of individuals and groups. He earned his degrees at UCLA, did postgraduate work at Stanford, and spent 5 years in psychology at the University of Wisconsin, Madison. In 1969 he returned to Stanford University to join the School of Education, where he is presently a professor in the Committee on Language, Literacy, and Culture, and the Committee on Psychological Studies.

counseling, and assessment, to name only a few. Educational psychologists seek to understand the process of schooling and learning, that is, how students learn, how teachers instruct, how achievement depends on motivation, the influence of social contexts, and the interplay of curriculum, instruction, and assessment. Their interests range from birth to adulthood, but are mostly centered around the institution of formal schooling. Because educational psychologists are interested in understanding phenomena associated with schooling, studying theory is an important goal shared with other scientific psychologists. Because they are often employed in universities, they conduct and publish empirical research. Because educational psychologists study children across the years, their work links with developmental psychology and the study of how individuals differ from one another. And because they focus on schools, they often involve themselves in practical applications like the development and evaluation of educational programs.

Several themes have emerged in the work of educational psychologists during the past century (Berliner, 1993). Perhaps foremost has been the measurement of individual differences: the development of reliable and valid tests of various human characteristics, including learning and achievement (Linn, 1989). Another significant theme is the study of the child in school environments. Thus, at one time, developmental psychology was difficult to separate from educational psychology, but in the 1940s and 1950s, as part of the war effort and its aftermath, educational psychologists played an important role in the design of instructional programs. Many of these were aimed at behavioral training (e.g., learning how to operate a radar system or repair an aircraft engine). In more recent years, educational psychology has played a critical role in the cognitive revolution (Lesgold & Glaser, 1989), in the development of curriculum that promotes thinking and problem solving in social situations (Resnick, 1987), and in the preparation of teachers to handle the new concepts of reflective instruction (Peterson, Clark, & Dickson, 1990).

Educational psychologists are a diverse group. This chapter describes the opportunities for our profession in a research university setting, but a doctorate in educational psychology opens the way to a wide variety of positions in academia (in schools of education and in other social science departments), in primary and secondary schools and other educational organizations (doing curriculum development, evaluation, and assessment), and in business (as designers of training programs and client-interface programs). In fact, you can find educational psychologists employed in virtually every field represented by the chapters in this volume!

Preparation for the discipline emphasizes an understanding of psychological principles, mastery of research skills, and connection with the various worlds of schooling. Within these constancies you will find a diversity of concrete tasks and personal styles. Some educational psychologists commune mostly with computers, examining, for instance, large-scale surveys to discover the relations between home background, teaching practices, and student achievement. Others develop and analyze tests and instructional materials, and connect only indirectly with schools. But you can also find those who spend a good deal of time with schools, teachers, and students, that is, those who do more "people work" than "paperwork." What binds our discipline together is a commitment to the scientific method for understanding individual human beings, with particular emphasis on the institution of schooling.

How best to introduce you to this field? The numerous introductions to educational psychology mostly offer beginning teachers the fundamental principles of the field. These introductions range from the theoretical and "researchy" to the very practical. The *Handbook of Educational Psychology* (Berliner & Calfee, 1996) offers a comprehensive overview of the field and is a resource for beginning graduate students and professionals. A recent collection of application-oriented volumes presents the more practical side of the field (e.g., McCombs & Pope, 1994).

You can find useful information in these resources, but I present a personal view of my career as an educational psychologist. My experiences may not be typical, but that's the point: Ask any two educational psychologists about their professional life, and you will find considerable variability. Next comes a sketch of how my career developed. Again, the point is that you can find many ways to move from "here" to "there."

A Week in My Life

What do I do? Where and how do I do it? How did I wind up in this situation? How do I like it? Why would I recommend it to young people thinking about a career in this field? These questions provide an organizing framework for this section.

To begin, I am a professor in the School of Education at Stanford University. My official responsibilities include teaching, research, and service. According to the university, I am supposed to give equal weight to these three areas. In fact, many weeks work out that way, as a week in early January illustrates:

Wednesday:

- 7:00 A.M. Check e-mail. Review plans for today's class.
- 8:00 A.M. Teach a 2-hour graduate course in research methods. Introduce NUD.IST, a new computer program for analyzing qualitative data (interviews and classroom observations).
- 10:30 A.M. Have a 2-hour meeting with six doctoral advisees to review their thesis work. I have organized a dissertation group in which students review and critique each other's work, which is preparation for the time not far ahead when they will be professors themselves. (Some things have to be learned by doing.)
- 1:00 P.M. Check correspondence, look over journal manuscripts, and write commentary on student papers from research methods course.
- 8:00 P.M. Check e-mail and review admissions folders for new students. Read page proofs for the upcoming *Handbook of Educational Psychology,* of which I'm coeditor.

Thursday:

- 7:00 A.M.. Revise my segment of a paper about best practices in reading and writing for a Bay Area school reform project. (The goal is to produce an easy-to-read document that is conceptually valid, has "punch," and navigates the shoals of reading's "great debates"about how to teach reading.)
- 1:00 P.M. Fax and e-mail my draft of the paper. Check in at the office.
- 2:30 P.M. Head off to San Francisco International Airport for a trip to Chicago and Omaha. (I have a tight schedule: Friday in Chicago, then to Omaha for a Saturday workshop with reading teachers. I have 3 hours in the air to work on a book I'm coauthoring with a colleague at the University of Nebraska.)
- 10:00 P.M. I arrive at Chicago O'Hare Airport on time! Reach the Ward home in Evanston at 10:45. Gail Ward, principal of a Chicago school, is managing tomorrow's workshop. Have a long talk with Gail and her husband John about schools. Suddenly it's 12:30 in the morning.

Friday:

- 8:30 A.M. Conduct a 6-hour workshop for 50 primary-grade teachers on methods for effective phonics instruction using cognitive techniques rather than rote practice.
- 3:30 P.M. Meet with school staff to discuss workshop follow-up. (It's a good discussion, but there are tough problems ahead.)
- 5:00 P.M. Go to O'Hare for the flight to Omaha, but a January snowstorm has canceled all flights. Check into the airport hotel. Wonder if I can reach Omaha tomorrow.

Saturday:

- 6:30 A.M. Go back to the airport; Omaha flight is on time. Hallelujah!
- 10:15 A.M. Conduct a 5-hour workshop for 40 teachers and reading specialists on phonics strategies—a rerun of the Chicago presentation, but in a different, much more upbeat context.
- 4:00 P.M. Meet with Omaha administrators to discuss implementation. Productive session!
- 6:00 P.M. Get back on the plane. Type up reports from the past 2 days. Take some time to work on this chapter.
- 10:00 P.M. Arrive in San Francisco. It's great to be home.

This week was busier than some, but was not unusual. Teaching is important in my life. Research threads its way through everything I do. Service is an integral part of my position in education. It's a great life, and I am privileged to have it. I work hard, and I feel that I make a difference both theoretically and practically. My real passion is research—generating concepts and data that can improve student learning in today's schools. Sometimes this passion is realized as I analyze data and write articles, sometimes in sessions with graduate students, and sometimes in the chaos of visits with schools, teachers, and classrooms.

The university is my home base, but I work a lot in school settings. My background is experimental cognitive psychology, but 20 years ago I shifted from laboratory studies toward action-oriented studies (Calfee & Patrick, 1995). My research is still experimental, but now spans years rather than weeks, and involves elementary schools rather than college sophomores. This shift means going on the road, fitting my schedule to school calendars, and dealing with the messiness of complex organizations.

My home base is a graduate program. Our students pursue master's or doctoral degrees. Some will become classroom teachers and administrators, but most will work in universities, state and federal organizations, or business and industry. The faculty offer courses in various topics, but our teaching takes place mostly through apprenticeships, which are intense interactions with a few individuals over 4 to 6 years. Our aim is to prepare students to be future leaders. Especially in the final stages of a dissertation, time pressures can be demanding and unpredictable, both for students and faculty. Evening phone calls of frantic questions about a statistical problem or how to reorganize a chapter are frequent.

University life is not quite what I expected. At the beginning of my graduate work, I imagined a calm and reflective future, filled with lectures to eager students in my areas of expertise and time to read and write, to commune with colleagues, and to reflect and think deep thoughts. It hasn't worked out exactly that way, largely because of my decision to conduct research in school settings.

The purpose of this personal scenario is to suggest the range of possibilities for an educational psychologist in an academic setting. Research-oriented universities expect faculty to publish, but also to prepare future researchers. Once a professor attains tenure, he or she has considerable freedom to set a personal agenda for teaching, for research, and for service. Some instruction takes place in regular classes, but much more happens through advisement and apprenticeships. Teaching-oriented universities place more emphasis on classroom instruction.

The task is to balance the number of students that the individual professor reaches with the depth of preparation. For the educational psychologist, this often means a trade-off in the amount of attention one can give to individual students and the career goals of those students. Preparation to become a classroom teacher often requires a course in educational psychology that covers the principles of learning and motivation. This course is one in a series of foundational courses for prospective teachers, and so the intensity of preparation is understandably less than for those students with a career in the discipline of educational psychology. Opportunities for direct impact on schools can be substantial for the educational psychology instructor who connects with new teachers. The researcher with only a long list of publications can just hope for eventual benefits. The instructor who translates abstract research into practical reality can see immediate results. As you consider a career in educational psychology, these are some of the trade-offs to think about. But it is always wise to keep your eyes open for opportunities rather than make firm decisions too quickly.

An Unpredictable Path: Preparing to Become an Educational Psychologist

Suppose you are thinking about becoming an educational psychologist. How should you prepare yourself? I provide a few guidelines, and then I demonstrate how varied a path is possible within these suggestions.

As the chapters in this volume confirm, many psychologists are interested in "people things." The discipline of educational psychology falls on the research end of the research–practice continuum, and requires an analytic frame of mind, even though much of the work centers around students, teachers, and schools. Whereas educational psychologists take the individual student as their point of departure, students are part of classrooms and teachers, who in turn belong to schools and districts. In the United States, these social systems are quite complex and interactive, so that educational psychologists often have to deal with practicalities and politics.

Research methods are the core of graduate training in educational psychology. Not too many years ago, this preparation emphasized experimental design and statistical techniques, but the past decade has seen the emergence of qualitative methods—observations, interviews, case studies, and even ethnographies—as significant parts of the researcher's toolbox. Educational psychology has always had an interdisciplinary flavor, and that tendency has increased in recent decades.

Finally, educational psychologists have to be willing and able to write. Whether it is conducted in a university setting or any of the other workplaces mentioned earlier, research matters only when it is published, either in archival journals, like the *Journal of Educational Psychology*, or as technical reports for client agencies. Educational psychologists must also be effective in group presentations such as conventions and conferences. Finally, many of us teach in universities and colleges, where we are expected to set the standard for quality of instruction. A demanding job! How best to prepare for it? My preparation, typical in its atypicality, suggests some important themes, but also demonstrates the variations.

BEGINNINGS

How did my professional life come about? Any personal narrative must be selective, but a prevailing theme in my experience has been the importance of taking advantage of unexpected opportunities. After a stint in the Air Force during the Korean War, I returned to UCLA to complete an undergraduate degree in psychology. My aim was a career in clinical psychology, but Allen Parducci's course in experimental psychology "hooked" me, and led to doctoral work in experimental psychology with top-ranked people in learning theory, research design, and statistical analysis. Although clinical psychology was no longer my focus, I continued to work in the area, which was a decision that proved valuable later in my career.

By 1960, my course work complete, I took a position as research associate at Stanford's Institute for Mathematical Studies in the Social Sciences (IMSSS), which immersed me in the emerging field of cognitive psychology. Patrick Suppes, director of IMSSS, was a renowned theoretician in mathematical learning theory who also had a practical streak. In the mid-1960s he and Richard Atkinson developed programs for computer-assisted instruction in mathematics and reading. A good deal of my early preparation for educational psychology came from actively "hanging around" these programs.

"THE KINDERGARTEN YEARS"

In 1965 I was hired as an assistant professor and moved to the University of Wisconsin, Madison. My assignment was to develop the program in mathematical psychology. The following year, Dick Venezky, a graduate of Stanford's linguistics program, arrived in Madison. He and I had met briefly at Stanford, and enjoyed each other's company. We applied to the Wisconsin Research and Development Center for a grant to investigate prereading skills in kindergarteners, which was the beginning of a collaboration that has endured for 3 decades. Our backgrounds were complementary. Today I understand linguistics because of Venezky's influence, and he knows cognitive psychology in part through our interaction. In 1965, however, our job was to learn more about how young children learn to read.

Reading research during the 1960s centered on "the one best method." Reading meant phonics, and researchers were looking for "teacher-proof" methods of instruction to improve performance on standardized tests. Venezky and I took a different tack. We actually talked with kindergarteners about what they thought about tests. We experimented with different formats and techniques. We discovered many conditions in which students failed, but it was more difficult to develop "clean tests" that supported optimal performance. We found that very young children, especially those from homes that had not introduced them to the alphabet song- and story-books, did much better on tests when given a little guidance and some examples. Their main problem often was that they simply didn't understand what they were supposed to do.

ADULT EDUCATION

In 1970, I returned to The Stanford Graduate School of Education. This job offer included an opportunity to spend 6 months in Israel with Venezky. The two of us studied schools. We observed lessons, talked with principals and teachers, and spent time with young students. We had time to read, think, talk, and explore. It was an education about education. Our view of reading began to shift from the individual toward the organizational, from students toward teachers, from cognitive models of the reading process toward curriculum and instruction as "mind-shapers," and from a laboratory view of reading skill toward an appreciation of the complex demands confronting a typical first-grade teacher.

On my return from Israel, I found that the education department at Stanford proved very different from a psychology department. The doctoral students were mature, experienced, and knowledgeable about the pragmatics of schooling. Colleagues spoke unfamiliar languages, but connections began to emerge. Cronbach's generalizability technique—a fundamental advance in test reliability—was linked to concepts of design and analysis. The Educational Testing Service asked me to assist with a large-scale study of beginning teachers in California to design student tests, teacher surveys, and classroom observations. This was life in the real world!

Stanford's graduate program in education attracts a wide array of talented students—some headed toward research careers, others straddling the gap between research and practice. Many took my course in research design and statistical analysis, and it was both a challenge and a treat to mesh theoretical ideas with the wide variety of dissertation topics. My experiences in Israel had shown that numbers were not enough; classroom practices were often better told as stories than as averages, as episodes rather than variances. Shirley Brice Heath joined the Stanford faculty in the 1970s, and her seminal monograph, *Ways With Words* (1983), showed the power of using qualitative information to support claims as rigorously as statistical tests.

My teaching responsibilities also included instructing students in the Stanford Teacher Education Program (STEP). STEP is an intern program in which students have part-time assignments in local high schools while completing their master's degree. The tension between theory and practice can be intense and obvious as students make their daily treks between campus and school, often hearing one thing in college courses and another from fellow teachers. An educational psychology course, in learning theory, motivation, classroom management, and so on, is typically part of the foundational requirement in teacher preparation programs. Because my background was in reading, I taught both educational psychology and the required reading course. STEP prepares high school teachers, who may have little interest in basic skills until they discover that their students cannot handle assigned readings. I learned a lot about the "in your face" challenges confronting today's teachers from these experiences.

BACK TO ELEMENTARY SCHOOL

The next significant turn in my professional career occurred in 1980 at a school in a middle-class Silicon Valley neighborhood during a visit to observe the reading program. My routine for classroom observation was simple. After watching a lesson, I asked students and teachers what they were doing and why. *Why* was the tough question because today's reading instruction is driven by activities more than concepts, by filling the day more than moving toward a goal. The principal called later in the week and asked if I would return to discuss some whys and wherefores: Why were reading and writing disconnected? Why weren't their students more challenged? Why were both students and teachers often bored by instruction? How could they reinvigorate their curriculum?

I offered to share some ideas about how cognitive principles applied to these questions, but warned that the answers would be best worked out through collaboration. The school faculty met with me and a team of graduate students for a week during the early summer. As the week went on, our discussions centered around the concept of *critical literacy*—the capacity to use language as a tool for problem solving and communication. Handling print was important, but it was the style of language use that was important, not whether it was speech or print.

The collaboration resulted in Project READ, a program to inform teachers about cognitive psychology, rhetoric, and the peculiarities of the English language, so that they could adapt their instruction to local contexts. Teachers could use prepackaged materials where it made sense, but also could make professional decisions when these were called for. For students, skills were important, but so was understanding. Individual competence mattered, but so did the capacity for teamwork.

During the 15 years since Project READ, my students and I have worked alongside elementary school teachers in hundreds of schools, refining and evaluating the program. From one perspective, READ is not a very "sexy" concept—it has no computers, no special materials, nothing obviously out of the ordinary. A visitor may notice that Project READ classrooms are noisier—that teachers seem to be doing less "teaching." The walls are hung with large sheets of brown paper that students use to develop *webs* and *weaves,* which are graphic diagrams for organizing and displaying their ideas. And if visitors ask students to explain what is going on, they can be amazed at the answers, which make sense and are delivered with considerable enthusiasm.

Over the years, READ has provided me a framework for conducting literacy research in a natural setting. From the outset, READ demonstrated that regular classrooms could be transformed into authentic learning environments rather quickly and cost effectively. Elementary School teachers are bright and caring people; given the opportunity to realize their potential, teachers can bring all students to their own potential.

This new career may appear far removed from my early laboratory studies of cognitive processes in reading, but the constancy is a focus on the interplay of language, thought, and literacy, and the formal use of language as an amplifier of human thought. Experimentation has been another persistent theme in my career. Whereas descriptive and observational research plays an important role in the behavioral and social sciences, researchers often understand a phenomenon best when we can change it.

Costs and Benefits

Mine has been a zigzag career, with some downsides, but many more upsides. The bottom line is an enthusiastic recommendation of an academic research career in the field of educational psychology to today's young people.

What are the downsides? One is the workload. The modern university does not allow the opportunity for quiet reflection that many people imagine, and most of us occasionally resent and resist the stress of continuing and overlapping commitments. Another is the financial payoff: Whereas most academic salaries allow a satisfying lifestyle, other careers might have put much more money in my bank account for the same time and effort.

The upsides have been personally significant for me. I grew up during the Great Depression, during which I worked on an assembly line and I was also unemployed. The stability of a tenured academic position lets a person take risks and wrestle with new problems where there is no answer at the back of the book, where research poses non-routine challenges, and where teaching means that last year's lectures won't work for this year's students. Some view tenure as a *sinecure*—"without care"—but responsible teachers care continuously, and tenure carries responsibilities as well as securities and freedoms.

Stanford is a research university, but teaching is also a priority. The faculty have a limited course load, and classes are small. On the other hand, expectations are high and advisement is intensive. In my courses, students submit a succession of papers during each quarter, and I typically prepare a two- to three-page critique for each draft, which is an investment of an hour per week for each student beyond class time. It is an intensive apprenticeship program and is impossible to "automate." The teaching costs are high, but the teaching rewards are substantial.

Like many educational psychologists, I spend a great deal of time working with schools, conducting workshops, and consulting with curriculum directors and administrators. This is my choice; I could write more, specialize in teacher preparation, or invest more effort in administrative and committee activities. Virtually all educational psychologists confront such choices because we are prepared for all of them. Nothing is worth teaching unless students can use it in a new situation. Teaching is about transfer. This advice applies to both teachers and students, and the best educational psychology programs provide graduates with generalizable skills and knowledge. To be sure, you have to figure out how to use what you already know to tackle each new problem. But never throw away a learning opportunity. You never know when you might need it later on.

Tomorrow's Road Map: Opportunities

How can this story help young people considering a career in educational psychology (Wittrock & Farley, 1989; Salomon, 1992)? As noted earlier, educational psychologists often find a place in research universities, but they also play major roles in research organizations like American Institutes of Research, RAND Corporation, Educational Testing Service, and SRI, to name a few. Teacher preparation programs in universities and colleges rely on educational psychologists for foundation courses in learning and motivation that provide novice teachers the skills and knowledge they need for the practicalities of classroom instruction. State, district, and federal organizations hire large numbers of educational psychologists to develop, implement, and evaluate instructional programs. Industries hire educational psychologists directly or hire them as consultants to handle similar tasks.

Times have changed since I began my career in the 1960s. The knowledge base has changed. Technology is now a major part of the picture. Educational psychologists once kept the holy grails of statistics and psychometrics. Now they have many other methodologies in their tool-kits.

Opportunities for a research career have also changed dramatically over the years. In the 1960s, the federal government was broadly committed to research and development, including in the behavioral, social, and educational sciences. Two ideals were leading our nation to world leadership in higher education: (a) cutting-edge college instruction enlightened and enlivened by cutting-edge scholarship, and (b) university contributions to basic research impacting all facets of national life. The past 2 decades have seen substantial reductions in these commitments, in both the "hard" and the "soft" sciences (real funding in social and psychological research has declined by 30% during the past 20 years; Smith & Torrey, 1996).

The 1960s were also a time of increased opportunity for college education, which meant more academic jobs. Economic policy was a driving force; a "smarter" nation would be more competitive in the world market. Social policy also entered the equation; the feminist and civil rights movements focused attention on inequities in educational opportunity for women and ethnic minorities from preschool through graduate work. This confluence was propitious for educational researchers. The job market flourished, and research funding was available for a broad range of projects.

By the mid-1970s, graduates found a job market with fewer openings. Many colleges, especially those in the public sector, have been relying on temporary and part-time positions to fill teaching slots. These have no employment benefits, no promise of tenure, and little expectation that the individual will conduct research. Today's graduates who locate tenure-track positions find opportunities for research restricted by heavy teaching loads and limited funding opportunities.

This tide is about to turn, however, and we will soon see renewed support for educational research and development, bringing greater opportunities for educational psychologists. One reason for hope comes from the nation's continuing search for a political middle ground in the role of the federal government. Another is the emerging demographic profile; after years of declining birth rates, schools are now bulging from kindergarten through college. From 1985 to 1995, the K-through-8 public school enrollment increased from 27 to 32.3 million, and is projected to reach 35 million in 2005. College enrollment rose from 12.2 million in 1985 to 14.5 million in 1995, and should exceed 16 million by 2005. More students mean more teachers, and more teachers mean more professors. The third factor is research funding. Whereas research support from the Department of Education has been flat over the past decade, agencies like the National Science Foundation and the National Institute of Child Health and Development are increasing funds to support basic and applied research on student learning and classroom instruction.

Preparation

How can you prepare for a career as a psychologist in education? First, a doctorate is usually required, which means 4 to 6 years of postbaccalaureate study. Fellowships and assistantships are available in many universities to cover tuition costs and some living expenses. The studies require hard work, especially in the methodological areas: research design, statistics, surveys and interviews, and qualitative techniques like ethnography and case studies. Evaluations of schools of education and psychology departments appear regularly in national publications. Graduates of highly rated institutions have better prospects in the job market, so start with the highest ranked, and then look over the bulletins to see how well each program matches your interests. Once you have identified several prospects, write or phone for additional information or check the World Wide Web site if one is available. Don't hesitate to call the institution for additional information and counsel. Talk with the department chair and individual professors.

A second word of advice is to search for people as mentors. I was fortunate. Along the way, one professor was excited about perceptual adaptation (Parducci), another stalked his classroom portraying multiple regression as the "patina on the plane" (J. A. Gengerelli), a young assistant professor challenged us to explore finite math equations (Atkinson), and an insomniac insisted that we all fully understand and appreciate the marvels of analysis of variance (Norman Anderson). These individuals had each mastered demanding domains and insisted that their students also strive for mastery. The lesson is that you should grasp every opportunity to search for tough instructors who can help you find out what you can learn. Do this when applying to an institution, while you are in the program, and after you graduate.

The third word of advice is to explore future possibilities. Educational psychology has made significant conceptual breakthroughs in the past 50 years (Berliner & Calfee, 1996). Scientific psychology applied to education is a significant discipline in its own right. Many in the field immerse themselves in laboratory studies of human learning and motivation. But others explore applications in a variety of real-world settings, such as schools, of course, but many other situations as well, including business, out-of-school programs, and even homes. For readers especially interested in the applied side of educational psychology, I strongly urge that you search out opportunities to connect with practice during your graduate program. Here my story has more to offer *a posteriori*. It was only during my visit to Israel in 1970 that I could immerse myself in genuine study of schools and could appreciate the enormous influence of contextual factors in shaping the learning of students, as well as teachers and all the other individuals who inhabit schools (e.g., principals, parents, and secretaries). For me, this occasion was accidental, but with limited funding, today's newcomers may need to be more foresightful.

The Jobs

What kinds of jobs are available once you have completed the course of study, and what are the salaries like? In 1989, more than two-thirds of the doctoral graduates were faculty of research universities throughout the country, in departments of educational psychology, but also in curriculum and teacher education—reading and language arts, science and mathematics, and special education [American Psychological Association (APA), 1990]. This category includes positions in state universities and colleges where the emphasis is less on research and more on teaching, especially courses in teacher preparation. The latter offer opportunities for research, but the demands of working with novice teachers, especially for intern programs that require school-based activities, mean that time is at a premium, and opportunities for reflection and writing can be limited.

Around 15% of the graduates in the APA survey were in nonacademic settings: federal, state, and school district positions; research laboratories and centers; and consulting firms. Several of my former students hold positions in major industrial settings, including Hewlett Packard and Apple Computer. The jobs include corporate training, design of systems for learning to use computers, and personnel evaluation and education. Graduates can find other business opportunities in companies producing educational software for home and school, which is a burgeoning industry for individuals with skill in the design and development of computer learning programs. Stanford graduates can be found in federal and state programs managing support activities, developing testing and assessment systems, and functioning as assistants in policy positions. One of my former advisees joined the Research Department of the Sacramento County Office of Education several years ago and now heads a multimillion-dollar enterprise providing professional development services for hundreds of area schools.

Educational psychologists often move into administrative positions, which reflects their combination of analytic skills and knowledge of human relations. Private consultancies attract the more entrepreneurial people, who survive by their talents at acquiring federal and state grants for surveys and evaluations of educational programs. The risks are greater in industry than in academia, but the rewards can also be substantial. Education has its own industries, including organizations like the Educational Testing Service, American Institutes for Research, and RAND Corporation. Closely related are semigovernmental institutions such as the network of educational laboratories funded by the Department of Education. In these organizations, educational psychologists conduct applied research, but the agenda tends to be driven by external contracts and demanding time lines, which leads to a frenetic pace.

Salaries

Monetary compensation varies widely across these different positions, and information is sketchy for jobs in private business. For academic positions, the American Association of University Professors conducts annual surveys of salaries. The 1995 survey (Hamermese, 1996) showed that the entering 9-month salary for new assistant professors averaged $30,000 and increased to $60,000 for full professors. These numbers apply to all psychologists; salaries in education schools were slightly lower at the top end. These positions typically lead to tenure and have good benefits and retirement packages. Civil service positions also carry job security, but are subject to the vagaries of politics and changing budgets. Salaries vary substantially, depending on the organization, but are typically stable, with increases based on time in the job. The salary schedules are public information, but you have to ask the organization. Positions in business and industry, as well as private consultancies, entail much less security, of course, and it is harder to find out what people are paid. There is no guarantee of tenure, and although salaries appear to be higher than in academic and civil service positions, the bottom can always drop out.

The real rewards, however, of a career in educational psychology go beyond financial return for many individuals who value the opportunity to do "people work," especially where the ultimate clients are learners. For example, textbook publishers play a major role in setting the stage for classroom curriculum and instruction, and the publishing industry employs many educational psychologists. My conversations with colleagues in textbook publishing reveal a practical side— "Whatever we do, it has to sell!"—but also reveal a concern about issues of learning, motivation, and caring for the ultimate clients: students, teachers, and parents.

Conclusion

The combination of hardheadedness and softheartedness, of science and practice, perhaps best characterizes the field of educational psychology. The individual with this preparation can move across a spectrum from statistical analysis to classroom narratives, from evaluating the effectiveness of a science curriculum to developing a program for character education, and from investigating eye movements in reading to inquiring about how children's literature fosters empathy. Our field has a distinguished past, and the future promises even more!

References

American Psychological Association. (1990). *Profile of Division 15 members: 1989*. Washington, DC: Author.

Berliner, D. C. (1993). The 100-year journey of educational psychology: From interest, to disdain, to respect for practice. In T. Fagin & G. R. VandenBos (Eds.), *Exploring applied psychology: Origins and critical analyses* (pp. 39–78). Washington, DC: American Psychological Association.

Berliner, D. C., & Calfee, R. C. (1996). *Handbook of educational psychology*. New York: Macmillan.

Calfee, R. C., & Patrick, C. (1995). *Teach our children well*. Stanford, CA: Stanford Alumni Association.

Glover, J. A., & Ronning, R. R. (Eds.). (1987). *Historical foundations of educational psychology*. New York: Plenum Press.

Hamermese, D. S. (1996, March–April). Not so bad! The annual report on the economic status of the professor. *Academe*, pp. 14–22.

Heath, S. B. (1983). *Ways with words*. Cambridge, England: Cambridge University Press.

James, W. (1899/1983). *Talks to teachers on psychology and to students on some of life's ideals*. Cambridge, MA: Harvard University Press.

Lesgold, A., & Glaser, R. (Eds.). (1989). *Foundations for a psychology of education*. Hillsdale, NJ: Erlbaum.

Linn, R. L. (Ed.), (1989). *Educational measurement*. New York: Macmillan.

McCombs, B. L., & Pope, J. (1994). *Motivating hard to reach students: Psychology in the classroom*. Washington, DC: American Psychological Association.

Peterson, P. L., Clark, C. M., & Dickson, W. P. (1990). Educational psychology as a foundation in teacher education: Reforming an old notion. *Teachers College Record, 91*, 322–346.

Resnick, L. B. (1987). *Education and learning to think*. Washington, DC: National Academy of Education.

Salomon, G. (1992). The nature and mission of educational psychology [whole issue]. *Educational Psychologist, 27*(2).

Smith, P. M., & Torrey, B. B. (1996). The future of the behavioral and social sciences. *Science, 271*, 611–612.

Wittrock, M. C., & Farley, F. (1989). *The future of educational psychology*. Hillsdale, NJ: Erlbaum.

Victor H. Vroom

Teaching the Managers of Tomorrow: Psychologists in Business Schools

3

Prologue

hortly after accepting Robert Sternberg's invitation to write this chapter, I attended an annual meeting of the Society of Industrial and Organizational Psychology. While there, I met a former student who is currently teaching in a business school. In the midst of a casual conversation, I mentioned my new writing task. His response was immediate: What do you know about teaching in a business school? I blanched and inquired what he thought I had been doing for the last 32 years! The ensuing discussion helped me to understand my colleague's position. My experiences in business school teaching were not representative of what he had encountered and presumably not what others might expect to encounter. Both Carnegie Mellon and Yale, the two business schools at which I have had my direct experience, have relatively small student bodies and are better known for their contributions to research than is the typical business school.

At that time, I considered withdrawing from this assignment. However, there were several deep convictions

Victor H. Vroom holds the John G. Searle Professorship in Organization and Management at Yale University. He received his PhD in psychology from the University of Michigan, after which he taught at the University of Pennsylvania and Carnegie Mellon University, before moving to Yale.

The author is grateful for comments on earlier drafts from Sigal Barsade, Donald Gibson, Arthur Jago, Chris McCusker, Jim Phills, and Cheryl Tromley.

that led me to continue. Primary among these is my belief that enlightened management of our organizations—private, public, and nonprofit—is of monumental importance to our society. Historically, business schools have played a key role in the development of tomorrow's managers, and there is no reason to believe that this role will be diminished in the years to come. Furthermore, I believe that the science of psychology has much to contribute to our understanding of the interplay of people, groups, and organizations and to helping future managers meet the challenge of unleashing the human potential in the workforce. Finally, I believe that confronting and studying real-world problems, such as those involved in the management of complex organizations, will lead to the development of more viable and more applicable theories of human behavior.

To meet my colleague's concerns about the representativeness of my knowledge of the domain of business schools, I decided to do two things. The first was to share with the reader the most salient facts about my academic background so that the reader might be able to assess any likely sources of bias. The second was to get to work on it immediately so that there would be ample time to obtain the reactions not only of my former student, but also of others with potentially different perspectives.

The latter step has been taken and I believe the chapter has been strengthened thereby. To the former—the autobiographical part—I now turn.

A Brief Personal History

I studied organizational psychology at the University of Michigan and received my PhD there in 1958. Because academic job opportunities for organizational psychologists were not abundant that year, and because my spouse had another year or more to finish her dissertation in clinical psychology, I elected to stay at Michigan as a study director in the Survey Research Center and a part-time lecturer in Michigan's psychology department. Two years later, I was offered an assistant professor position in the department of psychology at the University of Pennsylvania. For the next 3 years I occupied myself with teaching large undergraduate sections of introductory psychology, teaching doctoral courses in motivation and social psychology, and writing a book that subsequently was titled *Work and Motivation*. My career path was set. I intended to spend the rest of my academic life in a psychology department.

While at Penn, I had only limited contact with the Wharton School of Finance and Commerce. I had some friends there in the economics and sociology departments, but I never taught a course or even offered a seminar there.

Then, in 1963, for reasons that I will expand on later, my telephone began to ring with requests to consider moving to a business school. Among the most interesting were the Columbia Business School, the Stanford Business School, Carnegie Tech's Graduate School of Industrial Administration, and Yale's Department of Industrial Administration. There were some apparent advantages to this kind of career move. All talked of an immediate promotion to associate professor, a substantially higher salary, and contacts with field sites in which I could carry out my research.

Despite the economic advantages, I was ambivalent about a change in career. My conception of business education was that it was crassly commercial and its students were professional rather than academic. I had been trained as a psychologist and was unprepared for what I felt would be a wrenching change in my identity required by moving to a business school.

To reduce the risks involved, I made it clear to those who sought to induce me to move that I would consider only a joint appointment with a psychology department. This I felt would afford me easy access to colleagues who shared my discipline and a safe exit in the event that I found business school life unpalatable. That requirement proved unacceptable to Columbia and Stanford but manageable at both Yale and Carnegie. After a protracted decision process that reflected my ambivalence, I decided in 1963 to accept Carnegie's offer, and I moved to Pittsburgh as associate professor of industrial administration and psychology.

Now I have logged a third of a century in business schools. In that time, 9 years were spent at Carnegie and 23 at Yale, and sabbaticals were spent at the University of California at Irvine and the London Business School. I do not argue that all of these years have been fun and that a career in a business school dominates other choices on all relevant dimensions. Instead, I try to portray as accurately as I can advantages and disadvantages of such a career, to permit readers to assess its appropriateness to their interests and capabilities.

A Question of Nomenclature

Throughout this chapter, I use the term *business school*, although the reader should be aware of frequent use of other language. Recognizing the generic nature of management skills required in private, public, and not-for-profit organizations, similar departments at some other universities, including Yale, Northwestern, and the University of California at Irvine, refer to themselves as management schools. For some of these schools, the difference is largely semantic and the curriculum and degree granted (MBA) are essentially the same as those of a business school. At Yale, however, the difference is more substantive, and anyone referring to it as a business school will be made aware of the fact that an important norm has been violated: Instructors in virtually all courses use case material and examples taken from government and the nonprofit world as well as business. In addition, a course in politics is part of the core curriculum. Reflecting these curricular emphases, a substantial portion of the student body comes from and (to a lesser extent) goes to work in the public sector or for not-for-profit organizations. Appropriately, Yale is unique in granting the degree of Master of Public and Private Management (MPPM).

In the interests of simplicity, I use the term *business school* to refer to all educational institutions preparing people for management careers, and refer to students pursuing a graduate professional degree as *MBA students* even though their actual degree might be called Master of Management, Master of Science in Industrial Administration, or Master of Public and Private Management.

History

Although the discipline of psychology spans over a century, the role of psychologists in formal education in business and management began in the late 1950s. Its inception can be traced to a pair of reports prepared for the Ford Foundation and the Carnegie Corporation (Gordon & Howell, 1959; Pierson, 1959). Both reports were highly critical of the existing university programs designed to prepare people for careers in business. At that time, such education was largely conducted at the undergraduate level. Courses included secretarial science, bookkeeping, and office management. Academic standards were low, and the students were among the least able in the entire university. The courses' content was uninformed by the concepts and tools that were being developed in the social sciences. Business school faculty were frequently part-time managers, and less than half of full-time faculty had doctoral degrees. Curriculum content reflected undue emphasis on *institutional knowledge*, that is, revealing existing managerial practices, rather than the applications of methods of science to determine what the practices should be.

Unlike the profession of medicine, which depends heavily on a strong link with the biological sciences, or the profession of engineering, which depends heavily on knowledge from the physical sciences, the profession of management was a "tub on its own bottom," devoid of any substantial infusion of concepts, theories, or methods from the social sciences.

While the Ford and Carnegie reports were being written, I was a PhD student in organizational psychology at the University of Michigan. Michigan was then, and still is, known for its interdisciplinary work and its many research centers. However, the business school was notably absent from these activities. Even though I spent 5 years there—3 as a student and 2 on the faculty—I cannot recall ever entering the business school or even knowing anyone who did!

The Ford Foundation not only characterized the unhappy state of business education, but also set out to rectify it with a major infusion of funds designed to alter significantly the academic and research underpinnings of business education. Between 1954 and 1966, the Ford Foundation awarded more than 35 million dollars primarily to seven selected business schools, of which Carnegie Tech was one. The funds were to be used not just for the benefit of these highly select institutions, but for spreading the "gospel" to other universities around the country. On joining the faculty of Carnegie Tech in 1963, I became involved in planning and implementing three 10-day workshops in organizational behavior to which roughly 30 faculty members were invited. Where possible, faculty were selected in pairs—one from the business school and the other from a social science discipline of a given university.

In addition to these workshops, Ford gave research grants to faculty, sponsored a doctoral dissertation competition, and financed courses and workshops for faculty around the country. In the late 1960s the Ford Foundation extended its reach to management education in Europe. I recall fondly many trips to Brussels to give seminars on research methodology to professors in Louvain, Ghent, Brussels, and Liège.

The landscape of management education today is, in substantial part, a reflection of the vision portrayed in the Ford and Carnegie reports. Many distinguished psychologists moved their base of operations from psychology departments to business schools. In the 1960s, Donald Marquis and Mason Haire left their professorships in psychology at Michigan and Berkeley, respectively, for professorships in what is now called the Sloane School of Management at MIT. Bernard Bass left the psychology department at Louisiana State University for the business school at the University of Pittsburgh; and Lyman Porter left the psychology department at Berkeley for what is now the Graduate School of Management at Irvine.

Today, the relationship between the business school and the psychology department at most universities is very different from the one that existed back in the 1950s. At Michigan, many psychologists hold joint appointments between the business school and the psychology department, and although there are doctoral programs in both educational units, any student with interests in behavioral issues in organizations who did not take advantage of the resources in both places would be shortchanged.

Today, business schools are very different from psychology departments, but the differences are seldom ones of academic standing or quality of scholarship. To be sure, faculty in psychology departments may look askance at the "extravagant facilities" or less rigorous research methods found in the business school, and business school faculty may criticize the "lack of relevance" of much of what is taught and studied in psychology departments. These two parts of the university must be different from one another because they serve different functions in the larger university of which they are a part. The socialization patterns in both are strong and support the prevailing epistemology and values in that setting. Someone pursuing doctoral work in psychology and contemplating a career in a business or management school should be cognizant of such differences and carefully compare them to their own interests and propensities.

The Business School Atmosphere

THE STUDENTS

One of my favorite articles about business schools was written by Herbert Simon, a Nobel prize-winning economist who was also on the faculty at Carnegie. In "The Business School: A Problem in Organizational Design," Simon (1967) articulated the kinds of knowledge requirements for faculty and the organizational challenges for integrating the basic sciences and the world of practice. Rereading the article with today's eyes, after a long hiatus one readily sees that there is almost no consideration given to the education of students as a goal of the organization being designed. The issues addressed in the article are very relevant, but relevant to an organization primarily addressing the pursuit of new knowledge through research.

Simon's article was much more appropriate to the rarified atmosphere erected by the largesse of the 1960s. Today, any business school that ignores students does so at its own peril! In a climate that the Strategic Issues Committee of the American Assembly of Collegiate Schools of Business (AACSB) has termed a matter of "crisis and survival" (AACSB, 1992), business schools have come to recognize their students as "customers." Furthermore, these customers are primarily interested not in the disciplines of psychology, economics, or operations research, but in the professional practice of management. At many business schools, the largest number of customers will be undergraduate majors in business. At the more prestigious universities, the emphasis changes to students pursuing an MBA. They might also be executive MBA's who are pursuing an academic degree while working full time. In such programs the instruction may take place on a weekend or during evenings. In addition, business schools conduct nondegree programs for executives, ranging from short courses on particular topics or longer programs of 4 to, perhaps, 11 weeks in duration.

A common characteristic of all of these students is a principal interest in knowledge that is useful and that can be directly translated, in the short or long run, into managerial practice. They are a demanding lot, and will be insistent on getting "value for their money." Many MBAs will have left high-paying jobs in industry and are likely to be intolerant of education that is not perceived as relevant to their career goals. Many young assistant professors trained in psychology (or for that matter any academic discipline) have had a difficult time adapting to teaching students who are less interested in the faculties' academic credentials than in their general knowledge and practical experience.

On the positive side, management students in today's universities tend to be very culturally diverse and thus bring to the learning process a vast variety of backgrounds and work experiences. Individually and collectively, they have broad practical experience and a high degree of social and political awareness. Management education can provide a unique forum for testing theoretical ideas against a world of practical experience.

I recall my own difficulties in making a transition from teaching in the psychology department to teaching in Carnegie Mellon's Graduate School of Industrial Administration. Having taught introductory psychology and graduate courses in motivation and social psychology, I had lots of lectures of which I was very proud. However, I became painfully aware of the fact that the instructional methods and the content that had served me so well in teaching undergraduates and doctoral students were perceived as largely irrelevant and, by some of the master's students that I encountered there, as "intellectual masturbation." I don't mean to denigrate these populations. They were at least as bright as the best of the undergraduates and doctoral students that I had encountered at University of Pennsylvania, but appropriately, their interests were career interests.

How does one adapt to this new and demanding clientele? Fortunately, I had the benefit of a role model—specifically, Harold Leavitt—with whom I cotaught in my early years and from whom I learned the importance of understanding the managerial focus of my new constituents. I learned, particularly from Leavitt, the importance of *experiential learning.* By this term, I refer to learning experiences, such as role playing, films, simulations, cases, and the like, that directly involve students in acting out or thinking about how to deal with challenging managerial issues. The essence of such methods is that they were inductive rather than deductive. They started with specific events observable by all and moved from there to theory or concepts. In that way, students could see the concepts as useful in making sense of their immediate experience in a case or simulation and generalize from it to a broader range of situations.

I recall talking to a colleague, an economist, whose teaching evaluations had shown a tremendous increase in his effectiveness in the classroom over the last year. I asked him what had brought about this change. He replied that for his first 3 or 4 years of teaching, whenever he walked into a classroom, he mentally carried with him his dissertation advisor, and his lectures were designed to meet the critical demands and high academic standards of this person. His remarkable improvement came when he realized that he no longer had to please his mentor, and that the customer was, in fact, in front of him in the classroom!

The challenges of teaching students in a business school are perhaps greater than those found in other professional schools. The principal reason for this is that in most other schools the faculty have been trained, or in many cases practice, in their professions. Most faculty in medical schools are MDs. Most faculty in law schools have been trained as lawyers. Most faculty in schools of architecture are architects, and so on. However, currently in schools of business or management, many faculty members have been trained in social science disciplines. They are economists or mathematicians or statisticians or psychologists or sociologists. Others have done their doctoral work in fields like finance, marketing, or accounting. There are relatively few with MBA degrees, and as a consequence, faculty find it more difficult to understand the perspective that their students bring into the classroom.

There are ways to overcome this problem. Reading the *Wall Street Journal, Business Week,* or *Fortune* may be as important to your teaching effectiveness as reading the *Journal of Applied Psychology.*

THE COURSES

Naturally, the courses that a psychologist working in a business school would be expected to teach vary within the school and with the particular interests of the psychologist. In smaller schools, you are more likely to be expected to teach broad courses on topics such as principles of management, which would embrace things that you might have learned from psychology but also cover other disciplines at a very general level. More commonly, you might be expected to teach a course that could be entitled, "An Introduction to Organizational Behavior." As I write this, I'm looking out over my bookshelf, and I can spot at least a dozen textbooks that are frequently used in courses of this kind. They include material on topics such as perception, learning, motivation, and decision-making, which are, of course, familiar to psychologists. They also include chapters on groups, group dynamics, and leadership, which are perhaps more familiar to those trained in social psychology. In addition, they may include chapters on organizational change, careers in organizations, and organization theory, which will be somewhat less familiar to psychologists, but more familiar to those trained in sociology.

Advanced courses typically expand on the topics within the core courses. It is very common to find a course on interpersonal skills. Courses on managing organizational change and organization theory are also commonplace. Perhaps less common may be courses on race and gender in organizations, power and influence in organizations, and leadership.

Psychologists are also frequently involved in the teaching of courses on negotiations, a field that they share with game theorists and economists. They are also involved in teaching courses on the management of human resources. *Human resources* is a contemporary term for what used to be called *personnel,* and it, too, is a field in which economists, particularly labor economists, stake some claim.

It should be apparent from these examples that courses are not likely to correspond perfectly with those taught in a psychology department. You're unlikely to find courses labeled "Individual Differences," "Tests in Measurements," "Research Methods," "Cognitive Processes," or "Learning." Rather, courses correspond to practical challenges faced by managers in organizations.

YOUR COLLEAGUES

A former dean of mine once wrote that the field of management education can be compared to a three-legged stool. The legs of the stool correspond to the three academic disciplines on which the practice of management is based: economics, management science, and the behavioral sciences, including psychology and sociology. These three fields, or sets of disciplines, provide many of the concepts and the tools on which management education and practice rest. The top of the stool represents the functional areas of management. Among the most important functional areas are marketing, production or operations, finance, accounting, and human resources. You are likely to find many of your academic colleagues coming from and teaching in the areas represented by the legs of the stool. They might be economists, management scientists, and either psychologists or sociologists. Others might be more appropriately represented by the top of the stool. They might have received their training in marketing, finance, production, accounting, or human resources management. This plethora of academic disciplines and areas of inquiry represents a substantial challenge to a young psychologist entering into the field of management education. If your experience is at all close to mine, you will find people talking in very strange languages that are not obviously related to your own.

I recall vividly my own experience on arriving at Carnegie Tech and being assigned an office which was proximate to four others. One was occupied by someone who had been trained in applied mathematics and was interested in corporate strategy. In the second was a professor who had been trained in marketing. In the third was a political scientist, and in the fourth was an economist. My first reaction, which may or may not be yours, was to close my door and yearn for the days in which I was surrounded by psychologists who spoke the same language. It probably took 6 months or so before I ventured out of my office in a significant way and discovered that it was possible to get beyond the technical terminology, and once that was done, it was usually possible to find areas of common interests and shared intellectual inquiry. If this can be achieved, it can be tremendously rewarding, not just to the individuals, but also to the academic disciplines and the practice of management.

Let me return for a moment to the metaphor of the stool. If I were to revise the metaphor, I would add another level of the stool that is cross-functional in nature. It would correspond not with the subfunctions of management such as marketing and human resources, but to those areas of managerial activity that are intended to represent a synthesis of managerial functions. They include things such as general management, business strategy, and the management of change. These represent areas of increasing importance to managerial education, but do not correspond to fields in which most people are currently trained. They are sometimes taught by former businesspersons, or by scholars in one or more of the academic disciplines who are at a slightly more advanced stage of their careers.

Career Paths

The structure of positions in a business school is not different from that typically found in academic departments in the arts and sciences. For those with a PhD, the entry-level position is assistant professor. Promotion to associate professor for those who meet the institution's standards for promotion would typically occur after 6 years. The final step on the promotional ladder is professor, which typically follows several years of successful performance as an associate professor.

Moving up the promotional ladder is dependent on a thorough review of performance. Such reviews begin with a committee appointed within the department or, in smaller schools without a departmental structure, within the school. The committee is likely to be made up of faculty members at or above the level to which promotion is being considered. The committee reads your research publications, assesses the evidence of your teaching effectiveness, and evaluates the quality of your citizenship within the school, the university, and the broader academic community. The relative weights placed on these three factors vary across universities. Major research universities such as Harvard, Stanford, Chicago, and MIT place a much heavier emphasis on research than do teaching colleges such as Babson College in Wellesley, Massachusetts.

Some may disagree, but my experience has been that more attention is paid to teaching in business schools than in psychology departments. Particularly during the last decade, competition among business schools for the best students and for higher rankings in surveys such as that conducted by *Business Week* has resulted in greater attention to teaching quality among faculty.

Tenure may be granted at any of the three steps on the promotional ladder. Most frequently, it is granted at the associate professor level, but a school may have associate professors with and without tenure. Practices vary, and I even have known of tenured assistant professors and have occasionally heard of professors who were brought in from the outside without the immediate promise of tenure. In short, the granting of tenure is highly, but not perfectly, correlated with one's standing on the promotional ladder.

Internal committees are seldom, if ever, decision-making bodies. They make recommendations to be voted on by the faculty of the school at or above the level to which promotion is being decided. When promotion involves tenure or professorship, and often in promotions at lower levels, a committee solicits views from distinguished scholars in the candidate's field, whose letters attest to the impact of the person's scholarship outside the institution. Obviously, such letters are more likely to be informative about the quality of the candidate's research than about his or her teaching or citizenship.

In many educational institutions, the promotional review does not end with the business school. The ultimate decision may be made by the university president, the provost, or a university committee set up for this purpose. In rare instances, candidates who have passed all of the hurdles within the business school are turned down at this higher level.

My description of the multiple steps on the ladder and multiple hurdles in each review may suggest that teaching in a business school, or indeed academia in general, constitutes a very uncertain and hazardous career path. The probability of successfully climbing the ladder obviously varies with your talent and commitment, and depends also on the nature of the institution. For example, public universities have more certain promotional ladders than do the private Ivy League schools. The latter are highly protective of tenure, and successful candidates for tenure must demonstrate that they are better suited to the position than all others in their field who might be available for the position.

The uncertainty of promotional ladders bears comparison with the uncertainty that has crept into the careers of managers in the private sector over the last 10 or 15 years. It is no longer the case that someone who begins a career with IBM or General Electric can expect to end his or her career with that organization. As organizations downsize and reengineer themselves, managers shift from company to company and sector to sector. Similarly, faculty move from one business school to another and pursue new challenges, sometimes voluntarily and sometimes because they were denied a promotion. The major difference lies in the source of the career uncertainties. In the private sector, uncertainty results from economic factors such as mergers, restructurings, and the like. In universities, the origin often resides in colleagues' judgements of relative merit. If I work for AT&T and I am laid off, the cause probably lies in an economic reality. I am one of 5,000 or 30,000 who receive pink slips in order to reduce costs and make the business more competitive. On the other hand, if I work for the X Business School, am denied tenure, and am obliged to seek employment elsewhere, it involves a much more explicit judgement by others on my relative worth. Because such judgements are inevitably subjective, the processes are inherently more political.

Financial Rewards

It is a fact of life that psychologists in business schools get paid more than their counterparts in psychology departments. I would estimate the difference to be about 25 to 30 percent, and that difference remains relatively stable over the academic career.

It is also likely that as a psychologist, you would be paid less than a faculty member at a comparable stages in a career in finance or accounting. Academic salaries, like salaries in other fields, reflect market forces of supply and demand.

Salaries other than those for faculty who hold administrative positions are for 9 months. You can get compensated for the summer months (ie., get *summer money*) through extra teaching or research funded either internally or through external grants or contracts. Most schools finance travel expenses to professional meetings, particularly when you are "on the program," that is, presenting a paper or performing some administrative function. Another practice that is increasing in popularity is providing each faculty member with a standard budget to be used at the faculty member's discretion for professional expenses, including books, travel, society memberships, computers, and so on.

Business schools also allow faculty to use up to one day per week for outside consulting. Although faculty at all levels on the academic ladder have this benefit, those at more senior levels are likely to take advantage of it. Junior faculty find that they need all of their time to begin their research program and are less likely to have made the contacts necessary for consulting.

Professional Associations

A critical component of any academic career is membership in one or more professional associations. These organizations sponsor annual meetings in which colleagues present papers, share experiences, and sometimes share the latest gossip. They also reward academic and professional achievements.

Psychologists tend to join either or both of the American Psychological Association (APA) and the American Psychological Society. More directly relevant to the research and professional interests of psychologists in business schools is the Society of Industrial and Organizational Psychology (SIOP). This organization has come a long way in the last 2 decades. It was originally the Division of Industrial Psychology of the APA. "Organizational Psychology" was added to its name in the late 1970s, and a few years later it was incorporated as an independent society. At this time it has about 3,000 members and holds an annual meeting in April of each year.

SIOP is increasingly addressing managerial issues in its professional meetings, but it is much less likely to be a source of interdisciplinary exchange around management concerns than the Academy of Management. The Academy is much larger than SIOP, with 9,000 members, including 3,000 in the Organizational Behavior (OB) division. In addition to the OB division, there are divisions of organizational theory, organizational development, conflict management, business policy, marketing, and the like. SIOP also has an annual meeting in August. Furthermore, there are regional academies of management (Eastern, Western, Southwestern, etc.), each of which holds its own meeting.

Other organizations of potential interest, all of which hold annual meetings, are the Organizational Behavior Teaching Society, the Decision Sciences Institute, and the Institute of Management Science.

Advantages and Disadvantages

I have already alluded in previous sections to many advantages of a career in the business school for a psychologist. I have talked about the financial compensation, which is good, particularly in comparison with other parts of academia. I have also addressed the opportunities for consulting, which is valuable not just for its economic return, but also for enriching one's breadth of experience through exposure to real-world problems. I have referred, somewhat indirectly, to the fact that in the academic world one is somewhat insulated from the vagaries of the economy. To these substantial benefits I should add that teaching in a business school is likely to present rewarding opportunities for foreign travel. Many business schools have alliances with universities in Europe, Asia, or Latin America, and there are substantial opportunities, for those who are interested, to teach in other countries. On the same theme, some universities conduct executive programs or MBA programs in other countries, using facilities that either are their own or are rented from agencies in those countries.

One benefit that deserves special attention is the amount of freedom that faculty members enjoy—not just in business schools, but in all parts of academia. You will never be asked to punch a time clock, and as long as you meet your teaching obligations, attend faculty meetings, make yourself available to meet with students (usually during set office hours), and meet other committee obligations, you're free to work at home and schedule your life around your own priorities. In many institutions no one will question your decision to do large amounts of work at home, should that be your preference. The significance of this freedom for meeting child care obligations with a dual-career family should be apparent.

I should point out that this freedom is a two-edged sword. No one will tell you what to do until it is too late. You must be a disciplined self-starter, or else you will find yourself at the end of your contract without having met the promotional standards in your institutions. The moral is clear: Learn from your colleagues what it takes to climb the promotional ladder, assuming that this is in fact your goal. Set specific objectives for each time period of your contract, and focus on these objectives. Don't get sidetracked by the many potential distractions of the university until you are sure that you have more than met the standards to which you will be held accountable.

Another source of potential concern for a psychologist in a business school is the difficulty in "replicating oneself." Although doctoral programs exist in many business schools—certainly in those at large or prestigious universities—they don't produce psychologists. They are likely to produce PhDs in management, industrial administration, human resources management, or organizational behavior. But they do not train future professors of industrial or organizational psychology. Furthermore, these doctoral programs are likely to play a smaller role in your life than would be the case if you were teaching in the psychology department. Your primary responsibility is to educate students interested in management, not professionals in your own discipline. Accordingly, opportunities to teach doctoral seminars may be less abundant in business schools than in psychology departments.

Another frequent complaint that I hear from psychologists in business schools is the political bent of faculty who staff these institutions. However, intergroup conflict can certainly be found in any academic department. In psychology departments one can find experimental psychologists "at war" with the clinicians, physiological psychologists looking down on their nonphysiological brethren, and so on. Some psychology departments manage, with the aid of skilled leadership, to minimize or even avoid such conflicts. But unfortunately, not all institutions have been successful in this regard.

It is my view that the administrative challenges are even greater in business schools. It is all too common to find faculty members bonding with their parent academic discipline in the competition for resources. Thus, faculty in economics and finance have been known to make life difficult for those in organizational behavior, and vice versa. Such forces are likely to be maximized when disciplines or functional areas find that they can expand only at the expense of other disciplines or functional areas. Hopefully, the fairly recent trends for business schools to compete with one another for *Business Week* rankings, students, and in some cases survival as an institution will result in more cooperative behavior and awareness of shared goals and responsibilities within the department.

A final disadvantage (which may, in fact, not be a disadvantage at all!) is that in a business school you are likely to experience significant changes in your identity away from that of psychologist toward that of a scholar with broad interests in the potential contribution of the social sciences to management. The interdisciplinary and multidisciplinary endeavors that are frequently discouraged within psychology departments are encouraged and rewarded in business schools. I have observed countless young scholars gradually shifting their academic interests away from the theoretically driven to the problem driven, and from being psychologically relevant to being relevant to the world of managerial practice. So if you move into a business school, be prepared to be socialized and to have your interests changed.

Attributes Needed for Entry

I began this chapter noting the role of the Ford Foundation in promoting the movement of eminent psychologists and other social scientists into business schools. Naturally, such individuals need access to PhD students to further their own research programs. The predictable result was the establishment of PhD programs totally within the business school. Now newly minted PhDs from psychology departments seeking to enter a business school find themselves competing with their counterparts who were trained in business schools for entry-level positions.

More than a decade ago, Miner (1984) noted that the most valid and most useful theories of behavior in organizations have been authored by psychologists and have involved the process of motivation. However, Miner also expressed doubt that psychology would continue to be the influential discipline that it had been in the past:

> Yet, by its nature, this source cannot be relied upon to produce the successful theories of the field in the future. There are too many areas that need attention, areas in which psychologists have not done as well as with motivation. . . . In short, the legacy of the Gordon and Howell and Pierson reports is drying up. It

cannot be relied upon to fuel the organizational theories of the future. (1984, p. 303.)

Miner recommended the establishment of doctoral programs in *organizational science*. Although that term has not "caught on" as much as the terms *organization theory* and *organizational behavior*, his recommendation is reflected in many high-quality PhD programs that exist in business schools. However, even today, PhD students trained in psychology tend to be better trained in the quantitative aspects of research design and in statistics. They also have the advantage of a fairly coherent academic discipline, with a shared language and terminology that they can bring to bear on problems in many different institutional settings.

PhD students trained in psychology may also have certain disadvantages. They may be totally unprepared for life in a business school and for the teaching responsibilities which they will be expected to pursue. Over the years, I have quickly passed over the applications of many young PhDs or "to-be-PhDs" who looked as though they were capable of outstanding work in experimental psychology, cognitive psychology, or even industrial psychology, but who appeared to have no conception of what life in a business school would be like.

In reviewing applications from psychologists, I look for membership in the Academy of Management and for evidence that the candidate has taken courses in or had contact with professors or students in the business school. Of course, I look for a good background in psychology—particularly social psychology, because that field is more closely linked to the micro aspects of organizational behavior. It is helpful if the training in social psychology is accompanied by demonstrated research interests in organizational behavior, lest the candidate be perceived as unemployable in a psychology department and anxious to fit him- or herself into a business school. Probably the best preparation available within a psychology department for life in a business school can be found in a good program in industrial/organizational psychology with a strong emphasis on social and organizational psychology. Extensive training in industrial psychology, that is, job analysis, job evaluation, personnel selection, merit rating, and so on, is not, for me, a strong positive indicator. Such training would be conducive to teaching a small part of a course in human resources management, but would be seen as too technical and too specialized to interest many students of management.

Among the other attributes that are helpful in getting you a job at a good institution in the first place is some evidence in your academic vita of research activity prior to the PhD. This could take the form of published papers, but failing that, could include papers that have been submitted for publication that would be available to be read by the selection committee. Furthermore, the content of the papers should manifest an interest in exploring the connections between the discipline of psychology and problems of organizations and management. The search committee would also look for enthusiastic letters from professors with whom you have worked. It is always helpful if the endorsers are known to members of the selection committee, which typically means that they have a visible research productivity record themselves. The committee is also likely to look for evidence of your success in teaching, and because some universities do not permit teaching by nonfaculty members, it may be necessary for them to rely on your experience as a teaching assistant. It would also be helpful to your case if you had presented papers at academic conferences and, even better, that those papers had received some kind of award or acknowledgment within the profession.

Of course, the nature of the papers themselves is going to have a great deal of weight in the decision. If your record is otherwise attractive, you can expect that your papers—those that have been submitted as part of your application—will be critically read by members of the committee, who in turn will discuss the suitability of your candidacy. Typically, the selection committee will choose a short list of three to five candidates who will be invited to come to the university and be interviewed. As part of the interviewing process, you will be asked to give what is often called, colloquially, "a job talk." This is approximately a 1-hour talk, essentially on the subject matter of your doctoral research, that you will be asked to give before the faculty in the host institution. It is a very critical step in the process and should not be taken lightly. It is a good idea to rehearse your job talk well before giving it and to conduct a dress rehearsal before members of your own faculty who can help you to improve. If you are invited to several institutions, it is always useful to put those in which you are most interested toward the end of the process, so that you have had some practice before you make your presentations there.

You should be aware of the fact that the audience for your job talk may not be restricted to people in your own discipline. You may get questions from economists, from management scientists, and from those in functional areas whose perspectives and whose language and terminology may be quite different from your own. It is always helpful if your topic is, or can be made to be, relevant to some real-world issue, and not be solely driven by a problem that would be understood and seem to be relevant exclusively by those in academia. Thus, a problem-centered focus is really very helpful to establishing your suitability for a position in a business school.

Concluding Thoughts

The motivation for selecting a career does, and indeed should, rest not only on the intrinsic properties of the career but also on the broader social context to which that career contributes. Although it is true that business education has rarely been the most glamorous part of the academic world, events of the last decade have brought it closer to center stage in public consciousness. America's position as the world economic leader has been transformed into that of the world's largest debtor nation. *Cost cutting, downsizing,* and *reengineering* have become buzzwords reflecting management's attempts to compete efficiently in the new global marketplace. The keys to successful competition will be well-trained managers and the highly effective educational institutions that produce them.

I believe strongly that the job of educating managers cannot be left to the economists alone. Psychology and the other behavioral sciences have much to contribute to understanding the determinants of productivity (Campbell, Campbell & Associates, 1988). Such issues as the sources of the motivation to work, the dynamics of effective leadership, and the bases of teamwork and collaboration are both important to productivity and relevant to the conceptual and methodological lens of psychology. They represent the kinds of topics to which psychologists can make important contributions that, at the same time, will strengthen the underlying discipline (Vroom, 1983).

From a teaching standpoint, psychology has much to contribute to the education of managers. Studies of critical management skills (Margerison & Kakabadse, 1984) show that listening, managing conflict, and giving effective feedback rank very high in importance to success. These skills are eminently teachable, and the methods for doing so are well known and easily mastered by those with a background in psychology.

From my perspective, teaching in a business school is a noble profession—one filled with personal rewards and only a modicum of frustration—and one through which one's research and teaching can make organizations more productive and more satisfying places to work.

References

American Assembly of Collegiate Schools of Business. (1992).*Crisis and survival: A special report of the strategic issues committee* [Pamphlet]. St. Louis, MO: Author.

Campbell, J. P., Campbell, R. J., & Associates. (1988). *Productivity in organizations: New perspectives from industrial and organizational psychology*. San Francisco: Jossey Bass.

Gordon, R. A., & Howell, J. E. (1959). *Higher education for business*. New York: Columbia University Press.

Margerison, C., & Kakabadse, A. (1984). *How American chief executives succeed*. New York: AMA Publications.

Miner, J. B. (1984). The validity and usefulness of theories in an emerging organizational science. *Academy of Management Review, 9*, 296–306.

Pierson, Frank C. (1959). *The education of American businessmen*. New York: McGraw-Hill.

Simon, H. A. (1967). The business school: A problem in organizational design. *Journal of Management Studies, 4*, 1–16.

Vroom, V. H. (1983). "On advancing organizational psychology as a science." In R. A. Katzell (Chair), *Advancing industrial/organizational psychology as a science*. Symposium conducted at the annual meeting of the American Psychological Association, Anaheim, California.

II | CAREERS IN CLINICAL, COUNSELING, AND COMMUNITY PSYCHOLOGY

Jeffrey Young and Marjorie E. Weishaar

Psychologists in Private Practice

4

The Nature of Private Practice

INTRODUCTION AND DEFINITION

n this chapter we focus on private practice as a career for psychologists. Private practice is a multifaceted career that allows a great deal of autonomy and flexibility, but requires both clinical acumen and entrepreneurial skills. We discuss the range of professional services psychologists offer in private practice, the variety of work settings in which they function, how psychologists market their practices, and

Jeffrey Young, PhD, is founder and director of the Cognitive Therapy Centers of New York and Connecticut. He is also an adjunct faculty member in the Department of Psychiatry at Columbia University College of Physicians and Surgeons. Dr. Young received his undergraduate training at Yale University and his doctoral degree at the University of Pennsylvania.

Marjorie E. Weishaar is clinical associate professor of psychiatry and human behavior at Brown University School of Medicine. She received her PhD in counseling from the Pennsylvania State University. She did a clinical psychology internship at Brown and completed two postdoctoral fellowships. She has been in full-time private practice for 12 years.

The authors gratefully acknowledge the help of the following organizations and individuals in gathering information: the American Psychological Association Research Department and Practice Directorate, the Association of State Provincial Psychology Boards, Matthew M. Clark, PhD, Jayne Kurkjian, PhD, and John P. Wincze, PhD.

some of the additional responsibilities beyond clinical care. We also present the education and training requirements and personal attributes desirable for establishing and maintaining a private practice. Finally, we explore the advantages and disadvantages of pursuing this career path, including future trends in mental health care that will affect the outlook for private practice.

We define *private practice* as self-employment: Salary, wages, and fringe benefits are not provided by an employer. Psychologists in private practice typically generate their income by providing a combination of services (e.g., psychotherapy, testing, consultation), usually on a *fee-for-service* basis (i.e., they receive separate compensation for each service they provide, rather than a salary for working a set number of hours). Private practitioners may employ other professionals or paraprofessionals, or they may serve as *independent contractors* for other employers (i.e., they receive a relatively small percentage of their income from any single employer, who pays them for services provided on a part-time basis, without fringe benefits). Some psychologists have a part-time private practice, often in combination with other employment that is salaried. For example, some academic psychologists, or those employed by a hospital, also see clients in part-time private practice.

Private practice is a popular option for psychologists. Private or group practice was the most frequent institutional affiliation identified in recent surveys by both doctor-of-psychology (PsyD) respondents (40%) and PhD clinical psychologists (35%) (Hershey, Kopplin, & Cornell, 1991). (We discuss later the differences between these academic degrees.)

PROFESSIONAL SERVICES PROVIDED BY PRIVATE PRACTITIONERS

Psychotherapy

Private practice blends several types of work. However, psychotherapy is usually the major component. Psychotherapy can include individual therapy with adults, adolescents, or children; couples therapy; family therapy; or group therapy.

Hershey et al. (1991) report that PsyD psychologists in private practice spend 32% of their time providing individual psychotherapy; 17% of their time is distributed across group therapy, marital and family therapy, and behavior modification. For PhD psychologists, 35% of their time is spent in direct intervention activities (Norcross, Prochaska, & Gallagher, 1989a, 1989b).

A survey of 741 psychologists in private practice conducted by *Psychotherapy Finances* found that 97% provide individual therapy and 42% provide group therapy ("Fee, Practice and Managed Care survey," 1995). Group therapy can be time limited and focused (e.g., a 10-week assertiveness training group), or more open ended and broad (e.g., an ongoing group over several years for clients with interpersonal difficulties).

Psychological Testing

Psychological testing continues to be a major component of private practice. Although the percentage of psychologists and counselors in private practice who offer specialized testing has decreased in the past 10 years, 67% of them provide some testing ("Fee," 1995). Psychological tests include personality inventories, neuropsychological tests, intelligence tests, and vocational tests. Tests may be administered face to face by a psychologist (e.g., projective or individual intelligence tests) or may be self-administered and scored by computer (e.g., personality or career interest inventories).

Psychologists in private practice may also specialize in working with particular populations and clinical problems. Some of these are described subsequently.

Behavioral Medicine and Health Psychology

Behavioral medicine is the interdisciplinary field concerned with the integration of behavioral and biomedical science with techniques relevant to health and illness, and the application of this knowledge to prevention, diagnosis, treatment, and rehabilitation (Schwartz & Weiss, 1978). *Health psychology* is the application of psychology to the promotion of health, the prevention and treatment of illness, the identification of etiologic and diagnostic correlates of health and illness, and the analysis and improvement of the health care system and health policy formation (American Psychological Association, 1981).

Health psychologists work in the field of behavioral medicine. They use a variety of techniques, including biofeedback and hypnotherapy, to help clients manage pain, chronic illness, acute conditions, and surgical procedures. Psychoeducation also plays a large role in health psychology. For example, smoking cessation and behavioral weight control groups combine psychoeducation with psychological interventions. In addition, interest in pain control has grown considerably in the past few years, so that now 25% of psychologists in private practice offer some form of pain control program, and 31% work with chronic illness ("Fee," 1995).

Substance Abuse

Substance abuse is treated by 17% of psychologists in private practice ("Fee," 1995). This specialization is expected to be in increasing demand because of the high prevalence of addictive disorders in the general population and, especially, among psychiatric patients. Some aspects of the work, like detoxification, are more conducive to hospital settings than to private practice. However, private practitioners do conduct substance abuse screenings, provide interventions to motivate a client to acknowledge a substance abuse problem, conduct assessments of the nature and extent of the abuse, and assign clients (through "dispositioning") to the appropriate level of care (e.g., detoxification, structured rehabilitation). The psychologist also coaches the client through health care insurance requirements and provides guidance in maneuvering through the health care system. The independent practitioner may also work with a client's primary health care provider or psychiatrist to make sure that addictive medications are not prescribed to the client and to collaborate on a treatment plan.

Substance abusers who are stable in their sobriety are usually more appropriate for private practice treatment. The psychologist can help provide coping skills and prevent relapse. An additional focus is on physical wellness: nutrition, exercise, sleep, hygiene, and informing the primary care provider about substance abuse so that medical treatment does not jeopardize abstinence. Finally, the psychologist frequently works with a client's significant others. They may serve as sources of corroboration of the client's self-reported compliance, as codependents who reinforce the client's maladaptive behavior, or as valuable adjuncts to the therapy. Moreover, family and close friends often need psychological assistance themselves in dealing with the issues raised by the client's addiction.

Licensed psychologists do not need any additional certification to specialize in substance abuse. Certification as a chemical dependency professional is considered a paraprofessional certification. Training in substance abuse can begin in graduate school through research and training in an addictions lab. Students may then choose an internship that offers a substance abuse rotation to provide more specialized clinical training.

Divorce Mediation

Divorce mediation is directed at helping couples separate amicably, reach agreement on the distribution of money and property, and agree on child custody arrangements, without engaging in the traditional legal adversarial process.

Wellness Therapy

Wellness therapy does not focus on specific physical or psychological pathology, but views the person holistically. The focus is not on deficits, but on mind–body interactions and on personal growth through lifestyle changes. Such changes might include attention to diet and exercise, stress reduction, meditation, and enhancement of self-expression.

Sports Psychology

Sports psychologists help athletes prepare psychologically for training and competition. They help with concentration, motivation, attitude, and psychological readiness for athletic performance. Sports psychologists also deal with stress management and health issues.

Sexual Dysfunction

Sexual dysfunction is an area of specialization in which psychologists work with individuals and couples to resolve sexual difficulties. Some sex therapists also work with individuals with gender disorders and with sexual offenders. Clients with sexual dysfunctions are usually referred by urologists, obstetricians, gynecologists, internists, or other therapists, so that consultation with other professionals is frequent. Sex therapists also consult with schools on sex education programs or on how to deal with students with sexual problems or gender disorders. They also consult with residential treatment centers and schools for the developmentally disabled.

Sex therapists who treat sexual offenders often testify in court. Most of their referrals come from the courts or from the families of offenders. Additional certification for treating sexual offenders is not required for licensed psychologists, although the American Association of Sex Educators, Counselors, and Therapists offers certification.

Career and Educational Consulting

Career and educational consulting is usually practiced by counseling or educational psychologists who have received specialized graduate training. This type of practice includes interest and aptitude testing, vocational guidance, and job search strategies. Educational specialists also assess learning disabilities. Psychologists who specialize in career or educational counseling may consult with schools and businesses.

Forensic Work

Forensic psychologists emphasize diagnosis, evaluation, treatment, and testimony regarding criminal behavior, psychopathology, and the law. They provide expert testimony, psychological assessment, and consultation for law firms, courts, corporations, insurance companies, and government agencies. Forensic work involves such criminal and legal issues as evaluating insanity; judging competency to stand trial; assisting with jury selection, trial strategy, and eyewitness testimony; preparing for cross-examination; performing psychological autopsies; and assessing dangerousness. Forensic psychologists may also consult or testify in custody cases and in disability evaluations.

Supervision

Psychologists in private practice may supervise and train other therapists who wish to develop particular therapeutic skills or learn a new treatment modality. This can occur in solo practice, group practice, or one's own training center. Practitioners also provide consultation to other therapists on an as-needed basis to offer a second opinion about a diagnosis, respond to a specific assessment question, help resolve an issue in a therapeutic relationship, or recommend an alternative treatment intervention.

Supervision and training may also take place out of the office. Practitioners may provide ongoing supervision to the staff at a community mental health center or hospital, either on a contractual or fee-for-service basis. Such consulting arrangements are discussed in more detail subsequently.

Media Work

Psychologists may write articles or columns for newspapers, magazines, or professional newsletters in which they discuss psychological topics of general concern or those related to a current event. Some psychologists also write self-help books, or they may appear on television and radio talk shows to offer general advice and commentary or to respond to questions from the audience.

Workshops and Lectures

Many private practitioners offer lectures and workshops on innovative techniques and clinical problems to other professionals. These are often sponsored by a university, hospital, or professional organization. Of the PsyDs surveyed in the Hershey et al. (1991) study, 76% had conducted a professional workshop, 42% of which were national or regional workshops .

Psychologists in practice also present lectures and workshops to the public. These can be sponsored by the practice itself or cosponsored by a church or civic organization. Lectures might be on a current "hot topic" like attention-deficit/hyperactivity disorder, or on a more every-day topic such as time management.

Research and Publishing: The Scientist–Practitioner Model

The scientist–practitioner model of psychology encourages combining research and practice in a number of ways. Clinicians in private prac-tice may participate in research by being consultants on grants directed' by others. The clinician might help design a study, train or supervise therapists in a treatment outcome study, or rate therapy tapes to ensure adherence to treatment protocol. This kind of research is usu-ally administered by an academic institution or hospital.

Psychologists in practice also write professional articles, books, and book chapters. They may author scholarly articles for journals or may write practical books for clinicians. The use of scientific thinking in clinical work, the application of demonstrably efficacious treatments, and the awareness of methodological errors in both research and prac-tice all provide bridges between science and practice (Stricker & Trierweiler, 1995). Research and publishing help develop the scien-tist–practitioner by sharpening these skills.

Clinical psychologists with PhDs are more likely than PsyD hold-ers to have academic positions and, accordingly, more likely to have published a paper or article. According to survey data (Hershey et al., 1991), 87% of the PhDs had published, compared with 34% of the PsyDs. A larger proportion of PhDs had presented a paper at profes-sional meetings compared with PsyDs (86% compared with 40%).

EMPLOYMENT SETTINGS FOR PRIVATE PRACTICE

Self-employed psychologists may operate a solo practice, be a partner or owner of a group practice, serve as an independent contractor to a group practice, or consult with other institutions as a supervisor or by providing direct fee-for-service work.

According to Hershey et al. (1991), 68% of PsyD clinical psychol-ogists surveyed were in private practice; 40% of them worked full time and 28% part time (for an average of 11 hours per week). Forty-two percent of the PhD clinical psychologists surveyed by Norcross et al. (1989a) were engaged in part-time practice.

Solo Practice

Solo practice is the most common setting for psychologists in private practice; ("Fee," 1995). Holders of the PsyD degree tend to work for clinical institutions and agencies earlier in their careers and enter private or solo practice after 5 to 10 years of postdoctoral experience (Hershey et al., 1991). It also appears that fewer PsyD graduates since 1980 are identifying private practice as their primary affiliation, compared with those who graduated prior to 1980. There may be movement away from solo private practice into either larger group practices or HMO-type settings (see this chapter's section on HMOs and managed care). In contrast, Stedman, Neff, and Morrow (1995) noted that PhD clinical psychologists trained after 1980 went into private practice more rapidly than those trained prior to 1980.

Group Practice

Group practice may consist of several therapist-partners or of a therapist in partnership with physician. A survey of therapists (including marriage and family therapists, social workers, and psychiatrists, in addtion to psychologists) reported that most groups are fairly small, with an average of 10 professionals and 5 support personnel ("Fee," 1995). Groups tend to offer more services than solo practitioners; 90% have services for children, adolescents, and families. Group practices report fewer sessions per client and a greater percentage of income from third-party reimbursement than do solo practitioners ("Fee," 1995).

Independent Contractor or Consultant

Psychologists may also be independent contractors for medical group practices (e.g., work there for a day a week) or work for such a practice on a fee-for-service basis.

Direct service or supervision of staff may also be provided on a consulting basis to schools, hospitals, business organizations, and prisons. Group practices are more likely than solo practitioners to contract with companies, but they have an equal chance of contracting with school systems ("Fee," 1995).

In hospital settings (inpatient, intensive outpatient, and partial hospital), private practitioners may train or supervise staff in new therapeutic approaches or solve a therapeutic problem on an individual case. For example, second author Dr. Weishaar served as a consultant to several mental health centers in her state that were adopting short-term models of psychotherapy. In prison settings, psychologists often conduct assessments. In business settings, psychological consultants may conduct evaluations of work-site needs; offer workshops on interpersonal skills, leadership, or stress management; or assist with downsizing and job displacement.

OTHER RESPONSIBILITIES IN PRIVATE PRACTICE

In addition to providing professional services, psychologists in private practice must take on a variety of other responsibilities. An increasing portion of the psychologist's day is spent performing administrative duties as a result of the proliferation of managed care health insurance systems. Managed care refers to the services of third-party "middlemen" hired by corporations, including insurance companies, to control health care costs. Managed care companies attempt to control costs by limiting care. To accomplish this, they require extensive documentation, reports, and phone conversations with health care providers to justify additional treatment sessions for individual clients.

A recent survey found that managed care and other third-party programs account for 60% of the income of private practice psychologists ("Fee," 1995). Accordingly, more time is now spent filling out insurance forms and outpatient treatment reports. In addition, practitioners are devoting time to the collection of outcome data to demonstrate their effectiveness to managed care companies. Billing and collecting, keeping client records and notes, and responding to requests for records or treatment summaries are other administrative duties.

Maintaining relationships with third-party delivery systems occupies time to varying degrees, depending on which programs the practitioner participates in. Almost all clinicians in practice deal with traditional private insurers. Some psychologists are also involved with other programs, such as employee assistance programs (EAPs) sponsored by clients' employers. EAPs originally developed to treat substance abuse but now authorize treatment for a wide range of problems affecting workers and their families. According to the practice survey conducted by *Psychotherapy Finances* ("Practice Issues," 1995), 33% of psychologists provide EAP services. Also, 58% accept Medicare (for the elderly), 28% accept Medicaid (for the financially disadvantaged), 30% accept worker's compensation (for employees disabled on the job), and 46% participate in the Civilian Health and Medical Program of the Uniformed Services (CHAMPUS), for government employees ("Fee," 1995). A solo practitioner typically operates without administrative or secretarial help. Thus, interactions with third-party delivery systems may be especially time consuming.

It is common for a psychologist in private practice to consult with other professionals. Clients in need of medication must be referred to a psychiatrist, and the psychologist needs to be in collaboration and have good communication with the consulting psychiatrist. The psychologist might also consult with a physician about the interaction of a client's psychological and medical problems. Examples include eating disorders and substance abuse cases. Other therapists and counselors might also be consulted. For example, family therapists and school counselors may be contacted to coordinate care for a child. Sometimes a client is referred to an additional therapist or to a group while maintaining the relationship with the primary therapist. Groups for incest survivors, for example, usually require that clients concurrently be engaged in individual psychotherapy. In another example, a client may be referred to a second therapist for a very specific intervention such as relaxation training. Ideally, these therapists will consult regularly with each other.

Emergency coverage is a vital responsibility in private practice. Of psychologists surveyed ("Fee," 1995), 50% provided 24-hour availability by phone, and 36% said they provided crisis intervention. If a private practitioner is not going to be available, alternative arrangements for coverage must be made. Alternatives include having another clinician or group practice assume responsibility.

Finally, marketing is vital in building a client base and referral network. Many psychologists fail in private practice because they do not devote sufficient time and resources to promoting their practices. Some practices hire consultants or advertising agencies, but most take charge of their own marketing. This process may involve advertising in the Yellow Pages or in newspapers, volunteering to lecture or offer support groups for local community organizations or professional groups, appearing on radio or television programs, providing interviews or writing columns for newspapers, networking with other professionals who might provide referrals, developing and publicizing a narrow area of expertise ("niche" specialization), and volunteering to teach or supervise at nearby colleges, universities, or mental health institutions.

A TYPICAL DAY IN PRIVATE PRACTICE

It is difficult to describe a "typical" day in private practice because the nature of the work is so varied. In solo practice, the day may begin early and end late to accommodate client schedules; but the timing of psychotherapy hours is otherwise flexible.

The first author, Dr. Young, has an extremely diversified private practice and is probably not typical of practitioners. He provides individual psychotherapy with private clients; has an unpaid clinical appointment in a department of psychiatry; directs and owns two therapy centers that provide clinical services and training and employ other therapists; travels widely about once a month to offer workshops for other mental health professionals; supervises several other therapists; does media interviews on television and for popular magazines and writes self-help books for the general public; and engages in scholarly writing, including journal articles, books, and chapters for mental health professionals.

Because Dr. Young's practice is so diversified, it is difficult to describe a typical day. We instead focus on a day devoted to administering his therapy centers. During an administrative day, he usually works closely with his secretary. Together, they review new phone calls and correspondence and discuss practical problems that need resolution. For example, we recently had to resolve office space conflicts among the therapists, which arose because almost all evening office space was fully booked. As it turned out, some therapists were not using all the hours they reserved, while other therapists wanted to add hours. This required tactfully asking two therapists to cut back on the hours they reserved, without making them feel shortchanged or devalued.

During the same day, Dr. Young had to contact the beeper service because emergency pages were not going through, discuss plans to clean carpets and repaint rooms, review suggestions for revising emergency procedures with suicidal patients, review applications to hire a new therapist, obtain price quotations for printing course brochures for the center's training program, and lead a staff case-supervision seminar.

Dr. Weishaar is probably more typical of psychologists in private practice. She has a solo practice and a clinical appointment at a medical school where she trains psychiatry residents, psychology interns, and postdoctoral fellows. She also writes book chapters for edited volumes and has published a scholarly book. Some of her workdays are constructed around her child's school day. Some days involve early morning sessions, and two nights a week are devoted to seeing clients. A long day might involve seeing clients in the morning, teaching a seminar or supervising residents and psychology interns in the afternoon, seeing more clients later in the day, and attending a meeting at night. On the average, she offers one workshop or continuing education lecture per year, and twice a year travels to conferences or to attend advanced training workshops. She has 15 to 20 client hours per week, which is slightly less than the mode (20–24 clients) for therapists of all types in full-time practice ("Fee," 1995).

Education, Training, and Desirable Attributes

PRELICENSURE EDUCATION AND TRAINING

In order to have a private practice as a psychologist, one must have a state license as a psychologist. State licensure laws vary, and the details of state regulations are available from the Association of State and Provincial Psychology Boards (ASPPB), located in Montgomery, Alabama. All states and the District of Columbia require a candidate to have a doctorate (PhD, PsyD, EdD) from a department or school of psychology.

The major specialties for psychologists in private practice are clinical and counseling psychology, although in some states school psychologists are also eligible. Clinical psychologists receive either a PhD or PsyD degree; counseling and school psychologists receive either an EdD or PhD degree. Eligible candidates from all three specialties, with any of these doctoral degrees, take the same state licensing exam and carry the same legal title, psychologist.

PhD clinical psychology programs usually emphasize research at least equally with preparation for clinical practice and culminate in a substantial doctoral dissertation; they tend to be very difficult to get into. PsyD programs are designed for individuals who specifically want to practice psychology and are not particularly interested in quantitative research; clinical work is strongly emphasized.

Counseling programs are often part of a university's school of education and thus may be completely separate from the psychology department. These programs usually emphasize counseling and psychotherapy methods, but also require training in research methods leading to a dissertation. Counseling programs that offer a PhD rather than the traditional EdD often require more intensive research training.

Gaining admission to PsyD and counseling psychology programs is usually less difficult than to PhD clinical programs. All of these programs require at least 4 to 5 years of graduate work. PhD clinical programs are full time, but PsyD and counseling psychology programs (PhD or EdD) may sometimes be pursued on a part-time basis.

The ASPPB and the Council for the National Register of Health Service Providers in Psychology publish annually a list of programs entitled, "Doctoral Psychology Programs Meeting Designation Criteria." This booklet is used by many boards to determine the acceptability of doctoral programs from which applicants for licensure have graduated. School psychologists in some states (e.g., Ohio, Virginia) are permitted to take the licensure exam, but their practices are restricted to school psychology as defined by statute (ASPPB, 1996). Some states offer certification to master's degree holders, but they must be supervised by fully licensed psychologists. In most states, individuals with master's degrees in psychology are not legally permitted to have their own private practices.

In addition to a doctorate in psychology, candidates must have supervised clinical experience. In clinical and counseling psychology, the requirements for the doctoral degree generally include a year of internship. Some states explicitly require a doctorate in psychology from an American Psychological Association (APA)-accredited program and an APA-approved internship. Thus, these programs are highly desirable. The yearlong internship experience, however, is generally not sufficient for licensure. Many states stipulate that half to all of supervised experience be postdoctoral. States require between 1,500 and 4,000 hours (1 to 2 years) of supervised contact with clients (ASPPB, 1996).

Once these academic and training criteria have been met, a candidate may take the national licensure exam, the Examination for Professional Practice in Psychology (EPPP). Passing scores on the EPPP are determined by each state. If the EPPP is passed, the candidate may take the state exam, which may be written, oral, or both, depending on the state. The state exam sometimes requires the candidate to present a case study.

Since 1987, the EPPP (a multiple-choice test) has consisted of five knowledge areas. The first is problem definition and diagnosis and composes about 26% of the exam questions. It includes behavioral assessment; theories of personality, intelligence, psychopathology, and human growth and development; factors affecting behavior, such as individual and cultural differences; symptoms of physical diseases and psychophysiological reactions; and the effects of psychotropic and prescription drugs on behavior, affect, and cognition. This section also includes questions about tests and measurements of mental and intellectual functioning, personality, achievement, and other characteristics (ASPPB, 1995).

The second section, also about 26% of the exam questions, covers the design, implementation, and assessment of interventions. It requires knowledge of different intervention techniques and types of therapy. The third area, about 17.5% of the exam, concerns research design and statistics. The fourth area includes professional, ethical, and legal issues and makes up about 16.5% of the exam. The fifth area, about 14% of the exam, concerns the development and evaluation of intervention strategies designed to promote effective functioning in the social system. This section includes knowledge of factors affecting work life, consultation techniques, organizational structure, group dynamics, and performance evaluation (ASPPB, 1995).

POSTLICENSURE EDUCATION AND TRAINING

All but 12 states require licensed psychologists to take postlicensure training through continuing education programs (ASPPB, 1996). The number of credits required each year and their distribution across various categories of training vary by state. Attendance at regional and national courses, training workshops, professional conferences, and specialized institutes are common sources of postlicensure training.

Postlicensure training can lead to the attainment of diplomate of the American Board for Professional Psychology (ABPP). This certification is optional and identifies the holder as having achieved a high level of expertise in one field of psychological practice.

ATTRIBUTES FOR SUCCESS IN PRIVATE PRACTICE

A successful psychologist in private practice must have, first of all, very good therapy skills. Client satisfaction is the major determinant of continued business. Therefore, warmth, empathy, listening skills, and respect for clients and their confidentiality are basic necessities, along with the knowledge base of psychology.

A survey of psychologists in private practice found that *clinical confidence*, or certainty that one's professional style will be efficacious, was related to four factors: (a) clarity of goals, (b) belief that research and knowledge are available, (c) experience up to age 50, and (d) concentration on psychotherapy, as opposed to assessment and consultation (Glidewell & Livert, 1992). Confidence and a sense of competence in clinical work are necessary, as is a comfortable public persona to attract referrals.

Highly autonomous individuals do well in practice because they take the initiative, are often entrepreneurial, like to do things their own way, and have a relatively low need for collegial interaction. However, practitioners should be extroverted enough to network and speak in public. For a practice to grow, the therapist should be interested in marketing the business.

To maintain a practice, one must have good financial management skills and tolerance for financial insecurity. One must be organized and self-disciplined to juggle multiple demands and tasks. Administrative work such as scheduling, writing reports, completing forms, and returning phone calls must be done in a punctual manner. Although the work hours may be flexible in private practice, the flexibility is to serve clients' schedules and availability. Thus, those in private practice need to be willing to work evening hours, early in the morning, or on weekends.

Because of the demands of the job, therapists must be emotionally stable and well adjusted. They should be able to tolerate frustration and be patient when there is slow clinical progress. Finally, it is important that therapists have adequate social support at home and from friends and colleagues.

Benefits and Drawbacks of Private Practice

ADVANTAGES

According to several reports, psychologists in private practice are emotionally better off than psychologists who work in clinics, hospitals, and mental health centers (Glidewell & Livert, 1992). Compared with psychologists in academic positions, psychologists in private practice report substantially lower indices of job-related stress, lower indices of health-related concerns, and lower indices of mental health problems (Boice & Myers, 1987).

Advantages of private practice include the opportunity to focus on psychotherapy as the center of one's work; professional autonomy and independence from outside control (Tryon, 1983); higher income potential than psychologists in hospitals, clinics, or college counseling centers (Wicherski, Woerheide, & Kohout, 1995); entrepreneurial potential to diversify one's activities and add variety to work; a range of employment opportunities; the opportunity to work alone; time flexibility to set one's own schedule; job security, because one cannot be fired or forced to retire; and the tax benefits of self-employment. Private practice appeals to those who dislike working in a bureaucracy and who prefer working alone to working in teams or organizations.

DISADVANTAGES

Although private practice is often highly valued as an escape from institutional work, it has distinct drawbacks. The major dissatisfactions cited in a survey of 165 private practice psychologists were isolation, time pressure, and problems in the therapeutic relationship (Tryon, 1983). Common sources of work stress in private practice are maintaining the therapeutic relationship, scheduling, professional doubt, and work overinvolvement. However, these stressors often abate with more work experience (Hellman, Morrison, & Abramowitz, 1987). Psychologists with moderate caseloads report less stress than those with light or heavy caseloads (Hellman et al., 1987).

There are also financial disadvantages to private practice. These include the absence of a guaranteed salary or of fringe benefits, including health insurance, disability insurance, and retirement plans; the expenses of running an office; and collection problems. Managed care developments are reducing salaries of psychologists in private practice, and more than 20% of all types of therapists surveyed responded that they were taking "active steps" to quit practice as a consequence of managed care and practice trends ("Fee," 1995).

The solitude and autonomy of private practice can also feel like isolation, which includes a lack of team support for difficult cases. The emotional drain of hard-to-treat clients, combined with managing multiple roles, can lead to "burnout." Working during weekends and evenings inhibits recovery from stress, and boredom after many years of doing the same kind of work may also be draining. The responsibility to adapt one's practice to one's personal and professional developmental needs is constant, but so is the opportunity to do so.

INCOME DATA AND HOURS OF PRACTICE

Table 1 presents income data for psychologists in solo and group private practice. The data are further broken down by number of years of work experience. The data were collected by the American Psychological Association and are based on very small sample sizes (Wicherski et al., 1995).

Psychologists in private practice tend to earn higher salaries than those in government employment, hospitals, mental health clinics, and college or university counseling centers (Wicherski et al., 1995).

A larger survey reports the median income for psychologists in full-time practice as $75,000 ("Fee," 1995). When professional activities beyond psychotherapy are included, the median income for psychologists in practice is $81,000. Among part-time practitioners, the median income from psychologists' practices is $30,000.

Median fees that psychologists charge are $95.00 for 50 minutes of individual therapy and $45.00 for group therapy. Psychiatrists are the only mental health professionals who charge more: $120.00 for 50 minutes of individual therapy and $60.00 for group therapy.

TABLE 1

1995 Median Salaries: Private Practice Psychology in Selected Settings

Settings & Experience	N	Clinical Psychology	Counseling Psychology	School Psychology	Other Psychology
Individual Private Practice					
2–4 years	18	60,000			
5–9 years	65	72,000	55,000		65,000
10–14 years	116	75,000	75,000		60,000
15–19 years	110	75,000	74,000	68,000	95,000
20–24 years	91	75,000	82,000	110,000	75,000
25–29 years	57	70,000	95,000		
30+ years	14	79,000			
Group Psychological Practice					
2–4 years	5	53,000			
5–9 years	32	65,000			
10–14 years	60	71,000	69,500		80,000
15–19 years	61	75,000	70,000		95,000
20–24 years	37	85,000	60,000		96,000
25–29 years	11	73,000			
Medical Psychological Group Practice					
2–4 years	9	45,000			
5–9 years	16	66,500			
10–14 years	18	72,500	70,000		
15–19 years	17	100,000	60,000		90,000
20–24 years	9	79,000			

Note: Adapted from Wicherski et al., 1995. These salaries are based on very small sample sizes. Data are for doctoral-level, licensed practitioners. Salaries are for an 11–12-month time period.

Managed Care and the Future of Psychologists in Private Practice

According to the *Occupational Outlook Handbook* (U.S. Department of Labor, 1995), employment for psychologists of all types is expected to grow faster than the average for all occupations through the year 2005. However, the areas of job opportunities for clinical psychologists will be in health maintenance and preferred provider organizations and EAPs. If you choose to build a private practice in psychology, there are several health care trends you should understand.

Health maintenance organizations (HMOs) provide comprehensive health care to all enrolled subscribers for a flat fee. Under the staff model, HMOs employ providers, such as psychologists, directly. Under the group or network model, HMOs contract with providers based on a maximum fee schedule per service (usually much lower than the prevailing fee) or on a *capitation* basis (i.e., the provider receives a specified dollar amount per subscriber covered, regardless of how often services are used).

The majority of managed care organizations today use the preferred provider organization (PPO) model. Managed care companies provide financial incentives for clients to use a select panel of preferred providers. The PPO is based on a contractual arrangement with providers, in which health care is provided at a substantially discounted, negotiated rate (based on fee for service). Thus, the PPO serves as a broker between subscribers and providers. The purported main advantage to the psychologist is a steady flow of patients. In reality, this is often not the case, and providers complain that they may receive a very limited number of additional referrals; in return, practitioners have agreed to accept a lower rate for clients they might have seen anyway at a higher fee. To make matters even worse, it has now become extremely difficult to join managed care "panels" of providers. Thus, many private practitioners find themselves almost completely closed out of PPO plans.

Managed care is already dramatically changing the nature of clinical practice for psychologists by paying psychologists lower fees than other third-party payers do ("Fee," 1995), restricting the number of therapy sessions, and disallowing many claims. Specifically, psychologists in private practice reported the following changes: 65% have adopted time-limited techniques, 53% have attended training in time-limited techniques, 48% have had a reduced client load, 49% have changed their therapy approach, 64% have shortened the length of therapy, 63% have had a reduced income, and 53% have reported an increase in the number of disallowed claims ("Fee," 1995).

Group practices have been more responsive to managed care requirements than have solo practitioners ("Fee," 1995). For example, they have been more likely to adopt time-limited therapy techniques and to get formal training in these techniques. As a result, many have not reported reduced client loads. However, almost two thirds of group members report a decrease in income and an increase in the number of claims disallowed. Fewer solo practitioners report such changes ("Fee," 1995).

Growing competition is compelling private practitioners to demonstrate the efficacy of their treatments. Thus, efforts are being made to collect outcome data on client satisfaction. Competition is also forcing private practitioners to work more hours at more locations. Of therapists of all types in private practice, 85% to 90% have evening hours, and about 4 out of 10 work on weekends ("Fee," 1995).

Therapists in group practices typically see clients for fewer sessions than do solo practitioners. They are also able to offer a wider range of services. As managed care companies place increasing value on reducing costs by restricting the number of sessions, group practices will probably be favored, and many solo practitioners will move into group practices.

A survey of private practitioners who moved into a staff-model HMO found that 53% of the psychologists identified their increased caseload as the most stressful part of the job; 16% found limitations on the number of sessions most stressful (Austad, Sherman, Morgan, & Holstein, 1992).

The Practice Directorate of the APA has monitored the development of the managed care industry since its inception in 1987 and has found that efforts to control the costs of providing mental health care have produced a "marked decrease in the quality of these services. Ironically, they have not controlled costs" (APA, 1992).

The following predictions regarding the future of mental health care were made by the Practice Directorate in 1992: movement toward national health care, more cost control programs from state governments, and national regulation of the managed care industry (APA, 1992). Recent legislative initiatives at both the federal and state level suggest that these predictions are being borne out.

Corporations need cost control and improved quality of health care, providers want professional freedom to provide appropriate care, and clients want convenience and the ability to choose their therapist. In response to market forces, providers are forming groups and organized systems that self-manage care and, in some cases, contract with businesses, bypassing the middleman. The direct contracting between corporations and providers is called *integrated care*.

Another possible trend and current area of debate is prescription privileges for psychologists (DeLeon, Sammons, & Sexton, 1995). In the past decade, support has grown within psychology, particularly among practitioners, for psychologists to be allowed to prescribe medications. The federal government has developed a training model for psychopharmacology intended for postdoctoral psychologists, which has been implemented as a demonstration project and continues to operate despite strong objection by the American Psychiatric Association (Newbould, 1996).

Taking all of these factors into account, the occupational outlook for psychologists in private practice is likely to be negatively affected, although the magnitude of this negative impact is still difficult to predict. Some prophesy that the solo practitioner will become an extinct breed, whereas others remain guarded but more optimistic.

Summary and Conclusions

Psychologists in private practice combine many tasks in addition to psychotherapy. Private practice requires excellent clinical, organizational, and entrepreneurial skills and appeals to individuals who highly value professional freedom and the opportunity to design their own work life.

Private practice can be financially rewarding, but is also financially uncertain and can lead to burnout. Managed care trends of the past decade will probably further restrict salaries and limit the autonomy so valued by private practitioners. Nevertheless, psychologists preparing for private practice have a wide range of areas in which to work as consultants and are not limited to one work setting. Finally, the lengthy and demanding training required for licensure in psychology makes licensed psychologists highly competitive in the job market.

References

American Psychological Association, Division 38. (1981). Health psychology, *Health Psychologist, 3*(2), 6.

American Psychological Association, Practice Directorate. (1992). *Integrated care.* Washington, DC: Author.

Association of State and Provincial Psychology Boards. (1995). *Information for candidates: Examination for professional practice in psychology.* Montgomery, AL: Author.

Association of State and Provincial Psychology Boards. (1996). *Handbook of licensing and certification requirements for psychologists in North America.* Montgomery, AL: Author.

Austad, C. S., Sherman, W. O., Morgan, T., & Holstein L. (1992). The psychotherapist and the managed care setting. *Professional Psychology: Research and Practice, 23*(4), 329–332.

Boice, R., & Myers, P. E. (1987). Which is healthier and happier, academe or private practice? *Professional Psychology: Research and Practice, 18* (5), 526–529.

DeLeon, P. H., Sammons, M. T., & Sexton, J. L. (1995). Focusing on society's real needs: Responsibility and prescription privileges? *American Psychologist, 50*(12), 1022–1032.

Fee, practice and managed care survey. (1995, January). *Psychotherapy Finances*, pp. 1–8.

Glidewell, J. C., & Livert, D. E. (1992). Confidence in the practice of clinical psychology. *Professional Psychology: Research and Practice, 23*(5), 362–368.

Hellman, I. D., Morrison, T. L., & Abramowitz, S. I. (1987). Therapist experience and stresses of psychotherapeutic work. *Psychotherapy, 24*(2), 171–177.

Hershey, J. M., Kopplin, D. A., & Cornell, J. E. (1991). Doctors of psychology: Their career experiences and attitudes toward degree and training. *Professional Psychology: Research and Practice, 22*(5), 351–356.

Newbould, P. (1996). Psychopharmacology project continues despite psychiatry lobbying assault. *Practitioner Focus, 9*(1), 1, 13.

Norcross, J. C., Prochaska, J. O., & Gallagher, K. M. (1989a). Clinical psychologists in the 1980s: I. Demographics, affiliations, and satisfactions. *The Clinical Psychologist, 42*(2), 29–39.

Norcross, J. C., Prochaska, J. O., & Gallagher, K. M. (1989b). Clinical psychologists in the 1980s: II. Theory, research, and practice. *The Clinical Psychologist, 42*(3), 45–53.

Practice issues: Survey reveals therapists' marketing strategies. (1995, March). *Psychotherapy Finances, 21*(3), 3.

Schwartz, G. E., & Weiss, S. M. (1978). Behavioral medicine revisited: An amended definition. *Journal of Behavioral Medicine, 1*, 249–251.

Stedman, J. M., Neff, J. A., & Morrow, D. (1995). Career pathways and current practice patterns of clinical and counseling psychologists: A follow-up study of former interns. *Journal of Clinical Psychology, 51*(3), 441–448.

Stricker, G., & Trierweiler, S. J. (1995). The local clinical scientist. *American Psychologist, 50*(12), 995–1002.

Tryon, G. S. (1983). The pleasures and displeasures of full-time private practice. *Clinical Psychologist, 36*(2), 45–48.

United States Department of Labor. (1995). *Occupational outlook handbook, 1994–95 edition*. Lincolnwood, IL: VGM Career Horizons.

Wicherski, M. M., Woerheide, K., & Kohout, J. (1995). *Salaries in psychology, 1995: Report of the 1995 salary survey*. Unpublished tables.

Suggested Readings

Managed care: The industry is preparing for rapid growth in 1995. (1994, December). *Psychotherapy Finances*, p. 3.

Practice basics: A profitable sideline speaking to the corporate world. (1994, December). *Psychotherapy Finances, 20*(12), 8.

Kathleen L. Davis

Emphasizing Strengths: Counseling Psychologists 5

ounseling psychology is referred to as a health service specialty or as one of the applied specialties in psychology. As health service specialists, counseling psychologists work with people to help them improve their functioning in crisis situations, deal with long-standing psychological problems, or cope with developmental issues that people routinely encounter throughout the life span. Counseling psychologists directly or indirectly apply psychological theories and principles about human behavior, emotion, and cognition. Working with a client who is in therapy and serving as a consultant to an individual, group, or organization are examples of direct application of psychology. Conducting a workshop for managers that would benefit employees by improving the overall work environment is an example of indirect application.

Professionals within the applied specialties (e.g., clinical, counseling, industrial/organizational, and school psychology) engage in many of the same activities and have a lot in common with one another. They share the same foundations in psychological theory and science. For example, some clinical and counseling psychologists focus on psychodynamic principles in therapy and research, whereas others

Kathleen L. Davis is a professor in the Counselor Education and Counseling Psychology Unit of the University of Tennessee. She earned her EdD at the University of Georgia. Her primary research interests are professional issues in psychology and training psychologists. She has served as president and treasurer of the Division of Counseling Psychology of the American Psychological Association.

approach therapy and research from a cognitive–behavioral, gestalt, or humanistic orientation. Although all applied psychologists receive instruction in personality and intellectual assessment and use many of the same instruments, clinical psychologists tend to use more projective techniques (e.g., Rorschach and Thematic Apperception Test) than the professionals in the other specialties. It is very likely that counseling psychologists use more career development and vocational interest inventories, industrial/organizational psychologists make use of more personnel scales, and school psychologists administer more cognitive and intellectual tests in their work than others in the field do.

Clinical and counseling psychologists are among "the five largest psychotherapy-providing occupations" (Mariani, 1995, p. 13). Counseling psychologists emphasize using clients' strengths, which means helping clients to become aware of and to develop their potential abilities and interests. By sharing their observations and using therapeutic and assessment techniques, counseling psychologists help clients become aware of the skills and abilities that may be used to improve their functioning in a distressing situation or relationship. For example, while working with an adolescent boy who has a lot of anger toward his parents, the counseling psychologist may point out that the client exhibits very good problem-solving skills with his peers. The psychologist would ask the client to practice using the problem-solving skills with his parents. As the client reacts to his parents differently, they in turn are likely to treat him differently.

In facilitating personal and interpersonal functioning and reducing or relieving the distress that the client is experiencing, counseling psychologists tend to rely on three major roles: the remedial role, the preventive role, and the educative–developmental role (Gelso & Fretz, 1992). These three roles influence the counseling psychologists' work with people experiencing emotional, social, developmental, vocational, educational, or health-related difficulties. Counseling psychologists also use these roles in their consultation and interventions with organizations. It is important to note that the three roles are not mutually exclusive. In many instances all three can be implemented with the same client.

The *remedial* role is one of remedying dysfunctional behaviors of a client, couple, family, or group. The problem may be an immediate crisis such as guilt and depression because the client allowed a drunk friend to drive a car that was in an accident. Extreme possessiveness and jealousy from one spouse in a couple toward the other is an example of a long-standing problem that might require the counseling psychologist to take on the remedial role. Although counseling psychologists provide a variety of services and treat a wide range of psychological problems from severe pathology to relatively minor difficulties, many are likely to work with "normally" functioning people whose problems do not require long periods of hospitalization. As societal problems and other factors contribute to more distress among the general population, counseling psychologists are spending more time dealing with more severely disturbed people and working within the remedial role.

The *preventive* role is one in which psychologists help individuals, couples, and groups recognize and deal with issues before they become problematic. In this role, the counseling psychologist may help an elderly couple deal with issues of separation and death or meet with community leaders to develop plans and actions to prevent neighborhood conflict or violence.

Psychologists in the *educative–developmental* role provide informative and enhancing functions. Helping parents understand that their adolescent's seemingly strange behavior is "normal" and is an important part of establishing identity and separating from the family is an example of the application of this role. The parents also may be encouraged to enhance their strong support of the adolescent and be shown ways to do it. Other examples are marital enhancement groups, communication seminars, and relaxation-skills training. A counseling psychologist may be implementing the educative–developmental role by helping a cardiac patient comply with the medical regime necessary for recovery from surgery. The information and skills learned by the patient may also serve a preventive role in enabling him or her to avoid or prevent heart attacks in the future. As Gelso and Fretz (1992) stated, "Obviously, the distinction between the developmental and preventive roles is often subtle—a matter of degree rather than kind" (p. 6).

In enacting and fulfilling these three roles, counseling psychologists are *scientist–practitioners*. The term refers to the principle that there is a reciprocal relationship between psychological science and practice and that they continually inform each other in order to keep the discipline current. There are varying degrees of how much any counseling psychologist is scientist and how much practitioner. Many counseling psychologists view their work as mostly being that of a practitioner, and others see themselves doing predominantly scientific work. However, no matter what one's major identity, all embody in their work attitudes, thoughts, and behaviors that contain aspects of both science and practice (Pepinsky & Pepinsky, 1954). Counseling psychology scientists are researchers, implementers of scientifically established theories and techniques, readers of research articles in psychology, and users of such scientific procedures as observation, hypothesis testing, critical thinking, collection of data, and evaluation. Counseling psychology practitioners include therapists, program developers, consultants, and administrators. A therapist may notice, for example, that often minority group members report difficulties relating to the therapist when he or she uses traditional interviewing methods. The therapist confronted with this situation can review research related to beliefs about counseling, communication, and interpersonal relationship preferences of various minority populations. Then the therapist can begin to apply theory- and research-based methods to enhance a minority client's interaction during counseling. Or a university or college professor may do research on how to teach counseling skills and then use this knowledge to teach students in counseling. For some scientist–practitioners it is important to publish their research or present it at conventions; for others it is important to apply their scientific knowledge in working with their clients, students, and other groups

The Executive Committee of the Division of Counseling Psychology of the American Psychological Association (APA) approved the following definition of counseling psychology:

> Counseling psychology is a specialty in the field of psychology whose practitioners help people improve their well-being, alleviate their distress, resolve their crises, and increase their ability to solve problems and make decisions. Counseling psychologists utilize scientific approaches in their development of solutions to the variety of human problems resulting from interactions of intrapersonal, interpersonal, and environmental forces. Counseling psychologists conduct research, apply interventions, and evaluate services in order to stimulate personal and group development, and prevent and remedy developmental, educational, emotional, health, organizational, social, and/or vocational problems. The specialty adheres to the standards and ethics established by the American Psychological Association. (Division of Counseling Psychology, 1985, p. 141)

Counseling psychologists work in a variety of settings and with people of all ages and from diverse cultural and ethnic backgrounds. A number of surveys have been conducted that give a picture of the major employment settings and professional activities.

In 1986 two studies were published that reported similar results regarding the types of work and employment settings of counseling psychologists and the amount of time spent in these activities. Fitzgerald and Osipow (1986) had 351 members of the Division of Counseling Psychology answer questions about their jobs, such as what tasks they performed on the job and how much time they spent in each task. The other study (Watkins, Lopez, Campbell, & Himmell, 1986) surveyed 716 members of the Division of Counseling Psychology about their professional activities. Both studies found variability in the activities of counseling psychologists. The same six activities were reported most frequently by their samples, and there was minimal variability in the rank order. Table 1 summarizes the work activities of these samples.

These studies (Fitzgerald & Osipow, 1986; Watkins et al., 1986) reported that the settings in which these activities occur are also varied. More than one third of the respondents in both studies indicated that they were academics. Academics included administrators and professors at a university or college. Over 20% were private or independent practitioners, and between 13% (Fitzgerald & Osipow, 1986) and 18% (Watkins et al., 1986) were employed in university or college counseling centers. Approximately 5% were working in general and mental hospitals, another 3% were employed in community mental health centers, and 12% to 14% marked the *other* category. Other categories could include working in prison systems, the military, or government service.

The Fitzgerald and Osipow (1986) study found differences in the employment settings for those respondents who were younger than 40 years of age and those older than 40. Similar differences were found by Watkins et al. (1986) for those with less than 10 years experience and those with more than 10 years experience. More of the younger group or those with less experience were employed as private practitioners and by hospitals; fewer were associated with academic programs. It seems the younger professionals are more practice oriented and are finding or at least seeking jobs in the practice arena. Several recent surveys (Gaddy, Charlot-Swilley, Nelson, & Reich, 1995; Neimeyer, 1994; Wicherski & Kohout, 1995) indicated that the

Table 1

Professional Activities Reported by Counseling Psychologists

Activity	Percentage of Sample Engaged in Activity		Percentage of Time Spent in Activity	
	(Study a)	(Study b)	Median (Study a)	Mean (Study b)
Counseling/Psychotherapy	85%	74%	25%	27.5%
Teaching/Training	75	60	19	17.5
Consultation	71	61	10	7.3
Supervision	70	54	9	5.8
Administration	68	56	10	14.6
Research	67	50	7	8.0

Note: (a) Adapted from Fitzgerald and Osipow (1986) with permission of the authors. Copyright 1986 by the American Psychological Association. (b) Adapted from Watkins et al. (1986) with permission of the authors. Copyright 1986 by the American Psychological Association.

trends reported in Fitzgerald and Osipow (1986) and Watkins et al. (1986) continue (see Table 2).

Davis and Meara (1995) asked doctoral students in clinical, counseling, and school psychology programs what professional activities they would like to engage in after graduating from their programs. Unpublished data from this study indicated that almost 45% of the counseling psychology students preferred a position that was a combination of direct practice and academe. The next highest attraction (23.4%) was working for an agency. The description of *agency* included such settings as business, community mental health centers, hospitals, and public and private schools. Approximately 12% anticipated being in independent practice, both individual and group. (These percentages represent the ambitions and hopes of the students. They were not based on the availability of positions in the current job market or any projections about availability in future job markets.)

Why I Chose to Be a Counseling Psychologist

Few individuals declare at an early age, "When I grow up, I want to be a counseling psychologist." There is no reference to the occupation found in children's rhymes, chants, or games such as ". . . doctor, lawyer, merchant, thief. . . ." It seems to me that the decision to become a counseling psychologist typically is a complex one that has developed over a period of time and that has been influenced by multiple experiences. More often than not, the decision comes later in life, after college and after one has worked in a different occupation or perhaps had significant work or volunteer experience during college. I would describe my decision to become a counseling psychologist as typical for individuals in my cohort.

My college education emphasized more courses from mathematics and the sciences than from the humanities. My first job, which I greatly enjoyed, was as a mathematics teacher in junior high school. Part of my responsibilities included working with student organizations, and I found that I was interested not only in students' academic progress, but also in their social and emotional development. Chance often plays a role in career development, and when I was given the opportunity to attend a National Defense Education Act (NDEA) Institute to train as a high school counselor, I could combine my academic and counseling interests in my work and eventually earn a mas-

Table 2

Percentages of Counseling Psychologists in Selected Settings: Initial Employment

Settings	1988–1992 (Study a)	1993 (Study b)	1993 (Study c)
Academic	14.9%	21.6%	16.1%
Counseling Center	15.0	17.6	19.6
Independent Practice	15.7	13.7	15.6
Hospital	17.9	16.2	19.3
Community Mental Health Center	10.7	8.3	11.1
Business/Industry	—	*	0.4
Consulting	—	*	1.1
Schools	4.2	3.9	3.6

Note: * 9.3% for Business/Government and Other.
(a) Source: Gaddy et al. (1995). Copyright 1995 by the American Psychological Association. Adapted by permission of the authors. (b) Source: Wicherski & Kohout (1995). Copyright 1995 by the American Psychological Association. Adapted by permission of the authors. (c) Source: Neimeyer (1994). Adapted by permission of the author.

ter's degree. When some graduates had the opportunity to further their education at the University of Georgia, I eagerly agreed to learn more about psychology, development, and counseling and earn my EdD. I was able to study with Professor George Gazda, develop knowledge and skills related to group counseling and group dynamics, and learn about the newly emerging field of computer science.

Upon completing my EdD, I pursued both my counseling and academic interests as a professional counseling psychologist at the University of Georgia Mental Health Center and taught tests and measurements courses for the master's degree students in the counseling programs. I had the opportunity to be a scientist–practitioner at the service-delivery level. These experiences prepared me for my current appointment as a professor in an APA-accredited program and in a department that offers training for other counseling professionals such as counselor educators, guidance counselors, and community agency counselors.

If there is a moral to be found in this ordinary story, it is that we can help ourselves in choosing among educational and vocational alternatives by having a clear understanding of our preferences, interests, and strengths. By matching these with our feelings about the requirements and opportunities of a specific occupation and then factoring in the effects of those variables on our personal life, we are likely to be pleased with our decision.

Work Settings for Counseling Psychologists

ACADEMIC

The most obvious academic position for a counseling psychologist is as a professor in one of the 64 counseling psychology doctoral programs approved by the APA (APA, 1994). Many begin their academic careers in either a psychology department or a department in a college of education. Typically, one begins a university career as an assistant professor and usually remains in that rank for 6 years. After being tenured and promoted to associate professor for 6 to 10 years, many faculty members earn the rank of, and are promoted to, professor. This rank implies sustained and significant research and scholarly contributions to the field.

As has been previously discussed, the work of counseling psychologists is often applied, which is a reflection of the scientist–practitioner model. Professors' research projects may address such varying topics as (a) how men and women might differ, if at all, in the way they make decisions about their careers, (b) how best to train future counseling psychologists who are effective in assessing clients' problems, (c) what factors might support or refute a theoretical model of the effect of childhood relationships and events on the development of the adult's personality, (d) what model might best explain the development and effects of racial identity, and (e) what variables tend to prevent high school dropouts or violence. The results from the scientific exploration of these questions and many others could lead to the implementation of programs that would help clients.

It is not unusual for counseling psychologists who have proven their academic skill to become department chairs, deans, and vice presidents of student affairs or even provost, the highest academic officer in most universities. Counseling psychologists who are academics are sought after for these positions because of their training and expertise in understanding people and in managing complex organizations in which the needs of others, in this case mainly faculty and students, are of paramount concern. Their training in interpersonal skills, therapy, consultation, and program evaluation, in addition to their academic training and accomplishments, makes counseling psychologists in academia well suited for these positions.

Some counseling psychologists keep their hand in the area of practice, both to inform their research and help with the education of students. Most professors in counseling psychology supervise practicum or internship students in the university counseling center, the department's clinic, or a site in the community. Many see a few clients, either *pro bono* at a university clinic or in an independent practice for 2 to 8 hours each week. Other professors keep their skills current through consultation and program evaluation with local agencies on or off campus. Finally, there are some programs in which faculty have split appointments with the counseling center and are involved with both science and practice on a daily basis. In some sense many find these positions ideal, and students appreciate having such role models in their training. Those with split appointments have to be very good time managers.

There are a number of academic positions in programs other than APA-accredited psychology programs. Some counseling psychologists teach in other academic departments in a university (e.g., human resources, child and family services) or are program administrators (e.g., in university studies programs and advising centers). Many 4-year colleges and junior colleges hire counseling psychologists on their faculty. These psychologists may teach courses such as introductory psychology, personality, human adjustment, abnormal psychology, and human relations training. These individuals, too, often have an opportunity to work with the counseling center or provide outreach to peer counselors or resident assistants in the residence halls or to student leaders in other campus organizations. Some of these colleges or universities may offer a master's degree in counseling; part of the counseling psychologist's responsibilities may be in this program.

Most professors' salaries are paid on 9- or 10-month basis. Beginning salaries for assistant professors are approximately $34,000 (Wicherski & Kohout, 1995). Professionals in academic positions enjoy the freedom to set their own work schedules, except for teaching and committee responsibilities. The training of future counseling psychologists can be very labor intensive.

COUNSELING CENTERS

Most universities and colleges have a place where students can seek assistance with their problems that are causing or are a potential source of distress. Sometimes these are counseling centers, and sometimes they are university health clinics that have a mental health staff. As can been seen from the statistics reported previously, counseling centers are a primary and preferred work setting for many counseling psychologists. As with any of the settings in which counseling psychologists work, there is considerable variability in the professional services offered by these centers. In addition, the clients may include people from a wide range of ages, ethnic and racial backgrounds, cultures, and religious values. Some counseling centers restrict services to enrolled students, whereas others extend services to spouses, families, and university employees.

A counseling psychologist at a large university will have many clients who are dealing with developmental problems (i.e., identity formation, separation from family, selecting a career, selecting a mate, intimacy), as well as difficulties in interpersonal relationships and stress related to successful completion of their programs of study. An increasing number of students are treated for more serious mental disturbances, such as eating disorders and affective mood disorders. Most receive short-term therapy, which is a basic focus for many counseling centers.

Group counseling or group therapy has become a popular mode of treatment. Many counseling centers offer a number of time-limited focus groups (e.g., study skills, stress management, career decision-making), as well as time-limited therapy groups and a few long-term therapy groups.

Most counseling center personnel offer outreach programs in places on campus that students frequent. For example, programs on communication skills, cooperative living, or alcohol and drug abuse may be offered in the residence halls or the student center. A commuter campus in a large city may offer additional services. For example, such a campus may have many older students who are attending college while holding a full-time job. These students' concerns may be focused more on income, career, and marital and family issues than the issues already mentioned.

Many universities have academic programs in counseling, and the counseling center serves as a training site for doctoral interns and master's-level and doctoral practicum students. Often, supervision of these practicum students and interns is provided by the professionals in the center. Counseling psychologists also may have other opportunities to teach academic classes related to counseling psychology training or undergraduate courses in such areas as abnormal psychology, human adjustment, or personality.

Beginning salaries for counseling psychologists in a university counseling center are usually in the low 30s. The variety of activities and intelligent, verbal clientele make working in a university or college counseling center a very interesting and desirable work setting.

INDEPENDENT PRACTICE

Independent practice offers the counseling psychologist a great variety of activities. However, the two major activities are (a) provision of counseling and therapy and (b) business and management behaviors, such as client billing and office maintenance. The independent practitioner, whether in a group practice with other mental health service providers or in a solo practice without others, is running a small business and must have the knowledge and skill to be a business manager.

Counseling psychologists who are in independent practice provided individual, couple, family, and group therapy. Clients' problems may range from mild depression and stress due to recent relocation and job change or an adjustment disorder, which may require a few sessions, to a severe mental disorder, which may require long-term therapy. Structured groups in which 6 to 12 clients are working on the same general concerns (e.g., abusive relationships, eating disorders) are often a very popular form of treatment. Also, an hour of group therapy costs the clients less than an hour of individual therapy. As a service to society, independent practitioners usually have a few clients who do not pay anything or pay only a minimal fee.

If independent practitioners use tests, they are usually very short screening instruments. Usually diagnosis and assessment of a client need to be completed quickly. However, there are some situations, such as an evaluation of competency to stand trial or a rehabilitation evaluation, that require extensive use of assessment instruments.

Having a specialty for which the independent practitioner is well recognized and one for which medical and mental health professionals refer their patients is very beneficial because there will be a steady source of clients and income. For instance, people with bereavement concerns are often referred to Dr. Karen Swander in Knoxville, TN, because she has a reputation of helping people deal with the loss of someone. One specialty area for Dr. Jean Carter in Washington, DC, is career consultation—helping people examine possible career adjustments due to difficulties experienced as a result of changes brought about in therapy. Verifiable specialty credentials are becoming necessary if one is working with managed care companies.

With the advent of health care reform and managed care, some changes have occurred recently in independent practice. Although a few practitioners are able to have a caseload of clients who are personally able to fund therapy, most clients rely on their insurance to cover some of the expenses. This dependence on insurance payments affects the independent practitioner's income and, in some cases, the type of treatment offered the client. Short-term therapy is emphasized by managed care companies and employment assistance programs (EAPs). To receive reimbursement from insurance companies, independent practitioners submit credentials to become part of an approved list (called a *panel*) of providers of mental health services for each managed care company or EAP. The client is then given the name or names of independent practitioners that she or he can see for therapy. The managed care company determines the number of sessions the client can receive for each type of problem. The independent practitioner loses some autonomy as symptom management and crisis management become the focus of treatment.

Beginning salaries are extremely variable and are dependent on a number of factors, such as geographical location, hours worked, types of clients served, referral sources, and community contacts. The APA doctoral employment survey report (Wicherski & Kohout, 1995) states that more than two thirds of the 1993 graduates earned between $23,000 and $79,000 in group psychological practice; the average salary was almost $51,000. There has been an increase in the amount of paperwork independent practitioners are required to complete and a trend toward accepting lower fees with managed care companies. In addition, there is no income during the period when the independent practitioner takes a vacation or other times away from the job. However, there is still some independence in regard to the amount of time worked, the scheduling of hours, and so on.

COMMUNITY MENTAL HEALTH CENTERS

As with independent practice and counseling centers, working in a community mental health center (CMHC) gives the counseling psychologist an opportunity to directly apply therapeutic skills with clients who seek assistance in everyday functioning. Individual and group therapy and couple and marriage counseling are available. The large centrally located community mental health centers are disappearing, as most CMHCs are branching out with catchment area centers to make the services more accessible to those being served rather than have them travel to a central location.

Some community mental health centers are referral resources for health maintenance organizations (HMOs) and employee assistance programs (EAP), which means that insurance companies pay for treatment. A large number of the people being served by the CMHCs are those who are without financial resources or personal insurance. In these cases, there usually is a sliding scale for therapy payments, based on income or federal funds such as Medicare and Medicaid.

The counseling psychologist may be very active in the assessment of clients' problems, and will use a clinical interview and standardized test batteries. Program development and program evaluation, in addition to community needs assessments, are important parts of the position. The counseling psychologist with scientist–practitioner training has the skills to determine how well the needs of the community are being met and evaluate the quality of health service delivery programs. The comprehensive programs offered by some CMHCs usually contain educational and psychological components. Day treatment programs for people suffering from a severe psychological disorder, group therapy for sexual offenders, and workshops that train volunteers to work with the victims of a sexual offense are examples of the programs offered at some CMHCs. A few CMHCs may have residential programs for children and adolescents, with a self-contained school associated with the program. The counseling psychologist may work in individual or group therapy with the adolescents on such issues as impulse control, problem solving, and decision making.

Currently there is a trend in CMHCs for counseling psychologists to do less direct service and to supervise the work of master's-level counselors who counsel the clients and implement the programs. Some counseling psychologists are also involved in the administration of the center and the cases. The starting salary for beginning counseling psychologists is approximately $37,000 (Wicherski & Kohout, 1995). The beginning master's-level counselor earns about $22,500 in 12 months (Gehlmann, 1994).

There is a large range in the ages (children to elderly) the counseling psychologists may work with at a CMHC, which gives one the chance to watch development across the life span. There are opportunities to assess what programs are needed in the community, develop the programs, and then evaluate the effectiveness and quality of the programs, in addition to providing therapy and other services to those in need.

HOSPITALS AND MEDICAL CENTERS

Within a hospital or medical center, which may be private, public, or Veterans Administration (VA) facilities, counseling psychologists are found working in behavioral medicine, rehabilitation, family medicine, chronic pain units, psychiatric inpatient wards, and outpatient mental health, anxiety disorder, and substance abuse clinics. They also consult about patients on other medical units, in the emergency room, and in physical and occupational therapy. Usually counseling psychologists are members of teams that work together to evaluate and develop treatment plans, identify attainable goals, and treat the patients. Teams may comprise psychologists (e.g., counseling, clinical, health, neuropsychologists), nurses, psychiatrists, physicians, mental health counselors, and social workers. For example, Dr. Ellen Lent (personal communication, September 13, 1995) was a member of a managed care team in Michigan with a psychiatrist and social worker. The team evaluated people's mental health needs and made treatment recommendations to insurance companies.

Counseling psychologists provide individual, couple, marriage, and group therapy to patients. Some of these patients are being treated solely for mental health problems, such as mood disorders, anxiety disorders, eating disorders, somatization disorders, or suicidal or violent ideation or acts. Other patients are in the hospital or clinic for a medical disorder and are also dealing with depression, anxiety, substance abuse, sexual concerns, family problems, or insomnia. Dr. Cheryl Carmin (personal communication, September 12, 1995), in St. Louis, points out that there are fewer relapses and repeat visits to the hospital if psychosocial factors are attended to before a patient is released.

Personality assessment of a newly admitted patient is a common function in some services or units, such as psychiatry or rehabilitation. One counseling psychologist—Dr. Tim Elliott in Birmingham, Alabama—emphasizes the positive attributes of the individual, as well as acknowledging pathology, in his reports (personal communication, September 21, 1995). Many counseling psychologists lead staff development groups on communications skills, interpersonal relations, and burnout. They may also teach medical and psychology interns and supervise postdoctoral psychologists, interns, and master's-level counselors. Additionally, they may be expected to write research grants.

Beginning salaries for a 12-month contract are variable, depending upon location and setting. They tend to range from the mid 30s to the mid 50s. Although it is very demanding work and is sometimes more focused on crisis management, an attraction of this setting is the variety of activities (e.g., working with inpatients and outpatients, teaching, administration, and research) and the opportunities to develop educative interventions that take into account the diverse psychosocial aspects of patients' backgrounds. Psychologists who work in hospitals or medical centers usually have postdoctoral training.

SCHOOLS

Doctoral-level counseling psychologists perform a number of roles to facilitate the educational process in the elementary and secondary schools. In almost all roles, they rely on interpersonal and consultation skills with students, faculty, school administrators, parents, and the community.

In some school districts, they are assigned to an alternative school for children who have a record of difficulties. Others are assigned to more than one school and are members of crisis-management teams. No matter what the setting, counseling psychologists in schools are considered support staff for the primary mission of the schools: education.

On a daily basis, counseling psychologists engage in short-term therapy and behavior interventions with students to help them function more effectively in the classroom. In addition, they lead groups on adolescent problems, including such topics as relating to parents and others in authority, drug and alcohol abuse, anger management, and career development. Some schools with in-school suspension have counseling psychologists lead groups with suspended or troubled students in such areas as study skills, anticipating and recognizing trouble, and decision-making. Others may work with special education programs in the schools.

Counseling psychologists use interviews and assessment tools to diagnose emotional problems. Depending on the diagnosis, the student may be seen by the counseling psychologist in individual therapy or be referred to the school's guidance counselor or a family therapist outside the school. Counseling psychologists also consult with teachers and principals to assist them in recognizing the group dynamics in the classroom. They also work with teachers, students, and parents on programs to prevent students from dropping out.

Counseling psychologists are usually on call or are available for an emergency. In a crisis situation, they help defuse the crisis and try to respond to the needs of all involved. For example, if a shooting occurs in a school, counseling psychologists do not work only with the individuals directly involved (e.g., the perpetrator, the victim, and their families). They develop interventions with the student body and faculty members to reduce stress and promote a feeling of some control. The primary goals are to try to prevent similar situations from occurring and to restore the educational process.

There are numerous advantages to being a counseling psychologist in a school. Working in the elementary and secondary schools provides counseling psychologists with opportunities to be advocates for children and work with those who have disabilities. A creative person who enjoys problem solving may use these abilities to implement brief interventions and engage in triage. A month or more of vacation is another advantage of working in the schools. Dr. Harriet Arvey (personal communication, September 6, 1995) reports that the salary schedule in Houston for recently graduated counseling psychologists is approximately $35,000 on a 10-month contract.

INDUSTRY OR BUSINESS

In the world of business and industry, counseling psychologists hold either internal staff positions or external consulting positions. One with an internal position is a salaried employee of the company. One hired as an external consultant provides fee-based services as a member of a management or organizational consulting firm or as an independent contractor. According to Dr. Elizabeth Denton in New York (personal communication, September 8, 1995), the education and experiences that are found in most counseling psychology doctoral programs provide counseling psychologists with excellent skills that are valuable in working with organizations. Denton emphasizes the importance of training in one-on-one counseling, small-group facilitation, listening and interviewing skills, personality and career assessment, career development, and life span development of healthy, fully functioning individuals.

In comparison to other professionals who consult in business and industry, the counseling psychologist works primarily with the "people" functions most directly related to the employees of the organization. These functions include assessment, selection, placement, succession planning, team building, goal setting, and skills development. Such skill building includes communication and interpersonal skills, conflict management, problem-solving and decision-making skills, management of change, and working with and managing difficult people.

In reviewing the contributions of counseling psychology to business and industry, Gerstein and Shullman (1992) stated that most of the activities of counseling psychologists focus on human resources services. In addition to the services mentioned above, three integrated areas are organizational change, career development, and EAPs. For example, an organizational change may be a merger with another company or a major reorganization. This may involve downsizing, restructuring, or reengineering processes and functions, all of which significantly affect people in the company. The counseling psychologist can work with the employees, managers, and executives in accepting and adjusting to the changes that, many times, involve dealing with a new culture and new environment. The counseling psychologist may also "coach," on a one-to-one basis, executives or managers in the company. The psychologist helps executives become aware of their own and others' behaviors that detract from or contribute to the attainment of the company's goals. Counseling psychologists in organizations also teach managers how to lead and motivate people to perform their best.

A second major contribution that counseling psychologists in this area make is career development. These services may be provided to individuals and small groups or may be companywide programs. *Outplacement*, as an example of career development, is designed to help displaced employees reposition themselves. Outplacement counseling includes career and personality assessment; analysis of the client's work, experience, knowledge, skills, abilities and interests; training in resume writing; and teaching networking, marketing, interviewing, and negotiation.

Some businesses or companies have their own internal EAP manager, whereas others have an EAP that is managed by professionals outside the business or company. The counseling psychologist in an EAP may provide short-term therapy, crisis intervention, or educative and preventive programs. Preventive programs have been shown to be beneficial to the company by reducing absenteeism and lowering insurance costs.

A relatively new area of specialization for the counseling psychologist in organizations is violence in the workplace. Dr. Sandra Shullman in Columbus, for example, has consulted with company executives and developed preventive programs to help company executives identify early warning signs within the organization that might lead to violence. Together, they implement actions aimed at reducing the chances of violence and prepare strategies to handle a threat of violence.

As with individual practitioners, the salaries for counseling psychologists working in industry can vary greatly depending on many factors, including location and whether one is working for a business or consulting firm or is establishing his or her own consulting business. Establishing one's own consulting firm requires many contacts in the business world and can be very challenging for a period of time before one realizes a reliable income. According to a 1989 survey conducted by the Society of Industrial and Organizational Psychology, doctoral-level trainers entered the market earning an average salary of $45,000.

A Day in the Life of a Counseling Psychologist

As I stated previously, university or college counseling centers employ a large number of counseling psychologists. Therefore, I describe a typical day for a counseling psychologist in the counseling center of a large state university as follows:

8:25.   Arrive. Greet secretaries, colleagues, interns, and practicum students.

8:45.   Prepare for the day (e.g., get coffee, examine schedule, review case notes for day's appointments).

9:00.   Conduct ninth session with a 22 -year-old woman who feels very lonely and is depressed. (She has attempted suicide once and currently is on antidepression medication prescribed by the university psychiatrist.) Goals for today are to check on the effect of the recent change in her medication; evaluate how well she is implementing the plan to increase her contact with other people in the apartment complex, in the professional organization of her major, and in her classes; and introduce evaluation of therapy to date.

10:00.   Second session with a heterosexual couple dealing with stresses of school and differences in expectations about the relationship and responsibilities. Continue to focus on having them clearly state their own expectations, identify the source of the hurt and feelings of betrayal, and facilitate the negotiation.

11:00.   Supervise an intern who is counseling a 20-year-old male student with career indecision. The student is a junior who has decided to get out of pre-med (his father's and grandfather's profession) and change majors. So far the intern has addressed the client's fear of telling the father, asked the student what he would like to do instead of pre-med, and administered an interest and personality inventory. Intern decided to assess whether there is any underlying anger at the father, after the client alluded to anger last week.

12:00.   Lunch with a professor in the department of educational and counseling psychology.

1:00.   Attend case conference meeting. Dr. Jones is presenting a case for evaluation.

2:00.   Conduct a client intake. Resident assistant referred a second-year student who has been purging. The woman does not think she has a problem.

2:30.   Conduct another client intake: first-year male student who is thinking of dropping out of school. He is depressed and thinks his roommate is deliberately ignoring him.

3:00.   Write up case notes for the day, prepare for group, and consult with intern co-leader.

3:30.   Co-lead Adult Children of Alcoholics group, which has nine members.

5:00.   Review dynamics of the group with co-leader.

5:30.   Leave.

Personal Attributes

Some personal attributes are more important for some positions and professional activities than for others. In this case, unless students genuinely care about and like people, they will not be successful in or enjoy the many supervised counseling and therapy practicum courses in a counseling psychology program. Other important temperaments include the abilities to lead, communicate, and deal effectively with people. Academic and social intelligence, problem-solving ability, and emotional maturity are also essential to complete a doctoral program in counseling psychology and to be successful in the profession. Awareness and understanding regarding people from diverse cultural, racial, ethnic, and socioeconomic backgrounds and of different ages is essential.

Client change and research outcomes can take a lot of time. Therefore, patience and persistence are also important qualities. Likewise, good verbal skills—written and oral—are necessary for the communication of ideas, treatment reports, and the results of research. Scientific curiosity is helpful in formulating and verifying hypotheses about patients' behaviors and is essential for conducting scientific investigations.

The degree of interest one has in the various aspects of counseling psychology provides good information with respect to how one might wish to balance the science and practice elements of a counseling psychology career. If, as a college student, you think you may have some scientific or applied interests compatible with counseling psychology, you might reflect on how you might pursue a career in or enjoy some of the occupational settings that have been described in previous sections of this chapter.

Education and Training

The doctoral degree (e.g., PhD or EdD) is required to be a licensed counseling psychologist. Employment in many work settings I have described require a license. A license is definitely required for anyone who is going to work directly with people in a health-service function. Likewise, some states require trainers of health-service providers to be licensed. In many states the term *psychologist* is a restricted term; only those who are licensed may call themselves psychologists.

Although there are a large number of counselors with the master's degree, many of whom engage in some activities similar to the ones described in this chapter, they are not typically identified as or called counseling psychologists. There are mental health counselors, community agency counselors, marriage and family therapists, and school guidance counselors. These individuals may work with individuals, couples, families, and groups in counseling or assessment. Some are certified counselors or therapists, and some are licensed professional counselors. A few states license individuals with a master's degree in counseling or psychology as psychological associates or psychological examiners. Some master's-level counselors teach psychology or work in the counseling center at 2-year institutions or junior colleges or in high schools.

To become a counseling psychologist, a person first must earn an undergraduate degree. Although many earn the degree in psychology, students from a number of different majors (e.g., English, business, education, theology) with psychology electives are accepted into counseling psychology programs. It is highly recommended that students apply to programs accredited by the APA, because the course of study in these programs is recognized by almost all state licensing boards and internship sites, and often it is easier to make applications to sit for the license if an individual has graduated from an accredited program and had an accredited internship. Competition is very selective for these programs, and a high grade point average, strong recommendations, high Graduate Record Examination scores, and goals that are compatible with a program's goals are generally essential for admittance. Having experiences working with people and publishing research or making presentations at regional and national meetings generally are viewed favorably by selection committees and make the applicant stand out among all the others. Some programs require a master's degree, and some take a mixture of those with and without the master's degrees. In some programs, the master's degree is earned on the way to the doctorate. The master's degree in counseling or psychology contains a good preliminary course of study for many programs in counseling psychology.

It usually takes 5 to 7 years to earn the doctorate in counseling psychology. Often, students with a 2-year master's degree take less time. The first few years in a doctoral program in counseling psychology are spent in foundation courses in basic psychology, as well as more specialized courses such as counseling theories and techniques, supervised practicum, assessment, career development, statistics, and research. The advanced specialty courses and the dissertation compose the course of study in the later years. All counseling psychology programs require a 1-year predoctoral internship prior to graduation. It is very likely that a 1-year postdoctoral residency will be required in the future. Many states currently require 1 or 2 years of supervised experience after graduation and prior to passing an examination and obtaining a license.

Proficiency training in such areas as drugs and alcohol, health, neuropsychology, and psychopharmacology may be required for certification in these areas. After at least 5 years of experience, counseling psychologists may be able earn the diploma offered by the American Board of Professional Psychology in recognition of outstanding achievement and competence in the field.

Future Outlook

An increase in the number of requests for counseling psychologists and their skills will be dependent on the progress and resolution of current social, political, economic, and scientific events. Obviously, health care reform makes it difficult to predict the future of counseling psychologists and other professionals in the applied specialties of psychology. It does seem that more psychological professionals with master's degrees will provide direct services to clients. Counseling psychologists very likely will be more involved than they currently are with supervision of the master's level practitioners, program development, evaluation of the programs and workshops, and administration of EAPs, HMOs, and managed care agencies.

As people work more hours and increase the time they spend with impersonal machines, counseling psychologists' skills in teaching coping strategies will be in demand. As stressors in the workplace increase, counseling psychologists may be asked to design programs that lead to the development of workplace environments that reduce stress. Some workers may realize that they may not be as successful as they had hoped and need strategies for handling such a major disappointment. Other workers become depressed with their jobs and need help in preventing work stresses from negatively affecting their marital and family relationships.

In addition, more and more people are living longer and have to deal with health issues and new unanticipated problems in the personal, income, and family arenas. Helping senior citizens realize that these problems are normal and can be anticipated gives them a better sense of control over their lives.

It has been forecast that there will be a large number of retirements in the academic ranks in the late 1990s and early 21st century. If departments are able to fill these positions, there will be many open positions in the nation's universities and colleges. Social scientists have predicted that there will be great changes in the composition of the U.S. and world populations. Counseling psychologists have made significant contributions to the research on cross-cultural issues and have been leaders in theory development and the formulation of diversity identity. The knowledge and skills that counseling psychologists have developed in this arena will be greatly needed in the future.

Carol Kleiman (1992) stated, "Opportunities are best for those with doctorates in clinical and counseling psychology and in research..." (p. 174). The skills that counseling psychologists develop as a result of the training they receive should be in demand in businesses and industry, hospitals, health care agencies, and universities and colleges.

References

American Psychological Association. (1994). APA-accredited doctoral programs in professional psychology: 1994. *American Psychologist, 49,* 1056–1067.

Davis, K. L., & Meara, N. M. (1995). Students' perceptions of their future professional behavior. *Applied & Preventive Psychology, 4,* 131–140.

Division of Counseling Psychology. (1985). Minutes of midwinter executive committee meeting, January 18–19, 1984, Washington, D.C. *The Counseling Psychologist, 13,* 139–149.

Fitzgerald, L. F., & Osipow, S. H. (1986). An occupational analysis of counseling psychology: How special is the specialty? *American Psychologist, 41,* 535–544.

Gaddy, C. D., Charlot-Swilley, D., Nelson, P. D., & Reich, J. N. (1995). Selected outcomes of accredited programs. *Professional Psychology: Research and Practice, 26,* 507–513.

Gehlmann, S. C. (1994, May). *1993 Employment Survey: Psychology Graduates with Master's, Specialist's, and Related Degrees.* (Available from Office of Demographic, Employment and Educational Research, American Psychological Association, 750 First Street, NE, Washington, DC 20002)

Gelso, C. J., & Fretz, B. R. (1992). *Counseling psychology.* Fort Worth, TX: Harcourt Brace Jovanovich.

Gerstein, L. H., & Shullman, S. L. (1992). Counseling psychology in the workplace: The emergence of organizational counseling psychology. In S. D. Brown & R. W. Lent (Eds.), *Handbook of counseling psychology* (2nd. ed.; pp. 581–625). New York: Wiley.

Kleiman, C. (1992). *The 100 best job$ for the 1990s & beyond.* Chicago: Dearborn Financial Publishing.

Mariani, M. (1995). Beyond psychobabble: Careers in psychotherapy. *Occupational Outlook Quarterly, 39*(1), 12–25.

Neimeyer, G. J. (1994, August). *Council of Counseling Psychology Training Programs 1994 Survey of Doctoral Training Programs.* Report presented at the meeting of American Psychological Association, Los Angeles.

Pepinsky, H. B., & Pepinsky, P. N. (1954). *Counseling theory and practice.* New York: Ronald Press.

Watkins, C. E., Jr., Lopez, F. G., Campbell, V. L., & Himmell, C. D. (1986). Contemporary counseling psychology: Results of a national survey. *Journal of Counseling Psychology, 33,* 301–309.

Wicherski, M., & Kohout, J. (1995, April). *1993 Doctorate Employment Survey.* (Available from Research Office, American Psychological Association, 750 First Street, NE, Washington, DC 20002).

Ira Iscoe

Reaching Out: Community Psychologists

6

C linical psychology deals with individuals—their problems, their mental health, their relationships with others. Community psychology moves beyond the individual to deal with broad problems of mental health and human relations in community settings. How, for example, does a school program affect a targeted student population? What effect does unemployment have on the residents in both high- and low-income neighborhoods? How does community decision making affect neighborhood and city actions? How can persons acquire feelings of empowerment that enable them to shape their own future? Issues such as these are the core of community psychology.

How Community Psychology Began

Community psychology is a relatively young discipline. How and why it came about in part explains what it is. It grew out of clinical psychology, which itself was not recognized as a formal discipline until about 1945, when the Veterans' Administration, followed by the National Institute

Ira Iscoe is Ashbel Smith Professor of Psychology at the University of Texas at Austin. He earned a PhD in Clinical Psychology from UCLA in 1951 and was one of the organizers of the Division of Community Psychology (Division 27, APA).

of Mental Health (NIMH), gave financial support to academically based, PhD-level, clinical psychology training programs. World War II recently had ended, and the purpose was to find ways to help a broad spectrum of war-related mental health casualties. The emphasis was on diagnosis, treatment, and research in the area of mental illness.

Psychologists actively participated in the Joint Commission on Mental Health and Mental Illness set up by Congress in 1955 to get a better picture of the problems of mental health and illness in America. There was growing recognition that state hospitals were greatly over-crowded and largely ineffective in terms of treatment, and were "warehousing" not only severely mentally ill patients, but also elderly adults who were mildly impaired and children with a wide range of problems, not all of which were mental. In some ways, state mental hospitals had taken the place of the "county poorhouse" in housing people who, for the most part, would not have been there if there had been appropriate alternative settings.

Also in the mid-1950s, antipsychotic drugs became a significant force in the treatment of the mentally ill. The management of patients in hospitals became easier, and psychiatrists and psychologists recognized that many patients, with medication, would be able to live outside the hospital if appropriate facilities and support services were provided in the community. President Kennedy supported this philosophy and, in 1963, signed into law the Community Mental Health Centers Act, which mandated that the locus of treatment of the mentally ill change from state hospitals to community-based mental health centers.

This legislation set the community mental health movement in action. The 1960s were prosperous years for the United States, and the prevailing belief was that social problems could be ameliorated by spending money on them. Available funds helped the movement to grow. Little thought was given to the complexities of treatment in community settings. The community mental health movement for the most part ignored existing private and public agencies and their possible contribution to community-based care and treatment. It largely ignored the fact that mental health professionals were not familiar with the social pathology of low-income people in urban and rural settings.

As a result, although the Community Mental Health Centers Act led to the significant depopulation of state hospitals—or *deinstitutionalization*, as it was called—patients were released from the mental hospitals without adequate provision for their maintenance in the community. How were the people released from mental hospitals to be dealt with in the community? Who should be in charge? What were the ground rules? What were the priorities for treatment? What were the sources of needed personnel?

At the outset, each community mental health center was required to make provisions for five essential services: inpatient, outpatient, day care, emergency care, and consultation. However, communities were not prepared to deal with the severely mentally ill, and even professionals were not sure how people with mental illness were to be integrated into the community. Soon the county jail began to take the place of the mental hospital. (Sadly, the confusion of what to do with the severely mentally ill continues to exist today.)

This mental health revolution—placing the mentally ill in the community—created a need to educate psychologists to work in the area of community mental health. In May, 1965, a conference was held in Swampscott, Massachusetts, to develop that concept. I was one of the 36 clinical psychologists who, along with observers from NIMH, attended the Boston Conference, as it came to be called. This was the beginning of community psychology. A report on the conference describes the field's origin, philosophy, and goals (Bennett et al., 1966).

The conference was task oriented. The conference attendees recognized that drastic changes had to be made in the design, delivery, and evaluation of mental health services and that the ways of dealing with mental illness had to be expanded. We also recognized the need for a multidisciplinary approach for the acquisition of new knowledge and service delivery. Although we held diverse views on how to define and interpret the many changes in the field of mental health, we agreed on the need to expand the conference mandate and move toward the conception of a new field, then tentatively called *community psychology*. We also recommended that, rather than establish separate community programs in university psychology departments, it would be better at first to work this new field into existing clinical psychology programs and possibly social and developmental programs too. We urged that academic psychology programs dealing with abnormal behavior and problems of dysfunctional groups be moved from the laboratory of the university to the laboratory of the community in order to be in a better position for psychologists to carry on research and treatment.

At the conference we also tried to develop a working definition of this new field of psychology, but it may have been too early to do so. At that time we found that we were better able to explain what community psychologists should do than to provide a definition of the field. We listed the following activities in which a community psychologist should participate:

1. The study of persons in the community, including the effects of varying physical and social environments upon their func-

tioning both as individuals and as members of social organizations.

2. Assessment of the individual's reaction to planned change by varying methods of social interaction in a wide variety of human problems and concerns.

3. Basic research on the relationship between social–cultural conditions and personality functioning in order to add knowledge about the positive mastery of stress.

4. Examination of the effects of social organizations upon the individual, particularly those creating high-risk populations, and alternative social patterns that may serve to reduce their creation.

5. Facilitation of social–organizational change through modification of motivational and personality factors in the individual.

6. Evaluative research on consultation and other social change processes (Bennett et al., 1966, p. 23).

The enthusiasm generated at the Boston Conference led to a formal petition to have community psychology become a division in the American Psychological Association (APA). The petition was approved, and in September, 1966, the area became Division 27 of APA.

In 1975, 10 years after the Boston Conference, community psychologists met again. This time we gathered in Austin, Texas, under the sponsorship of the University of Texas community psychology training program (created in the years since the first meeting) and NIMH. More than 100 people attended. Here we reemphasized the need for psychology to move beyond clinical psychology and beyond community mental health. We placed increased emphasis on *ecology* (the interaction of human beings with their environment), prevention, crisis intervention, and the scientific study of the community. We examined a number of training models and proposed new ones. We also "passed the mantle" from the senior members, who had been the leaders at the first conference, to a group of young, enthusiastic psychologists with current training and diverse perspectives in this growing field.

In the years between conferences, a number of community psychology programs were developed, some free-standing within psychology departments, others embedded in clinical programs. The Austin conference served to further separate clinical from community psychology. After the conference, more community psychology programs were started separately from clinical programs, and the field began to expand and come into its own. In 1985 the title of Division 27, "Community Psychology," was expanded to "Community Psychology: Society for Community Action and Research" (SCRA) to better reflect the area's scope and mission.

Research, too, started to move away from clinical psychology and began focusing on prevention, the promotion of positive mental health, and the need to understand the problems of ethnic minorities and underserved groups. This focus continues today, as you can see if you look through the articles in the community psychology journals that have developed in the past 2 decades.

Becoming a Community Psychologist

I didn't begin my career as a community psychologist. There was no such field when I earned my PhD at UCLA in 1951. I started my career with a degree in child clinical psychology. I was convinced that as soon as there were more psychologists like me, parents would rear their children correctly, mental illness would become a rarity, frustrations of everyday life would be reduced, individuals would be better adjusted, the human condition would be greatly improved, and goodwill would be fostered throughout the world.

To start accomplishing these feats, I accepted a position as assistant professor of psychology at the University of Texas. There I taught graduate and undergraduate courses in abnormal psychology, behavior problems of children, and psychological assessment and supervised practicum students. The prevailing attitude at the time was that if clients and patients would only look at their problems differently, they could change their behavior to a more constructive mode. This approach, *psychic primacy*, gave little or no consideration to environmental conditions, socioeconomic–economic differences, and other cultural values.

The clinical program at the University of Texas—which, incidentally, was the first APA-accredited program in the southwest—worked closely with the public school system. We held weekly case conferences in which the teacher or principal presented the case, one or two of the clinical students presented the test results, and I, as chief guru, considered the inputs and suggested certain procedures, including referrals to other agencies. These agencies, of course, had waiting lists of at least 6 months and more than likely were not prepared to deal with severely acting-out 9-year-olds or uncooperative parents.

Realizing that there must be a more effective way to work with children and their families, I accepted a fellowship in 1960 to work on a community mental health project at the Harvard School of Public Health. Crisis intervention and consultation were paramount in the program. The goal of good crisis intervention was to foster more competent coping with mental health problems. Consultation was viewed as a means of expanding the skills of caregivers such as teachers, nurses, administrators, the clergy, and parents. The program also emphasized the use of community resources.

The effects of rapid intervention as opposed to long-term therapy reaffirmed my feelings about the need to change the direction of mental health services. The experience of spending a weekend in a run-down, crime-ridden, poverty-stricken neighborhood composed of mostly single-parent, fatherless families gave me a taste of the desperate struggle for day-to-day survival that some groups and communities face. Because many low-income families lived from crisis to crisis, it was easy to understand why they did not take kindly to long-term therapy. Courses in epidemiology, in which I learned the difference between such key concepts as incidence and prevalence, need and demand, and the necessary versus sufficient causes of a condition, helped me move away from a one-to-one viewpoint toward the need to understand the community, the value of community-based research, and the diversity that exists within and between various socioeconomic and ethnic groups. I saw that appropriate crisis intervention really could bring about constructive change.

Thus began my career in community psychology. I did not choose it so much as move into it by broadening my knowledge and outlook. But I did nothing unusual; seldom is there a direct path to a career. Although it is reasonable to select a general direction, we must be prepared for changes of interest and the acquisition of knowledge that might lead us to pursue different paths from where we began. Serendipity and an open mind play an important part in the directions a career may take.

A Day in the Life of a Community Psychologist

If you asked me to describe my day as a community psychologist, my response would depend on the day. Rarely are my days routine. My main activities are teaching, research, supervision, consultation, and planning. Let's see how that translates into what I actually do.

Today, for example, started with a phone call from a drug treatment program director who wanted me to recommend a student who could help him gather data for a project. A school board member called to ask me to serve on a new committee set up to reduce racial tensions in a middle school. Then I was on my way to an inner-city middle school, where I spend one morning every other week helping the administration and faculty deal with the enormous amount of social pathology they face while carrying out their academic responsibilities. Tomorrow I will attend the board meeting of a county juvenile detention center; sometime this week I will work with the Gray Panthers, a senior citizen group interested in bridging the generation gap.

Teaching has always been one of my primary and most enjoyable activities. This semester, for example, I teach a graduate interdisciplinary seminar called "Prevention: Myths, Realities, and Needed Research" and an undergraduate honors course on four critical problems of adolescence—juvenile violence, drug use and abuse, teen pregnancy, and school dropout. I encourage my undergraduates to conduct research projects, so in addition to lecturing, my teaching includes helping students with research design and working in the community. Undergraduates' vigor can be demanding, but their enthusiasm can make my day.

I also supervise graduate student research. Here, too, there is diversity. One student this semester is examining how people diagnosed with mental illness function when they are given probation instead of being sent to jail. Another is working in the area of risk-taking as it relates to HIV and other sexually transmitted diseases by surveying students at three ethnically diverse state universities. Another student is examining archival data to compare intensive family-based, community-oriented treatment of conduct disorders in children to standard, once-a-week, office-based treatment. Other doctoral dissertation topics this semester include the effects of discipline in early childhood on later aggressive behavior and early indications of school dropout as exhibited by middle-school children. All of this research is being conducted without grant support.

As you can see, my days are diverse. For me, they are satisfying and, though frustrating at times, generally rewarding. Overall, these varied activities lead to our understanding of the complexities of groups and communities and, in turn, to our ability to help them.

Career Diversity and Rewards

Would you like a career in a university? That is where you will find most community psychologists. Would you prefer working in a state or federal agency? You will find community psychologists there, too. A background in community psychology can widen employment opportunities and serve as an entry point for a variety of occupations.

TRAINING

Undergraduate preparation for community psychology usually starts with a major in psychology or one of the other behavioral sciences such as anthropology, sociology, or human ecology. It would serve you well to acquire beginning skills in statistics and experimental design. You also should gain experience in the field, perhaps doing volunteer work in jails, with the Salvation Army, or in a drug abuse program, to broaden your textbook knowledge and get an idea of what is actually involved in working in various communities. This should also help you get accepted into graduate study.

At the graduate level, you have to satisfy the core requirements of the psychology department at the university that you attend. Each program also has specialized courses and field-placement sequences designed to impart the goals of the training program. Advanced field training in one or several settings usually serves as the equivalent of an internship. The Division of Community Psychology for the present has chosen not to have APA-approved internships in order to foster flexibility and allow for growth, innovation, and a wider variety of experiences.

Opportunities for postdoctoral training are increasing. Such training allows you to gain specialized experience in your chosen area. Another path is to acquire a master's degree in public health. Equipped with a PhD in community psychology and a master's in public health, you will have more options and greater demand for your services. Master's degree financial support usually is available from approved schools of public health.

EMPLOYMENT OPPORTUNITIES

Graduates in our field are working in a wide variety of positions. Federal, state, and local departments of mental health, corrections, welfare, aging, and children and youth services frequently hire community psychologists as directors of research projects or consultants in evaluation research. School systems and private not-for-profit agencies increasingly are employing our graduates.

Community psychologists also serve as urban and rural planners, assistant city managers, and directors of programs and services that include city and county social services, city recreation departments, community-based halfway houses, drug and alcohol treatment centers, and HIV-reduction initiatives. Others have taken managerial positions in housing developments and senior citizen projects; some have gone into ethnic minority relations or become mediation specialists.

There a growing trend for community psychologists with an MA or PhD to work as independent consultants and contract with both government and private agencies. Some people trained in this area create their own jobs, such as designing or evaluating community rehabilitation and training programs or pursuing writing careers with a community mental health orientation. Others serve as adjunct faculty members and teach specialized courses that bring together theoretical knowledge with the realities of field-based programs and research.

REWARDS: FINANCIAL AND OTHERS

The question of salary is a realistic one. What salary can you expect after spending at least 4 years acquiring a PhD and possibly another year or 2 as a postgraduate? Although firm comparative figures are not available from all other areas of psychology, I have found that community psychologists in tenure-track academic positions can expect to start at the same salary as social and clinical psychologists. With increasing frequency, positions are posted that use such terms as clinical–community, community–clinical, and ecological psychologists, all indicating that university departments are seeking applicants with a knowledge and understanding of communities.

Starting salaries in colleges and universities in 1996 ranged from about $28,000 to $45,000 for a 9-month appointment, depending on the experience and teaching skills of the applicants. Summer teaching employment usually is available. State and federal agencies generally offer considerably higher starting salaries than do universities and colleges. Both universities and government agencies offer health and retirement benefits, and both traditionally offer periodic across-the-board and merit raises.

A career in community psychology can be an exciting one, whatever direction it takes. It offers the challenges and rewards of studying the interaction of human beings with their environments. It also offers the challenges and rewards of working with persons in other disciplines, collaborating in project evaluation, for example, or in designing and planning community projects.

Although the *Dictionary of Occupational Titles* does not yet list community psychology as a separate specialty, the skills of a community psychologist can enable you to function in a wide variety of settings, and your training in experimental design and evaluation heightens your attractiveness. Community psychologists often are in the forefront of social action, not as reformers or advocates, but as resources for helping to develop local leaders and for bringing together groups of people with different backgrounds, beliefs, and interests. With a knowledge of school systems, for example, we can help researchers in other areas of psychology, like social or developmental, gain entrée into the schools to conduct research. Increasingly, people in other fields respect and are finding need for the community psychologists' understanding of diverse populations and their needs.

Is Community Psychology for You?

For a person who likes variety and the challenge of the unexpected, who enjoys working with people and helping them work with one another, and who wants to have an impact on a community, large or small, a career as a community psychologist can be an exciting and rewarding one. The broad range of training required enables one to follow different paths, to be creative, to take advantage of technological changes and at the same time understand the effects of these changes on individuals and groups. For those interested in research, opportunities abound for advancing our knowledge of human interaction.

Community psychology is not yet well known, and ecological and prevention efforts tend to have low priority when it comes to obtaining support. These are disadvantages of the field. However, people in many fields are beginning to recognize that the community is the key locus for effective action and change and that the community decision process reflects a consensus of the need for certain actions.

Look at one major societal change that can be attributed to a community decision effect—the attitude toward and reduction in smoking. This change involved many stakeholders, or communities, and took considerable negotiation. Insurance companies, for example, view a ban on smoking as a money-saving action that reduces the danger of fires. Businesses see air-conditioning costs materially reduced by the absence of smoke in office and stores. Hotels have lower cleaning bills for carpets and draperies in nonsmoking rooms. Paramount, of course, is the public health approach that promotes the benefits of not smoking. But it took all of these diverse "communities" to bring about the change.

There are other examples. In the "war on drugs," advocates increasingly recognize that it is at the community level, not the state or federal level, that programs for the reduction of alcohol and drug abuse are most effective. It is at the community level that neighborhood rejuvenation takes place and that parents can have input into their children's schools. Even in higher education, there is increasing recognition that a university or college essentially is a community, and the input by students and staff is a crucial determinant of the success of the institution. Increasing emphasis on prevention—the reduction of mental illnesses, disease, and drunk driving are prime examples—also involves community psychology. There is no dearth of opportunities in community psychology for people who want to enhance the quality of life in some way.

There is, of course, no one personality type that leads to success in a given career. Nevertheless, over the years I have observed the attributes that are important for a community psychologist to have, and not to have. First, persons who require or prefer well-defined paths will be neither happy nor successful as community psychologists. Rather, they should have the following traits and abilities:

- Ability to tolerate ambiguity, function in a relatively unstructured environment, and be prepared to handle unforeseen developments.
- Ability and willingness to meet course and degree requirements, which are similar to and equally as demanding as those in clinical, social, and other areas of psychology. In other words, community psychologists must be prepared to know the field of psychology.
- Patience, optimism, and confidence in one's own ability.
- Willingness to examine issues from different angles.
- Ability to relate to stakeholders in a neighborhood or a research project. If you are working at a public school or in a community project, the old adage applies: If you work with them, you've got to eat with them.
- A sense of purpose. That is, know why and how you are involved in a project and what you expect the outcome to be.
- Belief in the coping ability of people. Understand that individuals and groups, disorganized as they may appear, have within themselves, with proper mobilization and guidance, the ability to cope more effectively with their problems of living.
- Ability to work for long-term goals without becoming discouraged. In a world in which quick returns and recognition have become the norm, this can be difficult.

▪ Respect for conventional wisdom before embarking on programs for reorganization or change.

Research makes different demands on a community psychologist than a psychologist in other areas. In a university laboratory, the researcher can readily obtain subjects and control variables; when the community serves as the laboratory, obtaining subjects becomes more difficult and controlling variables almost impossible. Community research calls for different experimental designs, as well as more time to acquire the data. Despite these differences, it is important to respect the methodology of science and to recognize that science allows more leeway than some people in academia will admit.

A skill not taught in university classes but important for a career in community psychology is the ability to construct a network of resources. Networking is a skill. It requires the ability to seek and establish relationships with people in the same and other fields that are mutually helpful and rewarding. With good networks, you can reach more people, have entry into different groups and communities, and accomplish more as a professional in the field. Relationships take time to build and care to maintain, but their rich returns are well worth the effort.

Learning More About Community Psychology

If you have read this far, you probably have more than a passing interest in community psychology. Would you like to meet and talk to some professionals in the field? Perhaps the best way to do this is to attend SCRA's national biennial meeting or one of its annual regional meetings. At these meetings, students, academics, and practitioners get together to exchange information, look at poster sessions, attend symposia, and participate in discussions and workshops. This is the occasion where community psychology students can meet their peers from other programs in addition to meeting faculty and leaders in the field. It is a time for learning about graduate and postgraduate programs, for previewing potential jobs, and for visiting and having fun.

Another way to get a feel for the myriad activities and interests in the specialty of community psychology is to do some reading. The *American Journal of Community Psychology* is the official journal of the SCRA and focuses on research and practice in the field. The *Journal of*

Community Psychology is also an excellent source of information about research and innovative programs in community settings. *The Community Psychologist*, a newsletter published five times a year, keeps division members informed about SCRA activities, new projects, special-interest groups, coming events, and the like. Its directory, with both alphabetical and state listings, is a good source of locating community psychologists throughout the country. These publications are available in most college and university laboratories.

Beyond that, you should review some of the readings listed in the references and in the suggested readings at the end of this chapter. Following are selections that in my view would be most interesting and useful to a potential community psychology student:

- Levine and Perkins (1996) provides an excellent historical and contemporary view of the goals and orientation of community psychology. It also furnishes examples of social movements and interventions and has an ecological, crisis-intervention, and prevention orientation.
- Iscoe, Bloom, and Spielberger (1977) deals with the Austin Conference on training in community psychology. Section II talks about the ideology of the field, especially in the articles by Sarason ("Community Psychology, Networks, and Mr. Everyman") and Kelly ("Varied Educational Settings for Community Psychology"). Section III deals with existing and proposed models for training and practice. Glidewell's chapter on "Competence and Conflict in Community Psychology" points out the demands and approaches needed at different levels of intervention and describes the clients or target populations. It can help orient you to the various roles played by psychologists at different levels of cultural preoccupation.
- Brickman et al. (1982) marks the entry of social psychologists into the field of social pathology and presents models for assessing causality as well as remediation. It is especially pertinent for the planning and evaluation of social and community interventions.
- Kessler, Goldston, and Joffe (1992) covers issues, theories, and activities in the area of prevention.
- Albee (1982), in a discussion of preventing psychopathology and promoting human potential, illustrates the crucial balance between positive resources and negative factors.
- Cowen et al. (1996) relates the theory, process, and outcomes of a longitudinal program of school-based prevention services.
- Tolan, Keys, Chertok, & Jason (1990) deals with the cutting edge of research in community psychology.

Summary

Community psychology, then, is many things, but chiefly it involves working with people in their own environment, the community in which they live or work or play. It is not a precise field or a neatly defined one, but for those of you who are challenged by the idea of learning about and helping improve the quality of people's lives, it can be an exciting and rewarding career.

References

Albee, G. W. (1982). Preventing psychopathology and promoting human potential. *American Psychologist, 37*(9), 1043–1050.

Bennett, C. C., Anderson, L. S., Cooper, S., Hassol, L., Klein, D. C., & Rosenblum, G., (1966). *Community psychology.* Boston: Boston University Press.

Brickman, P., Rabinowitz, V. C., Karuza, J., Coates, D., Cohn, E., & Kidder, L. (1982). Models of helping and coping. *American Psychologist, 37*(4), 368–384.

Cowen, E. L., Hightower, A. D., Pedro-Carroll, J. L., Work, W.C., Wyman, P. A., & Haffey, W.G. (1996). *School-based prevention for children at risk.* Washington, DC: American Psychological Association.

Iscoe, I., Bloom, B. L., & Spielberger, C. D. (Eds.). (1977). *Community psychology in transition: Proceedings of the National Conference on Training in Community Psychology.* New York: John Wiley & Sons.

Kessler, M., Goldston, S. E., & Joffe, J. M. (Eds). (1992). *The present and future of prevention: In honor of George W. Albee.* Newbury Park, CA: Sage.

Levine, M., & Perkins, D. V. (1996). *Principles of community psychology: Perspectives and applications.* New York: Oxford University Press.

Tolan, P., Keys, C., Chertok, F., & Jason, L. (Eds). (1990). *Researching community psychology: Issues of theory and methods.* Washington, DC: American Psychological Association.

Suggested References:

Allen, J. P., Kupermine, G., Philliber, S., & Herre, K. (1994). Programmatic prevention of adolescent problem behaviors: The role of autonomy, relatedness, and volunteer service in the Teen Outreach Program. *American Journal of Community Psychology, 22*(5), 617–638.

Bassuk, E. L., & Rosenburg, L. D. (1988). Why does family homelessness occur? A case-control study. *American Journal of Public Health, 78*(7), 783–788.

Betancourt, H., & Regeser., L. S. (1993). The study of culture, ethnicity, and race in American psychology. *American Psychologist, 48*(6), 629–637.

Bottoms, B. L., Shaver, P. R., Goodman, G. S., & Qin, J. (1995). In the name of God: A profile of religion-related child abuse. *Journal of Social Issues, 51*(2), 85–111.

Cairns, R. B., Cairns, B. D., & Neckerman, H. J. (1989). Early school dropout: Configurations and determinants. *Child Development, 60,* 1437–1452.

Cauce, A. M., Hannan, K., & Sargeant, M. (1992). Life stress, social support, and locus of control during early adolescence: Interactive effects. *American Journal of Community Psychology, 20*(6), 787–798.

Coie, J. D., Watt, N. F., West, S. G., Hawkins, J. D., Asarnow, J. R., Markman, H. J., Ramey, S. L., Shure, M. B., & Long, B. (1993). The science of prevention: A conceptual framework and some directions for a national research program. *American Psychologist, 48*(10), 1013–1022.

Cowen, E. L. (1980). The wooing of primary prevention. *American Journal of Community Psychology, 8*(3), 258–284.

Dishion, T. J., Patterson, G. R., Stoolmiller, M., & Skinner, M. S. (1991). Family, school, and behavioral antecedents to early adolescent involvement with antisocial peers. *Developmental Psychology, 27,* 172–180.

Holden, C. (1987). Is alcohol treatment effective? *Science, 220,* 20–22.

Iscoe, I., & Harris, L. C. (1984). Social and community interventions. *Annual Review of Psychology, 35,* 333–360.

Lavoie, F., Vezina, L., Piche, C., & Boivin, M. (1995). Evaluation of a prevention program for violence in teen-dating relationships. *Journal of Interpersonal Violence, 10*(4), 523–531.

Lefley, H. P. (1987). Aging parents as care givers of mentally ill adult children: An emerging social problem. *Hospital and Community Psychiatry, 38*(10), 1063–1070.

Price, R. H., Cowen, E. L., Lorion, R. P., & Ramos-McKay, J. (Eds). (1988). *Fourteen ounces of prevention: A casebook for practitioners.* Washington, DC: American Psychological Association.

Price, R. H., & Politser, P. E. (Eds.). (1980). *Evaluation and action in the social environment.* New York: Academic Press.

Price, R. H., & Smith, S. S. (1985). *A guide to evaluating prevention programs in mental health*. Washington, DC: U. S. Government Printing Office.

Rappaport, J. (1981). In praise and paradox: A social policy of empowerment over prevention. *American Journal of Community Psychology, 9*(1), 1–25.

Smith, G. B., Schwebel, A. I., Dunn, R. L., & McIver, S. D. (1993). The role of psychologists in the treatment, management, and prevention of chronic mental illness. *American Psychologist, 48*(9), 966–971.

Steadman, H. J., Morris, S. M., & Dennis, D. L. (1995). The diversion of mentally ill persons from jails to community-based services: A profile of programs. *American Journal of Public Health, 85*(12), 1630–1635.

St. Pierre, T. L., Kaltreider, D. L., Mark, M. M., & Aikin, K. J. (1992). Drug prevention in a community setting: A longitudinal study of the relative effectiveness of a three-year primary prevention program in boys' & girls' clubs across the nation. *American Journal of Community Psychology, 20*(6), 673–706.

Susser, M. (1995). The tribulations of trials—Intervention in communities. *American Journal of Public Health, 85*(2), 156–158.

Tableman, B. (1989). Installing prevention programming in the public mental health system. *American Journal of Community Psychology, 17*(2), 171–183.

Weissberg, R. P., & Elias, M. J. (1993). Enhancing young people's social competence and health behavior: An important challenge for educators, scientists, policymakers, and funders. *Applied and Preventive Psychology, 2*, 179–190.

Winett, R. (1995). A framework for health promotion and disease prevention programs. *American Psychologist, 50*(5), 341–350.

Billie S. Strauss

Treating, Teaching, and Training: Clinical Psychologists in Hospitals

7

Overview of What Clinical Psychologists in Hospitals Do

P racticing clinical psychology in a hospital is varied and exciting. The many activities in which clinical psychologists in hospitals engage include (a) providing direct service to patients, such as psychotherapy or psychological assessment; (b) supervising and instructing interns, students, or other health care professionals; (c) conducting research; and (d) administering or directing programs such as inpatient or outpatient services or psychology training programs. Clinical psychologists who work in hospitals must have a doctoral degree and a license to practice psychology independently.

Billie S. Strauss received her PhD in educational psychology and clinical psychology from the University of Chicago, her MA in educational psychology from Claremont Graduate School and University Center in California, and her BA in mathematics from the State University of New York at Binghamton. At present, she is chief psychologist in the Department of Psychiatry at Michael Reese Hospital in Chicago, associate professor of psychology in the Department of Psychiatry at the University of Illinois at Chicago, and in private practice.

How and Why I Became a Clinical Psychologist in a Hospital

Initially, I decided to become a psychologist because of two observations and my attempts to understand them. First, my roommate in college had some concerns about going home to visit her father and could not decide whether to make the visit. She told me about her concerns, and after we had talked for a while, she suddenly decided to make the visit and noted that her worries were not founded. In a sociology course, I discovered that when people talk about concerns, they begin to see these concerns in a new light and can make decisions they previously could not make. In particular, I became interested in learning how interventions in which people talk, such as psychotherapy, could result in change. Second, I noticed that my roommate was very different from me in interests, experiences, and study skills; we differed in the settings in which we lived and in our religious practices. However, we had the same number of siblings, our mothers had the same careers, and we studied similar subjects in high school. I wondered, how had we become different? My curiosity about the personalities and backgrounds of my roommate and myself, along with a social psychology course, inspired my interest in understanding differences among people.

I enjoyed engaging in a variety of activities and saw that, as a psychologist, I could combine clinical work, teaching, research, and administration. Moreover, I had been fascinated by psychological theory and by its practical applications and saw becoming a clinical psychologist as a way of integrating the two. The hospital setting of my career as a psychologist came about partly by chance and evolved over the course of many years.

In college I was a mathematics major. My primary interest was in number theory, a very theoretical subject. Although number theory was intriguing, I become interested in developmental psychology and change following psychotherapy through a sociology course. This led me to consider a career in counseling, to take a variety of undergraduate academic psychology courses, and to pursue a master's degree in counseling psychology, which I hoped to use to work with college students. I saw my task as helping students to make choices. Unfortunately, after receiving this master's degree, I found that I could not obtain a professional position and was advised to get a PhD. I pursued and completed a PhD in educational psychology, with a specialization in clinical psychology. During my doctoral study, my interest in integrating theoretical psychology with clinical application increased.

My first job after completing my PhD was at a multidisciplinary clinic located in a large hospital where we evaluated multihandicapped children, mainly those with cerebral palsy, spina bifida, mental retardation, and learning disabilities. I developed an appreciation of the wide range of individual differences among patients and began to work with very young children, school-age children, and adolescents. During this time, I also began training psychology interns, medical students, and pediatric residents as they rotated through my clinic. Because I saw so many and such different kinds of children, I developed considerable knowledge and competence in the area of psychological assessment and testing. In addition to intelligence and learning tests, I used personality tests and tests of social-adaptive ability for people of all ages.

After spending 5 years at this hospital, I moved to a temporary academic position in a psychology department of a university where, in addition to teaching courses and conducting research, I supervised students' psychological testing and psychotherapy and saw my own patients through a university-based outpatient clinic. My research compared responses on the Rorschach test of paranoid schizophrenics with those of nonparanoid schizophrenics. The following year, I accepted a position as associate director of this clinic and a faculty position that involved teaching primarily clinical courses in psychotherapy and psychological testing. I also broadened my research interests to include psychological testing and hypnosis.

During this time, I missed working in a hospital, and I accepted a position for several hours per week as director of geriatric psychological services in the inpatient unit of a hospital. This position involved evaluating older adults who were inpatients in the psychiatric unit of a hospital, mainly to determine whether they were depressed or suffering from dementia. I met with a team of psychiatrists, social workers, and nurses to set up a treatment plan for these patients. One patient who comes to mind as somewhat typical was in his 70s and had difficulty remembering to do basic tasks, such as turning off lights or buttoning his shirt. He also believed that his neighbors were going to take his possessions. After interviewing this man and his daughter, I administered several psychological tests to assess memory, judgment, concentration, comprehension of everyday circumstances, mood, and ability to cope with stress. My results suggested that he was in the beginning stages of a dementia.

After several years, I was offered the position of director of psychology training at that hospital and left the university. This position combined clinical work, teaching, research, and administration. My activities included total responsibility for the psychology internship and practicum programs; supervising interns and practicum students on their psychotherapy and psychological testing; teaching courses on psychotherapy, professional issues, and hypnosis; serving on departmental committees; attending case conferences; continuing my research; and having responsibility for outpatient psychological testing. Several years later, the outpatient clinic was reorganized, and I was appointed director of psychiatric outpatient services in addition to director of training. At this point, I was responsible for outpatient treatment and assessment conducted by psychologists, psychiatrists, social workers, psychiatric residents, social work students, and psychology interns and practicum students. Several years later, our chief psychologist resigned his position, and I was appointed chief psychologist. After moving into this position, I was in charge of all of the activities of clinical psychologists in our hospital.

What Clinical Psychologists in Hospitals Really Do

Clinical psychologists in hospitals may pursue a variety of activities, often in the course of one day. (See, for example, Hersen, Kazdin, & Bellack, 1983; Sundberg, Tyler, & Taplin, 1973; Walker, 1981.) The following section will give you an idea of what these activities may be.

PSYCHOTHERAPY

Clinical psychologists in hospitals may provide psychotherapy to patients who range in age from infancy to old age. Treatment may include individual, group, family, or couples therapy. Some patients are seen while they are inpatients, others while they are in a day hospital, and others while they are outpatients. Therapy may be supportive, may involve insight, or may be geared toward helping to relieve patients' symptoms. (See, for example, Balsam & Balsam, 1984; Brenner, 1982.)

Consider the following example of treatment that used the patient's understanding of her problem, provided support, and was geared toward treating a symptom. One elderly lady who was an inpatient in our psychiatric hospital was depressed because most of her friends had died or moved away. The patient smoked several packs of cigarettes a day, despite the fact that she had severe pathology involving her lungs. Her psychiatrist and the nursing staff asked me to see her to help her to stop smoking. The patient and I talked about how cigarettes had become her "friend" because so many of her friends had died. We used several strategies, including hypnosis, to help her to stop smoking and to manage the loss of these friends.

Another example involved a woman in her 40s who refused to talk, lived at home with her parents, and did not work or do chores at home. The treatment involved both consulting with a psychiatrist to obtain antidepressant medication and seeing a clinical psychologist for psychotherapy to help her deal with several disappointments in her life, including the death of a close relative and breakup of a relationship with a boyfriend. After several weeks of treatment, the patient began to talk more and worked on taking a bus herself and doing chores at home.

ASSESSMENT

Clinical psychologists who work in hospitals also may do diagnostic interviewing to determine a diagnosis and the type of treatment indicated, or they may conduct psychological testing. Psychologists use tests that evaluate cognitive ability such as intelligence or academic achievement, and personality and emotional variables such as depression or thought disorder. These personality tests include objective tests such as symptom checklists and projective tests through which the psychologist tries to assess particular conflicts and issues that are salient to a patient. Neuropsychologists may use tests to assess relationships between "brain and behavior."

Once, I was asked to test a high school student before she went to college because, although she did well in high school, she feared failure in college. She appeared to be a happy, bubbly person. The intelligence test and tests of academic achievement showed that she was of above average ability. Much to my surprise and contrary to my observations and the interview, personality tests suggested that she was depressed and angry. When I discussed these test results with the patient and her mother, the patient began to cry and revealed that she really did not want to go to college, but was afraid to disappoint her parents. I worked with the patient and her mother around this issue to help the patient make a realistic and free choice about whether or not to go to college.

Psychologists in hospitals also do assessment of infants. Some of the infants in our nursery are so physically impaired that they require placement in nursing homes. For example, some cannot breathe or eat without complicated equipment and need frequent evaluation of their pulse and blood pressure, so parents cannot care for them at home. To be placed in such institutions, children need a psychological evaluation. My evaluation of these children includes a comparison of their performance with that of normal infants on tasks that most infants can do, such as responding to the sound of a bell or a rattle, smiling in response to a smiling adult, or making infant noises.

Along with doing therapy or assessment, psychologists must do "housekeeping" chores, which include attending team meetings at which the psychologist and other members of the team such as social workers, psychiatrists, and nurses discuss the patient; writing reports of assessments; and writing notes in the patient's chart of time spent with the patient.

SUPERVISION AND TRAINING

Many hospital psychologists engage in supervision and training of junior staff, nurses, or other trainees (who have done psychotherapy or assessment of patients). Psychologists are involved either in individual or group supervision. The supervising psychologist may review notes or listen to tapes or sessions, and discuss cases with the supervisee. Sometimes senior clinical psychologists see patients with supervisees.

Psychologists also teach courses to trainees or department staff in areas of their specialization, for instance, psychological testing, child psychotherapy, group therapy, or psychopharmacology. For example, in my work at the hospital, I teach a seminar in clinical uses of hypnosis to psychology interns, psychiatry residents, and staff psychologists, psychiatrists, and social workers. This course includes lectures, discussion, reviewing patient cases, and my demonstration of techniques and my observation of students during class. Following the class, which involves 21 classroom hours over 6 to 8 weeks, I meet with interns, residents, and staff 1 hour per week in group supervision. During this time, I review students' sessions with patients with whom they use hypnosis.

Along with members of other professions who work in hospitals, psychologists may be present at what are called *grand rounds*, at which the entire department gathers to hear a case, research report, or other work in which the psychologist has been involved. For example, a social worker discusses the background of a patient who was hospitalized for psychosis, a nurse discusses how the patient reacted on the ward, a psychiatrist discusses how the patient responded to medication, and I discuss the psychological testing I did to determine the extent of pathological thinking.

RESEARCH

Some clinical psychologists who work in hospitals are involved in research. Projects may include topics such as assessing outcomes of therapeutic techniques, conducting surveys of psychologists or other health care professionals, and relating patients' responses on psychological tests to other of their characteristics. Many hospital psychologists also have academic appointments in medical schools affiliated with the hospital and, as such, may conduct research or teach in that medical school department. As part of my academic appointment, I served as advisor to a medical student. Some hospitals provide laboratories or equipment for research psychologists. When one of our psychologists studied tracking eye movements in patients and nonpatients, the hospital provided a room for equipment that he purchased with funds from a research grant.

Most psychologists keep abreast of their colleague's research by reading current psychology journals and attending functions for their own development. These functions may include courses, workshops, conferences, or other continuing education activities. Through these activities, psychologists monitor the most current developments in therapy and assessment techniques and in the field of psychology in general.

ADMINISTRATION

Psychologists with primarily clinical, teaching, or research positions sometimes have administrative responsiblities such as serving on hospital or departmental committees. A psychologist may serve, for example, on a hospital ethics committee that reviews ethical issues in all departments of the hospital. A psychologist also may serve on a department task force set up to review the services that are provided. For example, following concerns of some of the staff, I was on a task force that reviewed whether a depressed patient was discharged from the hospital too soon.

Some psychologists also function as administrators of clinical programs, psychology departments, or training programs. For example, a clinical psychologist may be director of a clinical service program, such as director of psychological testing services on an inpatient or outpatient unit, or director of neuropsychological testing services in a psychiatry department or neurology department. A clinical psychologist also may be director of a department clinical service that involves supervision of members of other disciplines, such as outpatient services, a partial-hospital program, or intake services. In these instances, activities may include keeping records of patients, meeting with or supervising staff, taking responsibility for financial aspects of these programs, or doing housekeeping chores such as noting attendance and hiring and evaluating staff.

Some clinical psychologists serve as directors of psychology departments or psychology training programs. Their activities include meeting with psychology staff and trainees; recruiting, hiring, and evaluating them; and meeting with psychologists from other hospitals in similar positions. In the case of directors of training programs, activities include determining the program of psychology trainees and meeting with psychologists from graduate academic programs to discuss students and various issues involving training in psychology.

Work Settings of Clinical Psychologists in Hospitals

Clinical psychologists in hospitals may work in a variety of settings within the hospital. Settings may be in units that serve patients with psychological problems or in those that serve patients with medical problems. In both of these settings, clinical psychologists provide, supervise, or do research on diagnostic interviewing, psychological testing, individual or family therapy, and group or milieu therapy. They also provide consultation to other hospital staff who work with patients.

In psychiatry, psychology, or behavioral health departments, psychologists see patients who have difficulty with their relationships with family, friends, teachers, bosses, or coworkers; difficulty with anxiety or managing stress; difficulty with moods, such as depression; difficulty making decisions; difficulty adjusting to new situations; learning difficulties; alcohol and drug problems; and difficulty thinking, as in psychosis. Settings in which psychologists may work also vary according to level of care needed—for example, there are inpatient units for patients who need a great deal of care, partial-hospital programs for patients who need less care and can live at home, outpatient services for patients who function independently, and intake services for new patients who need evaluation.

Psychologists may work in a medical inpatient or outpatient unit, seeing medical patients through that unit. The unit may include pediatrics, oncology, diabetes, HIV, and rehabilitation. Psychologists may be asked to see patients who need help realizing that they have medical problems, who do not comply with their diet or taking medication, or who seem unhappy or depressed for reasons independent of the medical problem. Psychologists also may be asked to do psychological or neuropsychological testing to provide psychotherapy for medical patients.

Academic and Other Preparation Needed

To be a clinical psychologist in a hospital, you first must become a licensed clinical psychologist. A licensed clinical psychologist must have a PhD or PsyD degree in clinical or counseling psychology from a university or professional school. To get admitted to graduate school, of course, you first need a bachelor's degree. Graduate programs have different requirements for undergraduate courses, but most require undergraduate courses in psychology and mathematics (including statistics). Graduate schools in clinical or counseling psychology should require that students take courses that will allow them to be licensed as clinical psychologists after they complete their training. Many graduate school departments are accredited by the American Psychological Association (APA; see APA, 1996). These require that students take courses in several areas: (a) biological bases of behavior, which includes courses in physiological psychology, neuropsychology, or comparative psychology; (b) cognitive and affective aspects of behavior, which includes courses in cognition or motivation; (c) social aspects of behavior, which includes courses in social psychology or groups; (d) history and systems of psychology; (e) psychological measurement; and (f) research methodology and techniques of analysis of data. Other relevant courses include individual differences in behavior, development, psychopathology or abnormal behavior, professional issues and ethics, and cultural and individual diversity.

In addition to academic courses, students must complete a dissertation, a comprehensive paper, or a series of papers, and fieldwork or practicum courses in psychotherapy and assessment (psychological testing or behavioral assessment). This fieldwork may be done in a hospital, an outpatient clinic or counseling center, or, in some cases, a private practice. Finally, most programs require a 1-year full-time internship, in which students work under supervision doing a variety of clinical tasks. Students who wish to work as psychologists in hospitals might want to do their internship and some of the practicum placements in a hospital.

Following completion of the doctoral degree and internship, a year or 2 of postdoctoral supervision is required before taking the licensing examination. Most states require that this postdoctoral year include 1 or 2 hours per week of individual face-to-face supervision. One of the accreditation bodies is considering, for accreditation of postdoctoral programs, requiring 2 hours per week of individual, face-to-face supervision plus 2 hours per week of additional education activities, such as group supervision, grand rounds, or seminars.

People who complete their postdoctoral hours in positions that are not official training programs must receive supervision and participate in training activities to get approval to sit for the licensing examination. Supervision must be paid for or provided by the hospital or facility for which the person works, so that people who are not yet licensed cannot hire someone to provide supervision.

Following the period of postdoctoral supervision, you are ready to apply to sit for the licensing examination as a psychologist. This is a national examination given twice a year. Results may be sent to any state, although each state has its own requirements to allow candidates to take the examination, and each state has its own score requirements. Most candidates study for the examination; some take workshops or use commercial study materials.

Following licensure as a clinical psychologist, you can work as a clinical psychologist in a hospital.

Financial Compensation

Financial compensation is highly variable. Today in the mid-1990s, many clinical psychologists in hospitals receive a salary that may range from a low of $30,000 to almost $100,000, depending on the hospital, location, seniority of the psychologist, and nature of the position. Some hospitals provide a base salary and additional income after the psychologist sees a certain number of patients or generates a certain amount of revenue. Salaried positions usually include benefits such as vacation, sick leave, holidays, and the options to purchase health insurance and retirement plans.

In a less usual arrangement, some hospitals hire psychologists through a registry or contract with them as consultants, so that they are paid an hourly fee only for hours worked. This arrangement typically does not include benefits, vacation, or holidays. In some cases, psychologists are paid only when patients come to their appointments.

In some hospital settings, psychologists see patients whom they bill privately.

Advantages and Disadvantages

For me, one of the major advantages of being a clinical psychologist in a hospital is the variety of tasks and available opportunities. For example, psychologists in hospitals do not need to choose between teaching courses, supervising students, seeing patients, or doing research, but can perform all of these. A second advantage of working in a hospital over having a private practice is the availability of support services such as clerical and administrative staff and services of the emergency room, security, medical clinics, and psychiatrists, particularly in working with difficult patients.

Psychologists who work in hospitals are also fortunate to have close association with other psychologists to provide professional stimulation and discussions. I also enjoy working with people in other disciplines, such as psychiatrists, nurses, and social workers, and looking at clinical cases, theories, and issues from a variety of perspectives. Working in a hospital also allows me the comforts of receiving a guaranteed salary, vacation, sick pay, and benefits. Finally, I enjoy the availability of continuing education opportunities, including rounds and seminars at my hospital, as well as activities at neighboring hospitals.

A disadvantage of being a clinical psychologist in a hospital is reduced autonomy in providing treatment. When a psychologist works in a hospital rather than having a private practice, the treatment policy, fee schedules, number of sessions, hours, and nature of the clientele are determined by the hospital instead of the individual psychologist. As a result of some of the changes that are occurring in health care today (particularly in mental health), psychologists in hospital settings may find that some services, such as psychological testing, may no longer be covered or may be covered to a lesser extent than they previously had been. Some insurance companies do not pay for services performed by trainees, and psychologists may have a difficult time finding patients for psychology trainees to see. Another disadvantage to working in a hospital is that as hospitals reduce personnel, the amount of work and responsibility assumed by psychologists increases (without commensurate increases in salary).

Although the disadvantages may be frustrating, I think the advantages of being a clinical psychologist in many hospitals outweigh the disadvantages and provide a rewarding professional experience.

How to Succeed as a Clinical Psychologist in a Hospital

Clinical psychologists in hospitals who are successful have several characteristics that are necessary for the various activities in which they engage. Attributes needed for clinical work include confidence and sensitivity, flexibility and persistence, and empathy and a realistically objective outlook (Wolberg, 1995). In addition, therapists must be sufficiently intelligent and motivated to meet educational requirements and examinations.

To work as a member of a team in a hospital, clinical psychologists must be able to get along with, respect, and enjoy working with others. Clinical psychologists need a certain degree of organization and motivation to complete administrative tasks and paperwork, and reasonable physical and mental health to endure occasional long hours and stressful situations. Finally, clinical psychologists in hospitals should enjoy doing a variety of tasks, including therapy, assessment, teaching, administrative tasks, and research, and should be able to shift easily from one activity to the next.

Opportunities for Employment

There is a wide range of opportunity in terms of age and diversity of patients seen, tasks performed and skills used, functions served, and departments in which clinical psychologists in hospitals work. Patients seen by psychologists in hospitals range in age from infants to older adults and may include people with many kinds of problems. Psychologists may work in departments of psychiatry or have medical specialities with inpatients or with outpatients. Psychologists may perform a variety of clinical services such as psychotherapy, diagnostic interviewing, or psychological testing; consult with or supervise other professionals or trainees; teach courses; and participate in team meetings, seminars, or rounds.

Psychologists also may conduct research. Research may involve clinical studies of patients or may occur in separate research labs. For example, a colleague and I are comparing results of art therapy techniques with psychological testing. We give the art therapy task (rating pictures of people and using crayons, scissors, and paste to elaborate on one of these pictures) and psychological tests (symptom checklist, rating scale, projective psychological test) to adult patients who are hospitalized on one of our psychiatric inpatient units.

Psychologists may perform administrative duties, including directing clinical programs; sitting on or chairing hospital, department, or program committees; or performing other administrative tasks. For example, I am a member of our department's policy committee and spent some time revising many of our policies, including criteria for admission to our hospital and policies about respecting patients' rights.

Psychologists work in hospitals at an entry level, middle level, or advanced level. Hospitals may be publicly supported or privately owned, and may be not-for-profit or for-profit. Some hospitals in which psychologists work are teaching hospitals in major medical centers; others are small community-based hospitals. These factors may influence career opportunities in that the importance of issues such as prestige, financial renumeration, and job duties (i.e., clinical, teaching, or research responsibilities) has an impact on the settings in which one chooses to work.

A Typical Day as a Clinical Psychologist in a Hospital

Because a career as a psychologist in a hospital can be so varied, typical days may vary according to the setting and function of the psychologist. I will give several scenarios based on my experience and my observations of colleagues.

The first example is from when I was a staff psychologist in a teaching hospital responsible for outpatient testing and therapy. On that day, I arrive at 8:30 and begin my day by listening to my voice mail and reviewing charts of patients seen by psychology interns the day before. The messages on my voice mail are from an intern who would like an additional hour of supervision, another intern who is not sure about scoring one of the psychological tests he gave, and a patient who would like an appointment. From 9:15 to 10:30, I hold a diagnostic clinic, in which I see patients together with psychology students called *externs* (second- and third-year graduate students doing a field placement conducting psychotherapy or psychological testing). I first see the patient with the externs for about 30 to 45 minutes; we try to find out why the patient wants therapy and what the patient's strengths and weaknesses are and assess what services would be of help. Following the interview, the patient waits outside the room while the externs and I discuss her or him. Next, the patient returns to the room, and one of the externs or myself gives the patient feedback about what is needed.

At 10:30, I supervise an intern on a therapy case. We discuss what the patient said and what the intern did, and together discuss the intern's interventions and thoughts about the cases. From 11:00 to 12:00, we attend grand rounds. Most recently, an attorney discussed legal aspects of providing mental health services. Other topics that have been presented at grand rounds include a psychiatrist discussing mind–body relationships; a psychologist discussing thought disorder; and a psychologist, social worker, psychiatrist, and nurse presenting the case of a patient who was in the hospital.

At 12:00, I read my mail and return phone calls while I eat lunch. From 12:30 to 2:00, I attend our clinical psychology seminar at which staff, interns, and externs rotate in presenting cases. Today, an intern presents the case of a child she has seen for several months. The child began to do poorly in school shortly after the family moved. We discuss why the child is doing poorly and make recommendations. After the seminar, I attend a meeting of the psychology staff. We discuss the progress of the interns and externs, a new psychological test that we are using, and the recruitment of next year's interns. At 3:00, I plan to write a report, but receive a phone call from an intern who is seeing a patient and has an urgent question. The patient is too disorganized to function at home and should be hospitalized. I help the intern to hospitalize the patient and discuss with him what is to be the next step in treatment. At 4:00, I return phone calls, read more mail, browse through one of the journals I received, and work on a report I am writing about the patient I saw earlier in the day. Finally, by 5:00, I go home. Later in the evening, I receive a phone call from the intern who hospitalized the patient to discuss the session with the patient. The intern says she will call again if difficulties arise.

My second example is from when I was a staff psychologist responsible for consulting to an inpatient service and a consult-liaison service that provided psychological services to the medical units of the hospital. My typical day was somewhat different: I arrive at 8:00 and see an inpatient I have been asked to treat for severe anxiety that is not controlled by medication. I have been teaching her relaxation techniques for the past several days, and she seems to be responding. After seeing the patient, I write a note in the chart and chat with several of the nurses. By 8:50, I am on my way to my office, where I respond to telephone calls and read the mail. There is an advertisement for a new book on psychotherapy that I am thinking of ordering. I receive a phone call from the patient's therapist, and we talk about the patient. At 9:30, I begin to test a patient to assess his strengths and the extent of his pathology. By 11:30, I complete the testing and rush off to attend a department meeting of all of the psychologists and psychiatrists. I have lunch with a colleague from 12:30 to 1:00; we discuss issues brought up at the meeting, including whether psychiatry residents and psychology interns are being sensitive enough to patients' needs. At 1:00, I score the tests I have given earlier and begin to write the report.

At 2:30, I receive a phone call from the nursery; the staff there would like an assessment on a 5-month-old baby as soon as possible. I see the baby until 3:00 and write a note in the chart. I return to my office to complete the report on the patient I tested earlier. At 4:00, I meet with staff nurses to discuss the assessment of patients as part of the nurses'continuing education program. At 5:00, I check phone messages and leave.

To Be or Not To Be (A Clinical Psychologist in a Hospital)

Working as a clinical psychologist in a hospital is a very rewarding and meaningful career, both because of the stimulation of my daily activities and because of the sense of contributing to the well-being of my patients and the professional growth of my students. I find having varying activities—therapy, assessment, supervision, teaching, research, meetings, administration—to be very challenging. Teaching, supervision, and attending case conferences and rounds provide a forum for discussing issues in clinical psychology and improving skills. Research is stimulating and challenging and provides professional growth. By supervising trainees and providing treatment and assessment of patients, I am furthering the skills of students and promoting growth and better mental health of patients.

References

American Psychological Association. (1996). *Book 1: Guidelines and principles for accreditation of programs in professional psychology. Book 2: Accreditation operation procedure.* Washington, DC: Office of Program Accreditation, American Psychological Association.

Balsam, R. M., & Balsam, A. (1984). *Becoming a psychotherapist* (2nd ed.). Chicago: University of Chicago Press.

Brenner, D. (1982). *The effective psychotherapist.* New York: Pergamon Press.

Hersen, M., Kazdin, A. E., & Bellack, A. S. (Eds.) (1983). *The clinical psychology handbook.* New York: Pergamon Press.

Sundberg, N. D., Tyler, L. E., & Taplin, J. R. (1973). *Clinical psychology: expanding horizons* (2nd ed.). New York: Prentice-Hall.

Walker, C. E. (1981). *Clinical practice of psychology.* New York: Pergamon Press.

Wolberg, L. R. (1995). *The technique of psychotherapy* (4th rev. ed.) Northvale, NJ: Aronson.

III | CAREERS IN DIVERSE ORGANIZATIONS

Douglas Herrmann

Rewards of Public Service: Research Psychologists in the Government

8

any psychologists spend their entire careers conducting research in the government. Many others work just for a while in government, devoting the bulk of their career to academia or industry. In this chapter I describe the personal and professional challenges that one faces in government research, for part or all of a career. It is my hope that my views here will provide students with a realistic sense of the variety of experiences that a psychologist may have while serving in government research.

What It Is Like to Work in Government Research

ORIGIN OF RESEARCH TOPICS

Government researchers investigate questions that originate in the will of the American people, as expressed at the

Douglas Herrmann was trained as an engineer at the U.S. Naval Academy (BS, 1964) and obtained an MS (1970) and a PhD (1972) in experimental psychology at the University of Delaware. Dr. Herrmann has been active in research on memory improvement and cognitive rehabilitation. He has published 71 articles and 7 books on various aspects of memory.

The author is grateful to his colleagues, Paul Beatty, Lindsay Childress, Linda Pickle, and Barbara Wilson, of the National Center of Health Statistics, for their valuable advice on the writing of this chapter.

ballot box and in polls. Thus, the questions investigated by government researchers are usually not conceived by them. This situation also occurs in business and industry, where research questions are formulated by higher level executives. This situation differs from the experience of researchers in academia, where the topics of research are typically conceived by professors who direct or do the research.

DIVERSITY OF RESEARCH EXPERIENCE

The most interesting aspect of being in government research is that researchers get to participate in many different research projects over a career, substantially more than a researcher experiences in business or academia. The diversity of government research contrasts with research in academia, where a researcher may investigate the same questions for most or all of a career. Investigations in business and industry also tend to last longer than investigations in government because business or industrial research often is concerned with the development of marketable products, a tedious process that may last up to several years.

One reason that researchers get involved in many research projects is that the duration of most government research projects is brief, lasting about a year. For example, a good deal of recent research has focused on the satisfaction of people who use the services of government agencies. This research has involved distributing questionnaires and holding focus groups. The collection and analysis of this data and developing reports on government satisfaction in many agencies took researchers about 6 to 10 months to complete.

Government research projects are, in part, brief because the research projects are aimed to provide the government and the public with information quickly enough to solve problems. Another reason that projects are brief is because shifts in public opinion lead political leaders or high-level bureaucrats to terminate an ongoing project and initiate a new project because the latter is of greater interest to the American people or to certain political leaders. For example, prior to the election of President Clinton, no federal research studied the cognitive processes that parents use to remember the immunizations of their children. After President Clinton's election, several investigations of parental recall of immunizations were initiated. However, a year and a half later, enthusiasm for health care reform waned, and most of the immunization projects were stopped or cut back.

SPECIALIZATION

Because the topics of research projects are constantly changing, government researchers inevitably become generalists. A seasoned government researcher is similar to the gunslinger in the Wild West who promised to "have gun, will travel," except that the government researcher's motto might be restated as "have research skills, will investigate." It is not unusual to meet government researchers whose careers have involved considerably different specialties. For example, a research psychologist colleague of mine whose entire career was in the military conducted investigations in psychopharmacology, personality traits, social psychology, verbal learning, neuropsychology, and psychotherapy. Such diversity is even more common among government researchers who have switched agencies. Such a diverse background would rarely be found in academia and would be found infrequently in business research.

In some cases, a government researcher will work on a project that lasts for a substantial period of time and thereby become a specialist. This occurs when the public continues to focus on a particular issue over an extended period. For example, many government researchers have devoted large periods of their lives to investigating issues such as the problems of the unemployed and the treatment of Alzheimer's disease. However, specialization is the exception in government research.

Government researchers not only experience a wide range of research problems in their careers, but they also come to use more kinds of methodologies than do researchers in academia, business, or industry. Government researchers conduct experiments and correlational studies. Sometimes the research will be conducted in a government laboratory, and other times the research will be done in the field. However, because it is usually applied to matters of public policy, government research probably involves more fieldwork, more correlational analyses, and less experimentation than research in academia and in business or industry.

Those government researchers that do specialize for a while are eventually shifted onto other projects and rarely return to the specialty they acquired. For example, a government research colleague of mine, who had studied perception in graduate school, investigated perceptual issues only briefly and subsequently investigated psychological aspects of health policy for several years, only to be switched to investigating financial aspects of such policy.

TEAM PLAYING

Once a topic has been handed to a government research group, a project is planned to address the topic. Because most topics are concerned with an applied problem (such as managed care of patients in psychiatric care), this planning usually requires a great deal of creativity. The implementation of the plan may be carried out by a single researcher, but it is more common for the plan to be carried out by a team of researchers. A research team is usually made up of specialists from several different disciplines. For example, one team that I served on consisted of three psychologists, a sociologist, one neuroscientist, one statistician, and one computer scientist. Because research teams are often multidisciplinary, the results of research are analyzed from the perspectives of several disciplines.

LOVE OF RESEARCH

Government research attracts and retains people who love research for research's sake. Researchers in academia and in industry love research pertaining to certain topics. If you present them with research on topics outside of their specialty, they are likely to yawn. Government researchers don't yawn when hearing about almost any research project. To the contrary, they sit up and listen eagerly to every detail. They love the process of seeking evidence and solving problems, no matter what the content.

Qualifications for a Job in Government Research

Most government researchers have a master's degree or a PhD. However, it is possible to start a government research career with a bachelor's degree as a research assistant. Research assistants who want to move up in the government usually find that they have to get a master's degree or a PhD.

There are many aspects of a government research job that should be considered before deciding whether it is for you. By way of illustration, let me tell you a little bit about how I got into government research and what I got out of my experience in the government. Afterwards I illustrate in more detail what government research is about and finally I suggest issues to consider if you are thinking about working as a research psychologist for the government, either in the short term or for a career.

My Background

I obtained my bachelor's degree from the U.S. Naval Academy in 1964. After a stint in the Marine Corps, I obtained an MS (1970) and a PhD (1972) in cognitive psychology at the University of Delaware, which was followed by a year of postdoctoral study at Stanford University (1972–73). Subsequently, I taught cognitive psychology for 16 years at Hamilton College, Clinton, New York (1973–1989).

While at Hamilton College, I became active in research into the improvement of memory and other cognitive functions of normal and brain-injured people. In the spring of 1988, I was invited to be a visiting researcher (supported under the Intergovernmental Personnel Act) in the Laboratory of Socio-environmental Studies at the National Institute of Mental Health (NIMH) to conduct research on memory improvement. While at NIMH, I learned that some federal survey agencies had become interested in the use of cognitive procedures (such as "think-alouds" and analyses of the comprehension of terms to be used in questionnaires) to pretest their surveys. I decided that the research programs of these agencies would broaden my background in memory and cognition, so in early 1990 I accepted the position of the director of a new cognitive lab at the Bureau of Labor Statistics (BLS).

BLS's cognitive lab performed a variety of fascinating cognitive analyses of potential surveys. The psychologists working in the lab were superb, and we got a lot of important work done. For example, we conducted investigations to guide the redesign of the Current Population Survey (the basis of the Unemployment Index) and the Current Expenditure Survey (the basis of the Consumer Price Index). These investigations involved asking people who might participate in this survey different forms of the questions that were being evaluated for a new form of the survey. The research effectively eliminated many defective questions from inclusion in the survey.

We also studied how interview errors affected a respondent's ability to answer questions (Miller, Herrmann, & Puskar, 1991). We were able to demonstrate that minor errors in presenting questions did not seriously affect the answers of respondents. Additionally, several of us developed a theory of the cognitive processes that interviewers and respondents engage in when participating in a survey interview (Mullin, Conrad, Sander, & Herrmann, 1994). This theory subsequently proved to be helpful to our lab and to other survey researchers in designing survey research and discussing research findings.

The cognitive lab at BLS functioned in many respects like an academic department. For example, we had a speaker series, and several distinguished psychologists presented lectures there. Similar to academia, government researchers routinely attend conferences and present papers. The conferences that they attend usually are different than the ones that academics attend. Instead, government researchers attend conferences related to the problem area in which they work.

For example, employees of survey agencies attend the meetings of statistical and survey organizations. In my first year in the government, I attended more conferences than I ever did while I was in academia. However, as in academia, travel to conferences depends on the availability of travel funds. In the past few years, opportunities to travel have decreased.

After I had been at BLS a little short of 2 years, the associate director of research and methodology of the National Center for Health Statistics (NCHS) invited me to come work for him as his special assistant on cognitive psychology. This position offered me more research opportunities than I had as a manager at BLS, so in 1992 I transferred from BLS to NCHS.

At NCHS I investigated a variety of interesting cognitive problems in survey research (Jobe & Herrmann, 1996) and epidemiology (Herrmann, 1995). For example, I codirected, with a statistician, a series of investigations into how people read statistical maps. Such maps illustrate, for example, increases in a disease's mortality rates by counties or states with increasingly darker grays, increasingly saturated hues, or different hues. Our research showed, for example, that people are more likely to correctly recognize the mortality rate of a disease in a certain region if the map employed grays or single hues rather than different hues (Herrmann & Pickle, 1996; Pickle & Herrmann, 1994, 1995). Finally, I initiated a pilot project to develop a national survey of cognitive functioning (perception, learning, remembering, problem solving) in order to measure the impairment in cognition resulting from diseases and disorders.

Why I Chose To Work in the Government

I chose to work in the government because it offered me the chance to engage in applied research and test my knowledge of cognitive psychology. By the time I entered the government, I had conducted basic research for more than 15 years. Additionally, I wanted the opportunity to participate in the investigation of problems that were important to our country. Probably because of the positive impact of my military training when I was young, I took extra pleasure in being able to once more make a contribution to my country.

When I entered government research, I did not expect to remain there for the rest of my career. My primary interests were in basic research and teaching; I knew that it was a matter of time before I would return to academia. I felt that experience in government research would make me a better teacher because applied research experience would provide me with valuable material for teaching. I also believed that experience in applied research in the government would help me become a better researcher. Thus, I decided that while I was in the government I would acquire as much applied research experience as possible and that, once I had gained enough of such experience, I would return to academia.

Financial Compensation

Salary had no bearing on my choice to work in the government. Across my six years in the government, my salary has ranged from $67,000 to $80,000. My salaries in academia have been comparable. It is sometimes suggested that the salaries are greater in the government than in academia. However, it is my impression that government and academic salaries are comparable as long as the researcher remains in research. If the researcher seeks administrative positions in the government, the salaries are higher; but this is also true in academia for those researchers who give up research and become a dean.

Alternatively, a researcher in academia has much more access to money-making opportunities outside of work than does a government researcher. In academia you can write books, be an expert witness in court, consult, and more. In the government, outside employment is possible, but you have to get permission to do so because of the potential for a conflict of interest between outside employment and the work you do for the government. Often the process of getting permission is onerous (filling out forms, securing the approval and signatures of various executives). Consequently, most government researchers give up doing outside work, or they limit the amount of outside work they do. If you hope to serve as an expert witness, write books (and be paid for it), consult, or do other kinds of outside work in your career, recognize that you may not be permitted to do these activities while in government employment.

The fringe benefits in the government are at least as good as they are in academia or industry. The government's retirement and medical programs are excellent. Vacation days increase with seniority (from 13 days a year after hiring to 30 days after 20 years' service). There are a variety of workday schedules (for 2 years I worked eight 10-hour days, one 8 hour day, and got my 10th day off). Also, most government researchers whom I know do not take work home at night.

Attributes Needed for Success in Government Research

A career in government research necessitates the attributes required of both basic researchers and applied researchers (Herrmann & Raybeck, in press). First, the government researcher should have an insatiable curiosity about both basic and applied research. The government researcher must enjoy basic research in general because basic research typically provides the avenue into understanding a new research project. The government researcher must enjoy applied research in general because, as mentioned often here, most government research is applied.

A second important attribute of a government researcher is a desire to work with others. Because most government research projects are conducted by an interdisciplinary team, government researchers need to enjoy others and like learning about other disciplines.

Third, the most important attribute of a government researcher is to be able to move easily from an ethereal to an earthy perspective and vice versa. Government researchers find it necessary to shift between these perspectives as they explain a research project to different audiences, such as members of congress, officials in the executive branch, or citizens visiting an agency. For example, a presentation of research on Alzheimer's disease will be done differently across these different kinds of listeners.

If you are the kind of person who is interested in science broadly, who enjoys working with professionals from a variety of disciplines, and who can readily shift from an elementary to a technical perspective, then a government research position might be right for you.

Range of Opportunities for Employment in Government Research

A wide range of research jobs exist in the government. There are positions calling for "hands-on" research, in which you run the subjects and do all of the analyses. However, these positions are uncommon. Most government research is conducted by contractors who are supervised by government researchers. By having government researchers work at a supervisory level, these researchers do not become too involved in any one project. Thus, government researchers remain flexible and are prepared to drop projects and pick up new projects without difficulty.

If you land a government research position, you will probably work as an *analyst*. With a psychology degree, you might also become a *psychologist*, a *social science analyst*, or even a *statistician*. As an analyst, you will conduct literature searches, supervise the research of contractors, and prepare reports on the knowledge and practice in particular problem areas. For example, the General Accounting Office periodically has psychologists studying the effectiveness of various mental health programs. The military periodically has its psychologists do research into the best measures of intelligence, in order to improve the tests used to recruit new military personnel.

Alternatively, if you like to carry out research that you conceive, you will find it hard to find a government job that will let you do this. Similarly, if you want to become a specialist in some area of psychology, you will probably have difficulty finding a job in government research that calls for specializing. However, if you can forego having your hands on research, and you enjoy supervising other researchers as they carry out your research project, your destiny may lie in government research.

How to Land a Government Research Job

Regardless of when you decide to seek a government research position, take your time. There are magazines that list job opportunities in the federal government (e.g., *Federal Career Opportunities*, *Federal Digest*). They can be easily found at magazine shops if you are in Washington, DC, or they may be ordered through the mail.

Landing a government job is easier if you have someone to help you. Seek out a friend who works for the government, if you know one. If not, seek out an alumnus (with the help of your career center) who works for the government. An alumnus who works for the government can provide you with valuable information about how to best present yourself in a job interview or on your resume.

If you get an offer for a government research job, look it over very carefully. Some offers are better refused in order that you can wait for a more suitable offer. Make sure that you are being hired at a level that is high enough for your education and experience. Don't take any action (quitting a job, arranging for a move) on the basis of a verbal offer. If you are presented with a written contract, go over it very carefully and ask lots of questions. Take it to someone with government experience, and ask this person to advise you. The formal and informal titles of government jobs are constantly changing, partly because the projects are constantly changing. Contracts have been nullified in some cases at the highest level, including the presidency, even after people have quit their jobs and moved to Washington.

If you obtain a written offer that is sound and the job is what you want, congratulations! You will have passed very stringent hiring procedures.

Preparation for a Government Research Position

If you decide that you want to pursue a government research career, I recommend that you consider working in basic research outside of the government for a few years before you start in government research. In most cases, entry-level positions in basic research are very hard to find in the government. If you begin your career in government research, you will probably not be promoted as quickly as you would had you begun in basic research elsewhere. Alternatively, many government researchers will regard your basic research experience as especially valuable in preparing you to understand the factors involved in an application.

A Typical Day in the Life of a Dual Research Career

If you were to obtain a government research job, a typical day might go like this:

The other day I got to work at the National Center for Health Statistics about 20 minutes before starting time. I checked my mail, read my e-mail, and listened to my phone messages. My mail included a manuscript that I had agreed to review for a journal. My e-mail conveyed a variety of chores of no great importance. My phone mail had messages from two different contractors who were conducting psychological research for the government. One message asked that I forward copies of the graphs that were to be included in a forthcoming technical report. The other message asked about how long subjects should be interviewed in a pretest of a statistical map. I answered a few e-mail messages and postponed replying to the contractors until later.

With immediate communications taken care of, I met with my summer research assistant. We were working on a project investigating how people use heuristics in answering survey questions. Such questions usually do not call for reasoning or problem solving. Instead, these questions ask about a person's behavior, for example, how often they do something (such as how often they visit the doctor). In principle, people supposedly answer such questions after checking their memory. However, research in recent years has indicated that people usually do not recall the information they give in their answers. Instead, they reason out their answers. My research assistant and I spent the morning checking the literature and trying to figure out the conditions under which heuristics are used in answering survey questions.

At lunchtime, I went to a local fast-food restaurant with a fellow researcher. We discussed various matters concerning the management of the research group in which we both worked. After lunch, I spent the afternoon writing a manuscript. This manuscript was concerned with what leads respondents to say that they recall the answer to a question or to say that they do not know truly or falsely.

The Pros and Cons of a Government Research Career

CONS

The greatest difficulty in government research is what it makes it exciting: politics. Because government research serves the public interest, many research topics are extremely interesting. However, as the public interest shifts, a government researcher has to quit many of the interesting projects. Prior to accepting a government job, it is important to carefully consider whether you will be happy having to give up working on interesting projects because the government's priorities change.

PROS

When anyone has chosen the right profession, he or she thoroughly enjoys the work. Washington, DC, is to an applied researcher as a candy shop is to a kid (Herrmann & Gruneberg, 1993). Many of the best labs in the nation are there. There are many opportunities for interagency collaborations. While working for the government, I maintained collaborations with colleagues in the National Institute of Mental Health, the National Institute of Neurological Disorders and Stroke, the National Institute for Aging, the National Institute for Alcohol Abuse and Alcoholism, and the Department of Veterans Affairs.

Government researchers are often the first scientists, or among the first scientists, to investigate a problem. For example, the first breakthroughs in psychological research on AIDS were made primarily by government researchers. Being among the first to investigate a problem often challenges government researchers to investigate psychological phenomena in ways that have not been tried before and to develop new theoretical perspectives. The opportunity to be first in the investigation of phenomena of importance to our society is what motivates many psychologists to work in government research.

The government researcher gets the broadest view of the entire research process, more so than basic researchers or applied researchers in industry. Basic researchers are often unaware that applications have been made on the basis of their findings. Applied researchers in business and industry are often aware only of the basic research that they apply while developing a product. However, government researchers are likely to see a project through: from relatively basic research, to initial applied research, to attempts at application, and finally to the impact of their research on public policy. If you love research for research's sake, value being involved in an important mission, and enjoy having the big picture of the research process, then government research may be for you.

EPILOGUE

In August 1995, I decided that I had learned enough about applied government research and that I was ready to return to teaching and basic research. Accordingly, I left government research to participate again in academic life, in the Psychology Department of Indiana State University (in Terre Haute, Indiana).

I anticipate that my 6 years of government research experience will help me considerably in the future in teaching and in research. My government research experience gave me a wealth of knowledge to use in teaching. This experience also has suggested many topics for my basic research.

I feel very fortunate to have served in government research. I expect to continue collaborating with colleagues with whom I worked in the government. Additionally, I hope that I will have the opportunity to work part time or full time in government research in the future. If you decide to make government research a part or all of your career, I am sure that you—like me—will be glad that you did.

References

Herrmann, D. (1995). Reporting current, past, and changed health status: What we know about statistics. *Health Care, 33,* 89–94.

Herrmann, D. J., & Gruneberg, M. (1993). The need to expand the horizons of the practical aspects of memory movement. *Applied Cognitive Psychology, 7,* 553–565.

Herrmann, D., & Pickle, W. (1996). A cognitive subtask model of statistical map reading. *Visual Cognition, 3,* 165–190.

Herrmann, D., & Raybeck, D. (in press). Basic and applied research cultures. In D. Payne & F. Conrad (Eds.), *Advances in basic and applied research.* Mawah, NJ: Erlbaum.

Jobe, J. B., & Herrmann, D. (1996). Comparison of survey cognition and models of memory. In D. Herrmann, M. Johnson, C. McEvoy, C. Hertzog, & P. Hertel (Eds.) *Basic and applied memory research: New findings.* Mawah, NJ: Erlbaum.

Miller, L., Herrmann, D., & Puskar, C. (1991). The effects of non-standard interviewer verbal behavior on respondent verbal behavior. Phoenix, AZ: American Association for Public Opinion Research.

Mullin, P. A., Conrad, F. G., Sander, J. E., & Herrmann, D. (1994). *Modelling the question answering process of survey respondents.* Washington, DC: American Psychological Society.

Pickle, L. W., & Herrmann, D. J. (1994). The process of reading statistical maps: The effect of color. *Statistical Computing and Graphics Newsletter, 5,* 1, 12–15.

Pickle, L. W., & Herrmann, D. (1995). *Cognitive aspects of statistical mapping.* (No. 18 of the Working Paper Series of the National Center for Health Statistics). Hyattsville, MD: National Center for Health Statstics.

Stephen F. Poland

Pathways to Change and Development: The Life of a School Psychologist

9

Beginning the Journey

A good way to acquaint you with some of the key issues you'll encounter as a school psychologist is to describe the circuitous journey, spanning over 20 years, that led me to become one. My journey illustrates a core aspect of the profession of school psychology: its focus on the facilitation of learning and development across a wide variety of settings with learners of all ages and cultural backgrounds.

My journey began with my decision to enter the Peace Corps. After training for the Peace Corps in inner-city Philadelphia and on the Caribbean island of Barbados, I was assigned to the island of Grenada, a steep, intensely green volcanic member of the Leeward Islands. I recall trudging the steep path each morning from the house I rented in the adjoining village of Grenville to the beautiful harbor of St.

After earning his doctorate from the Psychology in the Schools Training Program at the University of Minnesota, Stephen Poland returned to New Mexico to continue his rural and multicultural work. He continues to work extensively in rural school settings in the northern part of the state, where he provides school psychological services to Native American, Hispanic, and Anglo youngsters and their families. He also engages in the private practice of school psychology as part of a large managed care group in Albuquerque.

The author thanks Miriam Sagan for her editorial assistance in charting his course with this chapter. Thanks also to his colleagues in Division 16—Cindy Carlson, Jane Conoley, and Randy Kamphaus—for their helpful comments.

George's, surrounded by the bright red roofs made from the ballast of sailing ships, where the Anglican High School was located. In spite of the beauty of the setting, there were many times that year at the Anglican High School when I felt like giving up in disgust. The girls showed little if any interest in learning what I was told to teach, and I had no idea how to maintain effective discipline. The 10th-grade girls in particular seemed out to get me, and I became furious when I thought my authority was being challenged. I recall a very attractive dark-skinned young woman in my physiology class who was determined to ignore my discussions of evolution because her religious beliefs taught her that discussing alternative explanations for the origin of life on the planet was heresy. Much to my dismay, the senior girls in my physiology class failed to pass the end-of-the-year examination developed in England that in effect determined their final grade in the class. The exam was predicated on displaying competencies that would be necessary to get accepted to a college or university, something most of the girls I taught were never likely to seek. The teaching of the class focused on their passing the exam, not learning things relevant to life on the island. As the school year ended, I found myself proudly accompanying those senior girls, who had frustrated me so completely, to their graduation ceremony. I left my classroom experience in the West Indies appreciating how complex the process of schooling is, especially in culturally diverse settings.

I came back from the West Indies and worked as a substitute teacher in the Sacramento, California, public schools at the middle and high school levels. It was a pleasant surprise to enter classrooms filled with learning aides and textbooks, something missing from most schools in Grenada. In spite of the richness of resources in these classrooms, I found the classrooms I visited varied widely in their atmosphere concerning learning. In many classes, the children seemed eager to learn, especially as I shared some of my stories of the West Indies with them. In other classrooms, there was an atmosphere of doom. I vividly recall filling in for a frequently ill teacher and narrowly avoiding being trampled by the students as they mobbed the door when the bell rang. I had made the mistake of insisting that they remain a few minutes after class because of their misbehavior. The sense I had was that this class was a dead end for students who were so turned off to schooling that they were considered lost causes. I left the substitute teaching experience wishing I could hang around those classrooms as an invisible observer to tease out the factors in the students, the teachers, the parents, and the families that contributed to the great variability in these students' approaches to learning and the atmosphere of these classrooms. I wanted to meet with the teachers, those invisible presences in the classes I taught, to hear their stories of success and failure. Did they share the sense of futility and delight I had experienced as a teacher in the West Indies?

The summer of 1972 found me driving from Gallup, New Mexico, to Coyote Canyon on the Navajo reservation. The two-lane highway was nearly obscured by dust, and a young Navajo child seemed to materialize out of nowhere with his herd of sheep. There was a sense of unreality to the scene as I reached the school, a set of ancient flat-topped stone buildings and a rutted parking lot. I was even more disoriented when I entered a classroom and was confronted with severely mentally handicapped Navajo children, many of whom had until recently been in large impersonal state institutions, removed from their families, their communities, and their language and culture. Over time I came to love that community, those children, and the parents who cared so much, and I ended up staying 6 years.

Many of the students at the school had been given intelligence tests and scored at the lowest and most handicapped level. Yet it was evident that these young people had skills that were relevant to their culture. I recall a Down's syndrome child who could beat out complex rhythms on the drum, young women who learned to card and weave rugs from foster grandparents, and Yazzie, our survival artist who could go for days in very severe weather conditions with little clothing or food and would turn up in a distant town days later seemingly no worse for wear. Obviously, the intelligence tests were missing something that was very important. I left Coyote Canyon with a new appreciation of the cultural and social factors that shape the process of learning, and I was ready to seek training as a school psychologist because I had more questions than answers about the journey I had taken.

Training for the Profession

Your interest in school psychology may be a recent development, or it may be something you've had for many years. Although there is no single set of experiences that prepares you for this career, an interest in children and their schooling is a common denominator. In my case, the experience teaching in the West Indies and in California, as well as my 6 years in the Navajo Nation, kindled an interest in learning more about the process of schooling. If I had been asked as an undergraduate student in college if I would later become a school psychologist, I'm sure I would have said no. Although I felt as a child and adolescent that the schools and classrooms I attended were often oppressive and limiting environments, and certainly ones to which I hoped never to return, I now find schools to be some of the most exciting and challenging settings in which to work. Don't be surprised if your interest in school psychology comes late in your process of formal schooling.

So you have decided to apply for admission to a training program in school psychology. There are many programs around the country that train school psychologists at the master's, the specialist, and the doctoral levels. How do you decide which program to apply to and what level of training to seek? A good way to learn about exemplary training programs is to read the official journals of the professional organizations that represent the best interests of school psychologists.

The American Psychological Association (APA), a professional organization that represents the interests of psychology, considers the doctoral degree to be the entry level into the profession. Division 16, the Division of School Psychology, has traditionally represented doctoral-level-trained school psychologists who belong to the APA. The journal of Division 16 is the *School Psychology Quarterly*. It's important for you to know that most school psychologists in the United States have not been trained at the doctoral level and have earned the master's or specialist degree. Many of these professionals are represented by the National Association of School Psychologists (NASP). The journal of the NASP is the *School Psychology Review*. In recent years, there has been increasing cooperation between these professional groups in representing the best interests of school psychologists.

The history of the profession of school psychology over the last 20 years has seen a continuing discussion of the minimal level of training that is appropriate for entry into the field. At the present time, most school psychologists are trained at the specialist level, which requires 3 years of postgraduate work. As Cobb (1989) pointed out, the specialist level is now approaching the complexity of doctoral-level training. If you choose to enter the profession at the master's or the specialist level, you may decide at some point to continue your training at the doctoral level.

Doctoral training programs in school psychology involve a minimum of 4 years of full-time graduate study or its equivalent, followed by a yearlong internship. This training is based on the scientist–practitioner model for professional psychology. As a doctoral student, you will be socialized in this model as you complete your training, applying a research orientation to the practice of psychology and critically evaluating the techniques and interventions that you use to ensure that they are scientifically valid.

Your classes and seminars at the university or professional school will be at the graduate level and will include normal and abnormal development, the nature of exceptional learners, theories of how families and organizations function, and models for school consultation. You will learn techniques of assessment, including the administration of standardized intelligence and achievement tests and alternative methods of assessment and intervention such as individual and group counseling, parent training, and other skills. Additional areas you will study include the diagnosis of mental disorders, instructional psychology, statistics and measurement, the biological bases of behavior, and the ethics of the practice of professional psychology. Although this list may sound long—and it doesn't include all the content you will be exposed to—you will find yourself applying this knowledge to the supervised practical experiences you are engaged in on a daily basis, which will enliven the process of learning.

In most doctoral programs, from the day you enter your training program you will be involved in supervised experiences with children and youth. These field experiences or practica are in settings like schools, hospitals, and mental health clinics, and they will be offered at times in your training when you are acquiring skills related to that setting. For example, as you learn the many ways to assess learners, including observation, curriculum-based measurement, and individualized intelligence and achievement tests, you will assess children and adolescents in regular and special education classrooms. The goal of these field experiences will be to introduce you to the multitude of settings in which school psychologists work and to provide you with opportunities to practice and refine your clinical skills.

Because school psychology is a profession focused on the process of schooling, you will be evaluated in a variety of innovative ways. These include self-evaluation as well as evaluation by the other students, folios of materials to illustrate mastery of a content area, and evaluation by supervising professionals in schools and community settings. A major project in my graduate program, for example, involved doing a comprehensive assessment of a child, including interviews with his parent in the home environment and observations of his behavior at school and at home. In addition, there will be the more conventional methods of graduate school evaluation, including reports, research assignments, and written and oral examinations. At the completion of the course work and practicum experiences, you will take a preliminary written and oral examination requiring you to integrate the course content with the experiences you've had in your field settings. On successful completion of the exam, you will become a doctoral candidate ready to begin your yearlong internship and complete the work on your dissertation.

Predoctoral internship settings may range from the public schools to pediatric and mental health clinics. Some national training standards require part of the internship experience to be gained in school settings. You are provided at least 2 hours of supervision each week in the settings in which you work. At this point in your training, you will be performing the duties typically associated with the profession of school psychology. Although this training experience may sound daunting, in practice it moves quickly because you are involved from the beginning in direct work with children, their family and other caretakers, teachers, and adult learners, depending on the setting.

The formal degree is conferred when you complete the dissertation and successfully defend your work on that project. Dissertation projects vary considerably in content and approach. The project provides you the opportunity to function in the role of the scientist practitioner, carrying out a research project that addresses a question of significance to the field of school psychology. Dissertation projects have included the effect of mental imagery on performance, social information processing in socially isolated students, the effect of self-instruction on the completion of homework, and the impact of consultation on the ability of teachers to identify problems, to name just a few possibilities.

Completion of the degree means that you can apply for a credential to practice school psychology. Actually, by the time you complete the doctoral training program, you will probably have met the requirements for licensure. Because the practice of school psychology has traditionally occurred in school settings, and schools are regulated by state departments of education, the credentialing of school psychologists has been granted by education agencies. State requirements for certification vary widely, with most states not requiring the doctorate for practice. The license to practice outside of school settings is typically governed by state psychology licensing boards, and again there are considerable variations across states in these regulations. Many school psychologists, such as myself, hold credentials both from psychology licensing boards and from state departments of education.

Career Activities: The Ecology of Work and Setting

So now you have completed your graduate training and are ready to begin your work as a school psychologist. What is it about your professional approach that makes you different from the other psychologists described in this book? Although school psychologists share a common set of knowledge and skills with other professional psychologists, they differ because they provide psychological services that will facilitate the growth and development of learners throughout the life span. Let's begin our description of the activities a school psychologist might pursue to achieve this goal by considering the setting tradition-ally associated with the profession, the school. School psychologists believe that schools are where the action is, as far as children, youth, and families are concerned. The public schools have a zero-reject pol-icy concerning whom they serve, so you can work with children and their families in ways that are impossible in settings such as mental health clinics or private practice offices.

A useful way to conceptualize the multitude of tasks you may per-form in schools is to use the ecological viewpoint (Apter & Conoley, 1984). In this model, a child's behavior is the result of an interaction between the child's characteristics, such as age, sex, prior experience, or temperament, and his or her environment. To get an adequate description of the behavior of a sixth-grade girl, it is necessary to look beyond the girl's characteristics to consider how she responds to, and is responded to by, the teacher and the other children in the classroom. How is the classroom structured as far as her academic tasks are con-cerned, and what is the teacher's style of presenting material to her and other members of the class? Is she given frequent feedback about how she's doing, and how much time does the teacher have to indi-vidualize instruction? Is she accepted by the other children, or is she an unpopular child? Does the teacher view her as engaging and attrac-tive or remote and uninterested in learning what the teacher has to offer? Factors such as these color the child's' experience of the class-room and her attitude toward the learning process.

But it isn't enough to stop at the classroom door. To discover what a child brings to the learning process, you must go beyond the child and the classroom to learn how the child is influenced by the school, her family, and the community. Is the school a modern one with many learning resources, or are the buildings run down and poorly main-tained and the teaching staff demoralized by recent budget cuts? Are the girl's parents satisfied with their marriage and their roles, or are they engaged in marital conflict and faced with low-paying and stress-ful jobs? Does the community provide adequate resources for recre-ation and day care? Is the neighborhood safe from violence? How did the parents feel about their experiences in school? Were they success-ful students or labeled as failures? In conclusion, the ecological approach suggests that the behavior of a sixth-grade girl in her class-room is the result of the complex interplay of all these factors. How then is this approach used in your work as a school psychologist?

A fourth-grade boy, John, has been referred to you because he is not completing his assignments, and he is getting into frequent fights on the playground. There have been prior attempts to help

John succeed academically and avoid fights, and they have not been successful. Your first step as a school psychologist is to assess the situation in his classroom, and you decide to observe John. You choose a time when math is being taught, knowing that John is even less likely to complete his math assignments than his other academic subjects. He completes little work, and instead stares out the window and plays with a puzzle. John's behavior is in striking contrast to that of most of his classmates, who are working on their assignments. John's teacher makes a couple of attempts to get him to work, but John seems to ignore her efforts. You notice that the teacher is well organized and that the classroom is a pleasant environment in which to learn.

Later that day you interview the teacher, who is very frustrated at John's failure to respond to her teaching techniques. She has tried modifying his assignments with no success, and she believes his family situation may be contributing to his problems in school, for he often comes to school looking tired and unkempt. A review of the school records indicates that John was performing at grade level in most academic areas, including math, when he took the school district's standardized achievement battery last fall.

Your next step as a school psychologist is to consider the school environment outside the classroom. Because you want to know what triggers the fights on the playground, you observe him during lunch recess and discover that he spends most of his time with two younger boys. At one point he tries to grab a basketball from a group of fourth graders, and a fight is narrowly averted.

You meet with John's mother, who is also concerned about her son. She feels the school staff are not doing all they could to help her child at a difficult time in his life. She explains that her husband has been laid off from his job recently and that this has created conflict in the marriage as she tries to support the family with her low-paying job. She has not told school staff about this, believing that this isn't the school's business and that should this news get out, it will only make John's life more difficult.

You interview John to get his view of how he is doing at school and how he is treated by his teachers, classmates, and parents. John appears to be depressed, and his fights the result of his misinterpreting the actions of classmates toward him. You administer a standardized interview and a paper-and-pencil inventory to assess the level of his distress.

After all the information is gathered, your next step is to integrate this information in the form of a report that addresses the referral concern. These reports may be informal compilations of data, or they may be detailed written reports. The report is used as part of the decision-making process in the school to decide what interventions are most appropriate to use with John.

As a school psychologist, you are a member of a team of school professionals, including teachers and administrators, that makes decisions about children such as John. John's parents are important members of this team. As an expert in the team decision-making process, you have consulted in the past with other team members at John's school to ensure that their decisions are good ones. At the team meeting with school staff and John's parents, the team develops a plan, and members, including yourself, are assigned responsibilities to carry out interventions designed to assist John. You decide to include John in a group of children who are learning ways to cope with their depression and develop the social skills needed to make friendships and resolve conflicts without fighting.

In addition to providing direct services to John, as an expert in measurement you assist other team members in evaluating the effectiveness of their interventions with John. As an expert in consultation, you work with John's teacher in rewarding John for getting along with other students and completing more of his work. You help change the teacher's view of John as an apathetic child who hates the teacher to a depressed child who expects rejection and often acts to elicit this behavior from others.

Another area where you work with teachers at John's school is in staff development activities such as workshops. Teachers need to know how to identify students in their class who, like John, may be depressed and act out their depression in hostile ways. You are able to engage John's parents in a parenting group offered in the evening, with the school providing supervised child care for John and his brother and sister. In addition to parenting skills, John's parents learn how to assist him in completing his homework and improving his study skills.

At the school system level, you confer with the principal at John's school to ensure that there are policies to handle crisis situations such as the suicide of a student. As you move into the community meeting families such as John's, you work with other professionals and parent groups in the community to tackle such problems as the lack of appropriate child care or supervised after-school recreation. The school psychologist is in an excellent position to consult and help develop community-based programs to head off the development of problems in schoolchildren such as John. It should be clear that as a school psychologist, you have a multitude of ways to improve the process of schooling for children such as John.

What will your life be like if you decide to work in a setting outside of an elementary or secondary school? Pfeiffer and Dean (1988), in an edition of the *School Psychology Review* in which they were guest editors, focused on the contributions of school psychologists in non-traditional settings. They saw an expanding demand for the services of doctoral-level school psychologists. Contributors to that volume included Sandoval (1988), who described the role of the school psychologist in higher education. This might include many of the activities that school psychologists in elementary and secondary schools perform, such as counseling students with special needs and screening for students with learning problems. In addition, there would be the opportunity to consult with college faculty concerning their teaching and their relationships with students, advisees, and other faculty. Sandoval viewed the goal of the work of the "college psychologist" as increasing "the educational effectiveness of the institution." Other roles for school psychologists described by contributors to that volume included work in vocational rehabilitation facilities, in behavioral medicine programs, in departments of pediatrics and neurology, in day treatment and residential facilities, in community mental health centers, in private practice, and in business and industry. More recently, Talley and Short (1994) have described an expanded role for school psychologists as experts in health care. School psychology is a dynamic profession, with its practitioners contributing their expertise to an ever-widening variety of settings.

Pleasures and Challenges of the Profession

The greatest advantage I have found in pursuing a career in school psychology is the challenge to change and grow. School psychology is a very dynamic field that requires me to stay abreast of the latest developments in psychology and education. Rosenfeld (1990) described the ever-increasing pace of accumulation of professional knowledge and quotes Knowles's (1989) concept of the "competent person," one who is able to "sustain continuous, self-directed, life long learning." Most of us will need to make changes in our careers, and as an expert in the facilitation of growth and change, you will be able to use this knowledge for your own benefit. I am constantly learning new skills and competencies, consulting with colleagues to master a new technique, seeking supervision as I move into new areas of practice, and attending workshops and "retooling" myself.

Another advantage you have as a school psychologist is the opportunity to work in a multitude of settings with learners of all ages and backgrounds as well as cultural and social circumstances. School settings allow you to intervene with children who would never come through the doors of a mental health clinic because their families lack the financial resources, the motivation, or the knowledge to access these services. Most schools are "zero reject" service centers that are mandated to serve whoever comes in the door. The impact of your intervention is magnified in a school because you can work with children and their teachers, other school staff, and their parents. Parents may feel less stigmatized if their child receives the service from the school rather than a mental health setting.

Another advantage is the ability to do preventative work, working with entire classes or intervening with the school as a system to head off problems. In this way you are able to reach far more children. An example of such an intervention could be to help the school develop a "buddy system" to support students entering middle school, a time when many children experience increased stress because of stricter grading standards and less teacher support. As an expert in growth and development, you can help shape the institutions where children spend so much of their lives.

All careers have their challenging aspects, and school psychology is no exception. You may be faced with heavy caseloads of students with increasingly severe problems, and with schools facing increased economic pressures to cut back on services, your job may come to be in jeopardy.

Another challenge you may face is the tendency for some professionals, outside the field, to view school psychology as a second-rate profession. Professionals working in schools tend to be looked down on as having inferior training through their association with colleges of education. Because many school psychologists are trained at the master's or specialist level, they are thought to lack the professional status of other psychological specialists. As a result, school psychologists have been blocked in some parts of the country from getting reimbursed by third-party payers such as insurance companies for the services they provide.

Another problem with the evolution of the specialty is the focus on school psychologists as the gatekeepers of special education. Many school psychologists spend a great deal of their time testing children to see if they are eligible for special education services. The result is that the school psychologist has little time left to do the many activities they are trained to do, such as consulting with teachers and parents, designing intervention programs, and providing group and individual therapy to children.

I hope that you are not deterred from considering the profession because of these factors and that you see that the advantages far outweigh the disadvantages.

What It Takes To Be a Successful School Psychologist

Because school psychology is a career focused on optimizing healthy development rather than pathology, I hesitate to provide a list of requirements, fearing you may judge yourself harshly as not having what it takes. If you feel you lack some of them, don't despair. A central attribute for success in the field is the willingness to change and adapt, and you will find that these characteristics can be developed over time. Here's my list of recommended attributes:

1. Be passionately interested in children, youth, and their families. There is so much to learn about what constitutes healthy growth and development and what can get a learner "off track" developmentally.
2. Be a lifelong learner committed to keeping abreast of the latest developments in the fields of education and developmental psychology.
3. Look in an informed and skeptical fashion at the literature and research in education and psychology concerning schools and learners, and be willing to make your contribution to that literature with well-thought-out studies. In the field of education there is a tendency for educational fads to sweep the country without a sufficient base of research to support their widespread use.
4. Be responsive to serving an increasingly culturally diverse group of learners ranging from the gifted to those with severe handicaps, as well as their teachers and their caretakers.
5. Be self-reflective, continually aware of factors that might interfere with your successful work with a client and ready to seek out supervision or consultation to deal with any obstacles.
6. Be flexible in your approach toward problem solving. This would include the ability to establish collaborative relationships with students, parents, and other professionals. In this way, you can move away from always having to be the "expert" who knows all the answers to someone who can facilitate the problem-solving abilities of others and foster their self-reliance.
7. Always set the highest standards for yourself in your professional work and the ethical standards to which you adhere. As an expert in the process of growth and change, I'd have you set an example for other professionals in the way you conduct your life in honoring the capacity for personal growth and development in yourself and in others.

Financial Rewards of the Profession

What are the financial rewards of this challenging and demanding profession? The financial rewards of the career vary as a function of the level of training and the setting in which the school psychologist works. In a comprehensive survey of school psychology practitioners who were members of the National Association of School Psychologists and of faculty in school psychology training programs, Reschly and Wilson (1995) found that practitioner mean salaries during the 1991–1992 survey year were $37,587, as compared with university faculty mean salaries of $46,657. They found that whereas only 35% of the practitioners reported earning income in addition to salaries, 70% of the academics reported such income, including income from private practice, consultation, or royalties. On average, the supplemental income earned by the academics (mean = $14,697) totaled more than twice as much as the income reported by the practitioners (mean = $6,794).

When total income was broken down by level of training, the university faculty earned just under $57,000, whereas the doctoral-level practitioners earned $51,000 and the non-doctoral-level practitioners earned slightly less than $40,000. The authors pointed out that because non-doctoral-level practitioners are restricted in most states to practicing in schools, they are limited in their opportunities to earn additional income and their ability to advance in their careers, as compared with those school psychologists with doctorates.

A Typical Day in the Life of a School Psychologist

What is a typical day in the life of a school psychologist? The example I've created based on my experiences will illustrate that there is no typical day in a career where change and adjustment to change are defining characteristics. School psychology is an atypical career filled with atypical days. The community I have in mind for my example is somewhere in northern New Mexico about two hours by car from Albuquerque. The families in this community are lower middle class, and ranching and mining are the primary modes of employment. Students in the school are Anglo, Hispanic, and Native American.

After the long drive from Albuquerque, across the high desert country with snow-covered mountains in the distance, I pulled into the parking lot at the elementary school where I checked in each morning. The school, over 20 years old, seemed too large for its student population, the result of a downturn in the local mining economy a few years ago that led many families to leave the community. On entering the office, I found a message to meet immediately with the fourth-grade teacher, Mrs. Harrington. She was in the duty room, visibly upset as I walked with her to a corner of the room where we could talk privately. She told me that one of her students, who had been struggling with leukemia, died last night. Although the class had talked openly about the possibility of this child dying, the shock of the event was far more than she had expected. I arranged to meet with the class in the morning and to talk with Mrs. Harrington and her fourth graders about their feelings. The teacher had informed the school counselor, who would be meeting individually with students who were very close to this child to help them mourn the loss of their friend. I suggested that Mrs. Harrington start the day in as normal a fashion as possible, to give her students the comforting message that in spite of tragic events such as the death of a classmate, life goes on for the survivors.

I was scheduled to meet with Aaron this morning and found the thought reassuring as I struggled with my thoughts about the children in Mrs. Harrington's classroom. Aaron was a very bright midschooler who was failing a number of classes. He was a delight to work with, and I could count on him bringing me a new toy or project to talk about each time we met. The previous school psychologist had believed Aaron to be severely emotionally disturbed, because he would often break into tears in the classroom with no apparent provocation and he had no close friendships with students in his classes. He seemed to have a mental block when it came to doing open-ended writing assignments, and he would typically stare off or put his head quietly on the desk instead of completing his written work. Aaron came from a troubled family background, with a mother suffering from severe depression and a father who was often violent with his children. He was the kind of student who would not be seen by a psychologist in a mental health clinic, because the family saw mental health services as threatening and stigmatizing.

Aaron joined me at our scheduled time and proudly told me about his presentation in front of the parents' group the day before. I had discussed Aaron's writing block with his language arts teacher, Miss Napir, and she had agreed to let him use a tape recorder to record his thoughts about the writing assignments. He had done this on a recent assignment and used the computer in the classroom to write it. The result was an impressive paper that Aaron could share with others. Teachers such as Miss Napir, who collaborated with me in finding ways to help students like Aaron succeed, are a special source of pleasure in this work.

On my way to the fourth-grade classroom, Mr. Gordon, the elementary and middle school principal, thanked me for the material I had given him on how to design a transition program to assist students going from elementary to middle school. The middle school teachers were struggling with a seemingly unruly and irresponsible group of seventh graders and had asked the principal for help. I was aware of research indicating the difficulty many students had when they entered middle school, because of fewer close supportive contacts with teachers, stricter standards for grading, and less intellectually challenging work in typical middle school environments. The principal had been unwilling to blame all the teachers' problems on the seventh graders, and he was grateful for the insights into the environmental factors that might be involved. The parents' association at the school, upset at the lack of the seventh graders' progress, had suggested that a back-to-basics approach stressing stricter classroom discipline would help, but the principal had his doubts that this would solve the problem.

In Mrs. Harrington's classroom, the fourth graders sat quietly and said nothing. She had been asking them about their feelings concerning their classmate. I knew it was unrealistic to expect that many would speak in the group. I told them that although I didn't know their friend, I could imagine the confused feelings they would have. Their classmate had faced her illness in a very open fashion and remained active and alive up to the end; yet it seemed so unfair that a young life full of possibilities had suddenly come to an end. The children listened thoughtfully, and Mrs.Harrington seemed relieved that someone else could share her confusion. Before leaving the class, I told Mrs. Harrington I'd be available that day to meet with any child who was having a hard time, and she assured me the counselor was already talking to a small group of children who were closest to this child.

As I left Mrs. Harrington's class, I recalled my conversation a few weeks before with the superintendent, Mrs. Sanchez, about the pressing need for the district to have a plan to deal with crises. A middle school student who was alone in the boys' bathroom had discharged a pistol, and the bullet had hit the wall. Luckily, he wasn't hurt, although the bullet had passed near his head. He had been evaluated at the county mental health clinic and had not been found to be suicidal, yet he could easily have died or hurt someone else. I had recommended that the schools in the district develop a crisis response team that would include the school psychologist, counselors, teachers, administrators, and staff. I also suggested that procedures be developed for how to handle a traumatic event like the death of a student that specified how the students and staff would be notified, how classes would be conducted, and who would be available to meet with high-risk students. This was not the first time I had discussed this possibility with Mrs. Sanchez, but in the past she had been unwilling to acknowledge that such crises could occur. The discharge of the gun had changed her attitude, and she was willing to move ahead with a planning group.

As lunchtime neared, I prepared my notes for a meeting with Mr. and Mrs. Padilla. Their daughter Virginia had been referred for an evaluation for a suspected mental handicap because she failed to complete any classroom work and seemed to lack the skills needed to succeed academically. Virginia was a Native American child who, until a few months ago, had been living on a reservation in another state. She was placed with the Padilla's, who were distant relatives of the child's mother, because of concerns that she was being sexually abused by her parents. The little information I had from the file suggested that Virginia had been kept at home for many years and thus had little exposure to the culture of schooling. There was also a concern in the social service report that her mother had been drinking at the time of the pregnancy, so she might be a fetal alcohol syndrome child. I was concerned with the complexity of the case and the inappropriateness of assessing her ability with intelligence tests that relied heavily on exposure to a school environment. I could use a nonverbal intelligence test, but even this would be affected by cultural differences. In addition, the suspected history of abuse and the recent removal from her family could be contributing factors to Virginia's poor performance. The guardians were very concerned people who shared my concerns that their ward not be inappropriately labeled. They assured me they would soon be getting more information from the tribal social service agency on her early development, and I gave them a rating scale to assess the functional skills Virginia exhibited in their home.

After I finished lunch in the teachers' lounge at the elementary school, I searched for a fourth grader on the playground. Mary was a socially isolated child who withdrew into a world of fantasy at home and at school. She had already been retained once and was in danger of being retained a second time because of her poor academics. I often found her on the playground walking around in circles, "playing" with her imaginary companions, with whom she had long and involved conversations. My strategy was to encourage her to have real friends to supplement her imaginary ones, and I reminded her of this agreement if I saw her alone. Today I was delighted to find her playing happily with Sara, a classmate.

During the lunch hour, Ricardo, one of the students I counseled, had pushed the duty teacher who had told him to stop pushing another child. His mother had been called to school to take the child home, and I was called in to meet with the child, the parent, and the director of special education. Ricardo's mother was furious with the school for not being sensitive to her child's needs. She felt that her son had been picked on from the day he entered school and that his action toward the teacher was the outcome of his pent-up emotion. Ricardo was often caught between the school staff and his family. The special education director and I felt we needed to support his mother if we were to help Ricardo, and by the end of the meeting the mother seemed comfortable with a plan that would give her son time to cool off and calm down before he was sent to the principal. As we finished the meeting, I was aware that the duty teacher might feel unsupported and vulnerable, believing Ricardo needed more severe punishment to ensure that her authority was upheld. I wasn't sure how the principal would react and whether he'd feel we'd overstepped our authority, and I made a mental note to talk to the duty teacher and principal as soon as I could.

The rest of the afternoon was relatively calm. I was in the final stages of an evaluation of a student who was thought to be learning disabled in the area of mathematics and in need of special help. The assessment indicated a severe deficit in math skills in spite of normal intelligence. I would be meeting with the teachers and parents in two weeks to present my findings, and we would consider ways to address the deficit. I then met with Mr. Logan, a teacher whose job was increasingly stressful. I had begun meeting with Mr. Logan some weeks ago to talk about some students he felt were unruly and disrespectful; however, as we continued our meetings, it became clear that his personal issues were interfering with his objectivity in the classroom. Mr. Logan was nearly in tears today as he talked about his fear that his class could get out of control when he was observed by the principal next week.

As the day ended I met with Mrs. Harrington, who reported that her class seemed more settled and calm. I talked with her about the need to keep a close eye on her students over the next few weeks to make sure that they received the help they needed to move through the mourning process. As I walked out the door on the way to my car, I was greeted by a smiling Aaron, who told me to make sure to see him next week.

I hope this example gives you a flavor of how exciting and rewarding this occupation can be. This sample day represents only the experience of a school psychologist working in the public schools, but school psychologists work in such varied settings as colleges and universities, community mental health clinics, hospital clinics, and rehabilitation centers. Their life as a school psychologist is likely to be just as diverse and challenging as the example above. In sum, school psychology is an atypical career that provides you the opportunity to chart an exciting and rewarding course of growth and development for yourself and for your clients.

Continuing the Journey: Future Prospects

At the beginning of this chapter, I described a journey that began over 10 years before I began training as a school psychologist, and I ended over 30 years later with a description of a typical day for a professional school psychologist like myself. The journey I've described led me to a profession that seeks to understand the kinds of questions I've been asking for 30 years. How can we facilitate the optimal growth and development of learners and design learning environments in which children and their teachers can prosper? What role do caretakers and parents play in the facilitation of their children's growth, and how can parents be supported in carrying out this role? How do we involve children of widely varying cultural and social backgrounds in the classroom, and how can we design curricula to meet their needs? This profession addresses the needs of all learners, be they infants, the elderly, or ourselves. Few of us in this era of increasingly rapid change have the option of pursuing a career that will remain substantially unchanged throughout our adult lives. As we change and grow, we will need the help of the expert in facilitating growth and change, the school psychologist.

Although I don't have answers for the questions I posed for myself at the beginning of the journey, I know how to ask questions that can be broken down to workable size and how to collect the information I need to shed light on them, whether it be from data I collect in my work or by reviewing the significant research in school psychology. If I'd been a trained school psychologist when I was in the Peace Corps in Grenada, I would have consulted with the teaching staff to make the curriculum more relevant to the lives of those young women. If I had been a trained school psychologist instead of a substitute teacher in California, I would have conferred with the teachers in those classrooms to find ways to make the classroom and school climate a more productive one for learning. And if I'd been a trained school psychologist at Coyote Canyon, I would have found ways to measure the skills of those Navajo youth that related to their home environments.

My journey doesn't end here. I continue to grow and develop as a school psychologist, and I'm currently involved in new roles. In addition to the work I do in rural schools in New Mexico, I work in a private-practice clinic in Albuquerque, I supervise individuals who are delivering school psychological services, I evaluate children and adolescents at a psychiatric hospital, and I serve on the hospital committee that oversees the work of psychologists. I also have served as treasurer of the Division of School Psychology of the American Psychological Association. So there is plenty of room to grow in this profession.

And what about the future? In 1995, a celebration was held at the convention of the American Psychological Association (APA) in New York, marking the 50th anniversary of Division 16, the organization within APA that represents the interests of professional school psychology. What path will professional school psychologists follow over the next 50 years? Jane Conoley (1992) has given us some suggestions about where the field may be headed. As schools increasingly become the focus for the delivery of a wide variety of psychological services, she sees a movement away from the traditional role that many school psychologists have had of testing children and placing them in special education classrooms. Instead, the school psychologist will be an expert in accessing and linking the many settings in which learners reside. Efforts to reach out and address the needs of families through collaboration with agencies in the community, establishing parenting groups and consulting with parents, and accessing social supports for families in the community will accelerate. More time will be spent collaborating with other school professionals in facilitating their professional development and working in teams to solve schoolwide problems. The major focus of activity will shift away from individual children to the prevention of problems for the school community at large. Conoley sees the school psychologist of the future as having the skills to move readily among various roles and levels within the system.

As our society moves into the 21st century, the challenges to the profession will be great. The ecological framework encourages school psychologists to develop a coherent view of the process of development and change across all the settings of child, school, family, and society. This unified vision will allow us to create environments that will truly facilitate optimal human growth and development from birth to old age.

References

Apter, S., & Conoley, J. (1984). *Childhood behavior disorders and emotional disturbance: Introduction to teaching troubled children.* Englewood Cliffs, NJ: Prentice Hall.

Cobb, C. T. (1989). Is it time to establish the doctorate entry level? *School Psychology Review, 18* , 16–19.

Conoley, J. (1992, August). *2042 : A prospective look at school psychology.* Paper presented at the annual meeting of the American Psychological Association, Washington, DC.

Pfeiffer, S. I., & Dean, R. S. (1988). School psychology in evolution. *School Psychology Review, 17,* 388–390.

Reschly, D. J., & Wilson, M. S. (1995). School psychology practitioners and faculty: 1986–1991–1992. Trends in demographics, roles, satisfaction, and system reform. *School Psychology Review, 24,* 62–80.

Rosenfeld, S. (1990, April). On educating the school psychologist. *The School Psychologist , 44,* 1–2.

Sandoval, J. (1988). The school psychologist in higher education. *School Psychology Review, 17,* 391–396.

Talley, R., & Short, R. (1994, Summer). A wake up call to school psychologists from school psychologists. *The School Psychologist, 48,* 1, 3, 15.

Mary L. Tenopyr

Improving the Workplace: Industrial/Organizational Psychology as a Career

10

I became an industrial psychologist quite by accident. I had just gotten married and moved to Los Angeles with my new husband. I then responded in person to a newspaper job advertisement. The company I applied to would not even give me the slightest consideration for that job, because I was a woman. As I was leaving the company's employment lobby almost in tears, the interviewer called me back and asked me what I had done on my last job. I responded that I had been writing job knowledge tests. Thereupon he told me to wait, because he had a position opening for which they just might take a woman. Thus, I started on the path to becoming the person in charge of personnel testing for a major defense contractor and began a career as an industrial psychologist.

Industrial/organizational (I/O) psychology is a relatively small discipline within psychology as a whole, yet it is considered by many to be a highly rewarding field in a number of ways. The work is highly varied and may involve content from many other areas of psychology. In fact, Robert M. Guion (April 1990, personal communication) has referred to industrial/organizational psychology as "general psychology practiced in a business or industrial setting."

Mary L. Tenopyr is the director—measurement and selection systems strategy and planning in the Corporate Human Resources Department of AT&T. She is past president of two divisions of the APA and the author of numerous research papers and articles.

The activities of an I/O psychologist may involve matters as diverse as developing selection tests to be administered to job applicants, doing research on the configuration of the controls in an airplane cockpit, or redesigning an organization so that the people in it will function more effectively. Not every I/O psychologist does all such functions, but there is considerable overlap in most psychologists' work (e.g., a person who is a specialist in selection may work at times on designing organizations).

After two job changes, I was at a reception when a prominent psychologist who worked for AT&T remarked as I passed by, "I'd hire Mary Tenopyr if I could get her." I casually replied, "Try me." This began my 24-year career at AT&T.

My first assignment at AT&T started with a problem: Management was concerned about the high failure rate in training of customer service representatives. I immediately started problem diagnosis and concluded that the representatives were not being hired according to the right standards. So I obtained cooperation to do what is called a *test validation study*. This involves testing job applicants, not using the test results in hiring, and then following up on the applicants after they get on the job and gathering measures of training success and job performance. After a sufficient number of people have been hired, one does statistical analyses to determine whether people who did well on the test also do well in training and on the job and vice versa. This type of study is called a *criterion-related test validation study*. I am happy to say I solved the problem with the service representatives in this manner. This is but one example of the types of problem-solving work I have done.

A word might be said about the name of the field. The term "industrial psychologist" connotes someone working on a factory floor trying to make an assembly line more efficient; however, many different types of business and government organizations employ industrial psychologists. For example, these psychologists are employed in banks, insurance companies, civil service departments, and military research organizations. The traditional core of activities of a person who serves primarily as an industrial psychologist are personnel selection; appraisal of employees' job performance; analysis of jobs to determine what the job duties are and what employee knowledge, skills, and abilities are necessary to do the job; and development of assessment centers, which are collections of simulated work situations in which employees are observed to determine job abilities. An important, relatively recent addition to the activities of the industrial psychologist is preparation for litigation activities that arise in connection with complaints under the various federal, state, and local civil rights acts.

Whereas the industrial psychologist is concerned largely with individual behavior, its assessment, and its improvement, the organizational psychologist has the same concerns but focuses on whole organizations, such as a company's purchasing department. The activities of the organizational psychologist may be subsumed under the relatively new subdiscipline known as *organizational development*. The scope of work in this specialty has changed from time to time and is still developing.

Borman (1995) has made tentative identification of two other subspecialties in I/O psychology. One of these deals with individual development whereby persons are coached on actions they may take to improve their job performance and promotability. Psychologists in this subdiscipline usually work with high-level managers. Another specialty deals mainly with employee compensation in terms of salaries and with labor relations.

Industrial Psychology

Much of what industrial psychologists do in business is to benefit directly the economic well-being of the employing organization. No activity probably has so much immediately discernible economic benefit as carefully selecting employees for jobs. The work, however, is fulfilling in that one applies one's knowledge to practical problems and sees the effect of solutions immediately. It is extremely gratifying to see how one's work solves problems and helps others. The psychologists' main role here is to capitalize on individual differences, to provide the instruments that enable this careful selection, and to design systems and policies to facilitate administering and scoring the instruments and maintain records of the scores and their results.

The psychologist has the responsibility to ensure that the instruments, whether they be tests, interviews, or job simulations, yield valid results. By *valid* is meant that the results can be used to predict accurately some measure of job success of interest to the employer.

In addition to the type of study previously described, in which the best selection procedures are selected through statistical analysis in a criterion-related study, the psychologist may also develop selection procedures strictly on the basis of the content of the job. A technique called job analysis is used to determine what people actually do on the job. Then, a group of subject matter experts is assembled and taught how to write test items. The psychologist edits the items, probing the writers to ensure that the items are technically correct, are at the appropriate level of difficulty, and have only one correct answer. The test is then assembled and tried out.

Implied in this description of just one major duty of the industrial psychologist's job are a number of characteristics necessary for success as an industrial psychologist. First, it is necessary in diagnosis and job analysis to have interviewing skills and to be able to grasp quickly sometimes complex organizational matters and jobs. One must have the social skills that enable one to get the cooperation needed to conduct the study. In these times of limited budgets, adding new job responsibilities for anyone, such as providing special supervisors' ratings for criteria, may require strong persuasive skills. Knowledge of statistics and use of personal computers is important. Although skill in quantitative methods is desirable for all I/O psychologists, for those in the industrial specialty, such knowledge is mandatory.

Another example of the work of an industrial psychologist is the development of a performance appraisal system for an organization. There is considerable research on how to develop the forms on which the actual appraisal is recorded, but the success or failure of a performance appraisal system depends very much on how the system is viewed by the managers and other employees in the organization. In developing an appraisal process, most psychologists have found that the optimal strategy is to form a team from all of the departments of the organization and let that team do the development work. Because many employees are dubious about the worth and fairness of appraisal programs, it is usually necessary to do considerable internal marketing of a new system. The team can develop and implement the marketing strategy, too. In this situation, the psychologist serves in three capacities: as an expert consultant, as a team facilitator, and as a marketer.

The skills needed for these multiple roles overlap those needed in organizational psychology. The industrial psychologist must have a knowledge of the subject matter of performance appraisal, but more than that must have highly developed social skills, the ability to facilitate the work of a team, and skills at preparing and presenting promotional material both orally and in writing.

Another group of the industrial psychologists' activities that requires yet a different set of skills is preparing for and participating in litigation (Borman, 1995). The psychologist serves as an adviser to the company's attorneys and teaches them about selection and associated research and statistics. The psychologist usually serves as an expert court witness and must learn to persuade judges and juries that his or her work was done correctly. For this endeavor, the psychologist must learn a great deal about the extant civil rights laws. All competent industrial psychologists attempt to build compliance with the laws into their research and development efforts. However, even the most carefully crafted work is subject to legal challenge. It is often necessary to give one's labor attorney a great deal of assistance before the trial. The psychologist must learn the techniques of writing legal depositions and acting as an expert witness.

My day is not typical for an entry-level industrial psychologist, as I am a manager with other psychologists reporting to me. Nevertheless, it can give prospective industrial psychologists some idea of what life in business is like. My typical day starts early in the morning. I come into the office about 45 minutes early and immediately read my electronic mail; then I answer those messages requiring attention. I glance over my "to do" list and add things. I peruse the *Wall Street Journal* to see whether it contains any articles pertinent to my work or relevant to psychology. Then the day starts in earnest. At the official time for starting work, I usually initiate a few telephone calls or return some calls from others. After that, every day is different, and certainly the work is not boring. Every day involves meetings with other psychologists; we talk about progress on projects and interactions with our customers, the people who supervise the jobs for which we provide the means of selecting employees. Also, we often discuss technical problems in psychology as they relate to our work. I frequently meet with the people in our labor relations and legal departments about matters involving our unions and problems involving civil rights litigation, respectively. Meetings with the customers are also a regular thing. Sometimes I meet with them to determine their needs, to try to get them to provide subjects for research, or to make progress reports on our work. Although not every day provides it, I often get some welcome quiet time to review the other psychologists' research reports or read a journal article or two.

Presented here has been just a sampler of the likely duties of an industrial psychologist. From these examples, it should be apparent that the work of an industrial psychologist is highly varied and requires a number of different kinds of knowledge, skills, and abilities. The industrial psychologist must be a well-rounded person capable of doing duties ranging from solitary work with mathematics to team direction and marketing.

Organizational Psychology

Organizational psychology is a rapidly developing, diverse subdiscipline of I/O psychology. It is far less easy to define than the industrial side of the discipline, because the area is evolving so rapidly. Basically, whereas industrial psychology is concerned with differences among individuals, organizational psychology involves working with groups of individuals. The core of organizational psychology is an activity known as *organizational development*, which is a planned intervention into an organization to improve its effectiveness. For example, people in two departments are feuding so much that neither department serves the organization well. The psychologist in this case carries out an intervention and acts as a change agent who diagnoses and classifies problems, identifies courses of action, and recommends changes (Muchinsky, 1993, p. 445). Although knowledge of behavioral science is necessary for full capability as a change agent, it is apparent that people with only a smattering of knowledge of psychology sometimes serve as change agents.

A change agent serves a client that may be an individual, a work group, or a multigroup organization. The change agent must be supported by someone of authority within the organization and have ready access to the people who have to implement any changes the agent recommends. One of the most important functions of such an agent is to build trust among many people. The agent's sponsor and clients have to trust him or her, and the agent has to help build trust among the individuals and groups in the client organization. Building trust can be a trying task in some organizations in which there is animosity among individuals or work groups, and it is extremely rewarding to see, for example, people who were not working well together start working as a team.

An organizational psychologist may also work with organizations to improve business processes in ways such as removing steps from a paperwork-processing procedure. Another function might be working with an individual manager to provide him or her with increased awareness of others' perception of his or her style and its impact on the functioning of subordinates.

The psychologist may develop measuring tools such as customer satisfaction surveys that measure satisfaction with the work of the whole organization or with individual performance within the organization. Also, the organizational psychologist may design and use attitude surveys that measure employees' satisfaction with the company and its various programs. He or she may then develop procedures and programs designed to improve satisfaction and morale.

In recent years, some organizational psychologists have assumed more technical functions in an effort called *reengineering*. This involves doing broad studies of how certain work gets done and changing the work processes by assigning some work to computers and other work to humans.

Many companies are interested in having people work more as team members than as individuals. The skills of the organizational psychologist may be applied in promoting teamwork and designing methods to ensure that teams function effectively.

As can be determined from this small sample of activities of an organizational psychologist, this psychologist spends considerable time working with people, either individually or in groups. A background in social psychology is highly advisable. However, the organizational psychologist must also have technical education in the design of surveys and other types of measuring instruments. As computers become more a part of the workplace, the interaction between computers and people is a matter of concern in designing and reengineering work flows and processes. Consequently, computer literacy is becoming a requirement for people aspiring to be organizational psychologists.

Education

There are essentially two levels of education that can gain one employment in I/O psychology. These are the master's level and the doctoral level. As pointed out by Koppes (1991), master's-level individuals do not compete with PhDs for jobs. The two groups do different types and levels of work. Nevertheless, there appears to be some market for the services of people with master's degrees. As of 1990, there were 200 departments with approximately 520 terminal master's programs identified in *Graduate Study in Psychology and Associated Fields* (American Psychological Association, 1990). About 8,000 master's degrees, almost twice the number of doctorates, are awarded annually.

The master's degree in psychology is given little credence within organized psychology. In 1947, the American Psychological Association adopted the policy that the entry level for the independent practice of psychology is the doctorate. The question of the official status of master's-level degree holders has been debated periodically ever since. Nevertheless, the policy of the association remains the same.

A student with long-term interest in the field would be well advised to seek a doctorate. A 1993 survey of recent recipients of doctorates indicated that over half of these individuals felt that the doctoral degree was essential in obtaining employment. Another 25% suggested that the doctorate was helpful in getting a job (Wicherski & Kohout, 1995). In fact, 92.5% of the members and fellows of the Society for Industrial and Organizational Psychology have doctoral degrees in I/O psychology or a related field.

Students should also be advised that in most states it is necessary to obtain a license from the state if one is to offer psychological services to the public. In many states a license is also required if one works for a company and does not make a public offering of services. Uniformly, a doctorate in psychology is required to obtain a license.

One might well ask whether, particularly in the case of the study of organizations, a business school department-of-management degree might be appropriate. Most business schools now offer curricula in organizational behavior and organization development. If the main interest is obtaining a job with a corporation or consulting firm specializing in organizational development, a business degree might be appropriate. However, if one chooses a teaching career path, one will have great difficulty getting an academic appointment in a psychology department if one's degree is in business. One's options in the academic world are thus limited. Also, if teaching in a business school is an objective, one will find that many business departments accept degrees in psychology.

Also, in academia, psychologists with expertise in areas such as psychological measurement or testing, which is usually part of an industrial psychology curriculum, can often find teaching jobs in departments of education. The opposite is not true; education degrees are often not acceptable in psychology departments.

If one is considering a career in the academic world, a doctorate is practically essential. According to Howard (1990), 39% of the I/O doctorates were in academic positions, as opposed to 6% of those holding master's degrees. On the other hand, those with master's degrees were more likely to be employed as house psychologists (47% vs. 26% of doctorates). Howard also reported that the I/O doctorates tended to specialize in the more challenging I/O activities such as leadership research.

Consequently, a doctoral degree from a psychology department can give a person more options in academic employment than degrees awarded by some other, allied departments.

Opportunities

The Society for Industrial and Organizational Psychology, Division 14 of the American Psychological Association, has a membership of 2,729 professionals. The organization is characterized by a high proportion of White males. In a 1989 survey, Howard (1990) reported that respondents to a society survey were 96.5% White. It has been difficult to recruit minorities into the field, because African–American and Hispanic psychologists have generally shown a disproportionate interest in the health-care subfields of psychology and tended not to be highly represented in traditional research/academic areas (Howard et al., 1986).

One of the most notable developments in the employment of I/O psychologists has been the rapid increase of women in the field. In the decade from 1970 to 1979, 19% of the new doctorates in I/O psychology were awarded to women. This percentage more than doubled in the years from 1980 to 1989, to 39%. Thus, it seems that the white male domination of the field is rapidly waning. It appears that women are moving into the field at a rapid rate. The failure of the field to attract more minorities needs more study in the present environment.

Employment prospects, regardless of race, gender, or ethnicity, seem to be good. In the 1993 APA survey (Wicherski & Kohout, 1995), 92.9% of the new I/O doctoral graduates had found employment approximately 6 months after graduation. This can be compared with 73.8% of the health-care-services psychology graduates who had found employment in a similar period. Similar data for master's-degree recipients do not appear to be available.

It appears that those I/O psychologists who majored in either I/O psychology or psychometrics (testing) have found employment in the varied work settings (Howard, 1990). Those who studied psychometrics were more likely than others to work for government organizations, probably because testing and other forms of measurement are used extensively in both civilian and military settings. Howard also found that those who studied organizational behavior most often assumed academic positions. Borman (1995) has pointed out a recent pronounced trend for work to move away from psychologists working within organizations to external consultants. Corporate psychologists seem particularly vulnerable in cases of restructuring or downsizing, and many have lost their jobs. However, there appears to be considerable work for consultants. Perhaps employers with budget problems find it less expensive to contract with consultants on a project basis, rather than maintain full-time psychologists on the payroll and pay benefits such as health insurance, as well as full-time salaries. Thus, there may be more employment opportunities with consulting firms than with regular corporations now. It appears that job security with consulting firms may have markedly improved.

Also, Borman (1995) has noted that the organizational aspect of I/O psychology has grown markedly in terms of both activity and employment. It probably can be safely said that organizational development and personnel selection are on a par as the most active areas of practice for I/O psychologists. This is true for both nonacademics and academics who consult on a part-time basis.

In terms of who actually does the practice, as opposed to teaching and research work, it is apparent that internal corporate consultants and consulting firm personnel are each doing one third of the practice work, with other groups doing the remainder of the work. Thus, a person who wants to apply the knowledge base of I/O psychology in practice is advised to seek employment with a corporation or a consulting firm.

One last thing should be said about opportunities in I/O psychology. Few nonpsychologists do selection work, because most employers recognize the technical aspects of the area. However, many nonpsychologists may be found doing organizational development work. Often people take organizational development courses in business schools and apply the techniques taught them in business. If this trend continues, there may be more persons attempting to find jobs in organizational development than there are opportunities for employment. Also, one must recognize that human resources practices in business can be faddish, and newer areas such as organizational development may not have the staying power over decades as traditional industrial psychology work has had. Consequently, anyone planning to make a career in organizational development should obtain some breadth of knowledge and skills so that he or she may do other types of work.

Salaries

Salaries for I/O psychologists are relatively good, especially for PhDs going into business or industry settings. Academic starting salaries are generally lower. In 1993 (Wicherski & Kohout, 1995), the median starting salary of $52,000 for those with doctorates going into business and industry was the highest salary among those for all other types of entry doctoral positions and settings. The starting salary for doctorates going into consulting firms was lower, at $44,000. By way of contrast, the starting salary for doctorates going into psychology departments was $35,000.

Master's-degree holders in 1992 started at a median salary of $42,000 (Gehlmann, 1994). Kohout and Wicherski (1994) reported a median 11–12-month salary of $58,000 for master's-level respondents to an American Psychological Association survey concluded in 1993. This salary was the median for individuals of all ages and levels of experience. Another example of pay for master's-level psychologists is the median of $46,500 for those with 5 to 9 years of experience. A survey of I/O psychologists regarding 1994 income (Zickar and Taylor, 1996) reported a median salary of $59,500 for master's-degree psychologists of all ages.

However, in 1994, holders of I/O doctorates had a median income of $71,000. For men at both degree levels, the median salary was $75,000, whereas for women the median salary was $58,500. There also exists a significant differential between people employed in the New York City metropolitan area and those in other areas of the country. The median salary for PhDs in the New York area was $85,000; elsewhere the median was $70,000.

Summary

The job of an I/O psychologist can be rich and varied; such psychologists can find employment in a variety of settings. Certainly, the PhD is the preferred degree. Individuals with master's degrees do a different kind of work than PhDs, but there is enough of both types of work to afford employment opportunities for people at both educational levels.

References

American Psychological Association. (1990). *Graduate Study in Psychology and Associated Fields*. Washington, DC: Author

Borman, W. C. (1995, April). *The practice of I/O psychology: What are we doing and how well are we doing it?* Presidential address, Society for Industrial and Organizational Psychology Annual Conference, Orlando, FL.

Gehlmann, S. C. (1994). *1993 employment survey: Psychology graduates with master's, specialist's, and related degrees*. Unpublished research report. Washington, DC: American Psychological Association.

Howard, A. (1990). *The multiple facets of industrial–organizational psychology*. Bowling Green, OH: Society for Industrial and Organizational Psychology.

Howard, A., Pion, G. M., Gottfredson, G. D., Flattau, P. E., Oskamp S., Pfafflin, S. M., Bray, D. W., & Burstein, A. G. (1986). The changing face of American psychology: A report from the committee on employment and human resources. *American Psychologist, 41,* 1311–1327.

Kohout, J. L., & Wicherski, M. M. (1994). *Salaries in psychology, 1993: Report of the 1993 salary survey*. Unpublished report. Washington, DC: American Psychological Association.

Koppes, L. L. (1991). I/O psychology master's-level training: Reality and legitimacy in search of recognition. *The Industrial–Organizational Psychologist, 29,* 59–67.

Muchinsky, P. M. (1993). *Psychology applied to work.* Pacific Grove, CA: Brooks/Cole.

Wicherski, M., & Kohout, J. (1995). *1993 doctorate employment survey.* Unpublished report. Washington, DC: American Psychological Association.

Zickar, M., & Taylor, R. (1996). Income of SIOP members in 1994. *The Industrial–Organizational Psychologist, 33,* 63–69.

Anne E. Beall and Ted W. Allen

Why We Buy What We Buy: Consulting in Consumer Psychology

11

T his chapter presents perspectives on consulting in consumer psychology from two authors of different genders, ethnic backgrounds, and age groups. Despite these differences, and despite the fact that we studied at different universities with different concentrations, we have surprisingly similar goals and experiences in the field of consumer psychology. We both began our career paths with a strong interest in human behavior and a healthy enjoyment of the research process. Early in our careers we realized that we particularly enjoyed solving "real-world problems" and wanted to do research that would have an impact. One of us took the circuitous route of becoming a professor at the University of California at Los Angeles before managing marketing research in a Fortune 500 company, whereas the other joined a nationally recognized consulting firm directing marketing research projects for a wide variety of companies. Today, as consumer psychologists we conduct research

Anne E. Beall received her PhD in social psychology from Yale University. Her interests include consumer values, belief systems, and the effect of brand perceptions on purchase behavior. Dr. Beall is also a specialist in identifying key consumer segments in telecommunications markets. She is currently senior project manager at National Analysts in Philadelphia, Pennsylvania.

Ted W. Allen received his PhD in cognitive psychology from the University of Michigan and his MBA in marketing from the University of North Carolina. Dr. Allen's interests are in the processing of marketing information, in particular the impact of emotions and information-processing experience on marketing-related decision making. Dr. Allen is owner and principal consultant for Ted Allen ET AL.

and analyze data to help organizations solve marketing problems and meet the needs of consumers.

In this chapter we present our perspectives on the field and discuss the reasons why we find this career so challenging and rewarding. We have divided this chapter into several sections on the basis of the questions likely to be asked by those unfamiliar with our field. We first discuss the nature of our occupation, then the challenges and rewards of our work, and finally the skills that consumer psychologists need.

What Is Consumer Psychology?

Consumer psychology is roughly defined as the study of people and the processes they pursue as they purchase and consume goods and services. This definition is both broad and rich, given that everyone, whether rich or poor, young or old, in a capitalist or socialist economy, is a consumer. We all purchase, or have purchased for us, the food, clothing, and shelter necessary for personal survival and the personal items, recreation, transportation, education, and information (including advice from expert accountants, lawyers, etc.) necessary for functioning in modern societies. With so much of human behavior focused on the purchase and consumption of goods and services, the field of consumer psychology is fertile ground for the exploration of a wide variety of human behaviors.

Fundamentally, consumer psychologists are interested in many of the same questions that intrigue other psychologists. We seek to know, as in other fields of psychology, how attitudes influence behavior (and vice versa), how groups influence individuals, how goal seeking leads to plans and plans influence behavior, how information is processed, and what models best explain human thoughts and actions. The settings where we work (i.e., business, government, associations, and academia) and the issues we study are as broad as any field of psychology.

For example, some consumer psychologists study the influence of peer groups on behaviors such as altruism, greed, and delayed gratification, whereas others study the influence of childhood experiences on later consumptive behavior (e.g., hoarding, sharing). Some consumer psychologists study the factors influencing value systems and how those value systems are expressed in purchasing behavior. Others study emotional behavior, the growth of emotional attachment to products, and the influence of emotions on purchasing behavior. Still other consumer psychologists study the behavioral structures and information-processing styles likely to predict consumer behavior. In each case, the goal is to understand the processes by which consumers search for goods and services, decide which goods and services to purchase, and consume the items they purchase.

Consumer psychology differs from other types of psychology because its objective is to help organizations understand how consumers think, feel, and act toward them and their products and services. Generally, the questions that organizations want to answer are questions about themselves as seen through the eyes of the consumer: "What do consumers think about us? What is their image of our organization? How did they arrive at that image? Why do people have a negative image of our products? What could we do to become more appealing? How could we better serve our customers? How much are consumers willing to pay for our services? How large is the "market" for a particular product under development? How could we rearrange our organization to become more efficient and effective for consumers? Why do consumers buy our products for a while and then stop?" All these questions are ones that consumer psychologists might help an organization answer.

The answers provided by the consumer psychologist's research are crucial for the continued existence and growth of most organizations. Organizations that do not serve their customers soon fail. Even traditional monopolies such as the postal service and telephone utilities cannot hope to preserve their status if they fail to serve the ever-changing needs of their customers. Thus, it is critical that organizations understand their customers and organize themselves to meet the needs of those customers (Berrigan & Finkbeiner, 1992). Consumer psychologists provide the necessary information about the customer and help organizations develop their strategies for creating and delivering products and services and for interacting with consumers.

Executives use this research to plan the structure of their organizations, the logistics they will use to serve their customers, the training they will provide to customers and employees, the advertising and communication procedures they will implement, and the products and services they will offer. For example, suppose a company found that customers were having problems with a certain product. Information that consumer psychologists collect could be used to determine whether the company should design and launch a new product to replace the outmoded one, or establish a toll-free help desk to assist customers who are having problems with the current product. Other options are to establish a program to train consumers in product utilization, send communications to customers about using the product, or restrict sales of the product to a market segment best suited to the product's features.

Most major banks, restaurants, foundations, associations, hospitals, and retail stores, and even the U.S. government, conduct research about consumers with the help of psychologists. Typically, these organizations will combine the services of an internal research department with those of external consultants hired to help them meet their research objectives. Larger and larger portions of the organizations' research budgets seem to be spent on outside consultants from specialized research firms. These outside consultants are usually teams that include at least one consumer psychologist. More and more, the internal researchers are consumer psychologists as well, although all too often they are managers with too little training in either psychology or research. Clearly, as more organizations realize the importance of understanding their customer, the position of consumer psychology will take on greater importance.

What Are the Duties of a Consumer Psychologist?

Consumer psychologists help organizations answer their marketing questions by either conducting research or applying basic principles and findings from the field of psychology. The majority of consumer psychologists design and manage research projects (such as surveys or focus groups) and then help organizations interpret the results. To demonstrate how a consumer psychologist might approach a typical business problem, let's suppose that a company wants to know if, and how, it should introduce a computer that is voice activated.

The first step for a consumer psychologist would be to translate the business question into a research question. We might generate a number of research questions, including the following: Is anyone interested in a voice-activated computer? Who would use this type of computer? Has anyone purchased similar equipment in the past? For what kinds of functions could this computer be best suited? How many people would be interested in the computer because of their own intrinsic characteristics (e.g., disabilities) or because of their need to perform certain functions? All of these research questions could shed some light on how the business question might be answered.

Given these research questions, we would design a research study to address the questions within the constraints (e.g., time, funding, resources) of the organization. At this point a variety of options are available. We might consider (a) an analysis of the organization's current customer database to determine if purchasing habits directed at a product's features might indicate customer interest in the new product, (b) an analysis of external census data concerning people with injured hands or poor keyboard skills, (c) an observation of computer users to determine how they might use the product, (d) a survey to ask consumers directly about their interest in the product, or (e) some combination of these options.

Once we have established how to answer the questions (i.e., which of the options to use), the question of what source we will use must then be answered. If a database is being considered, we must determine what database fits the business situation and the analyses being considered. If an observation or survey is being considered, we must determine the person or group who should be surveyed or observed.

If a survey is used to gather data, we may need to know the details of the company's plans for the product to select the appropriate sample. Continuing our example, if the voice-activated computer has been specifically designed for a specific segment of the population, such as elderly people who have access to computers, then this group will be used in the sample. If the product is for a more general audience, the questions might be asked of people who own personal computers and who use them at least once or twice a month. Another possible group is people who own personal computers and who have experienced difficulties using the mouse and keyboard. If the company has a favorable image or a set of loyal customers among particular groups, these segments might be most amenable to this product and therefore should be interviewed. The last possibility is that we may want to ask Americans in general about their ideas and thoughts about our computer because it might be suitable for anyone. As always, the extent of this research is going to be limited by the available time and funding.

One of the most important, and most difficult, functions of the consumer psychologist is to ensure that the data collection procedures provide the necessary information. First, the data collection instrument must provide accurate and reliable data. In a survey situation, we have to design the project so that a representative group is sampled and then design the questionnaire so that the respondent provides truthful answers about relevant items. Next, the design of the project must be robust enough to accommodate changes in the market or study conditions that may occur during data collections, such as a competitor introducing a similar product or bad news about the company that might temporarily influence answers.

A real-life example of this problem occurred in research conducted for Duncan Hines. Duncan Hines wanted to determine the amount of demand for their soft-centered cookies before introducing the product nationwide. They introduced their cookies into a test market to assess the appeal of the product. Researchers had to analyze how many cookies were sold and then estimate demand for the cookies in the entire country. Before the analyses could be completed, Nabisco, Frito-Lay, and Keebler had used the Duncan Hines test cookies to develop their own products. By the time Duncan Hines introduced the cookies nationally, their competitors had introduced their own versions. Thus, the environment had changed so much that research results from the test market no longer applied (Hiam & Schewe, 1992). Clearly, designing research studies on such issues requires perseverance, an ability to plan for potential problems, and a method of solving them when they occur.

Consumer psychologists must worry about the consumer (and things going on in his or her head), the direction the organization wants to take (and its resources), and the events taking place in the market. To fail to achieve a proper weighting of these three factors in designs and analyses will almost assuredly result in a failure of the project. However, the fun and the challenge of this work is balancing these practical concerns with the theoretical and methodological ones.

After the data have been collected and analyzed, we must identify the strategic implications of the findings and make recommendations. At this point, we must translate the research findings into business implications. For example, suppose our research into the voice-activated computer showed that the people most interested in the computer were individuals who (a) had major physical disabilities, (b) had inadequate typing skills, or (c) used their computers intensively for simple repetitive tasks (as commodities brokers do). Another group with a large interest was sophisticated computer users who wanted leading-edge technology. We would then evaluate the size and financial attractiveness of each group and probably recommend different marketing programs for each of these segments. The communication media to reach these groups would have to be different. The company might go through physical therapists and doctors to reach the disabled but would need to go through trade magazines to reach the brokers and specialists. The messages would also be different because the company would need to communicate the different benefits of the computer to each group.

What Is a Typical Day Like?

Because our work focuses on research, a typical day varies depending on the stage of our research projects. At the beginning of a study, we meet with executives and managers to understand the nature of their business, their needs on this project, and the role that research will play in their decision making. We might confer over several days or perhaps weeks to ensure that we gain a thorough understanding of their business and their objectives. At this point in the process, we are working on Deming's principle that "those who would help us must know us." The more time we can spend getting to know the client, the more helpful we will be. Thus, a typical day at the beginning of the project is spent in meetings where we probe the clients for their needs and objectives.

The next phase of the project involves designing the research plan and the specific instruments we will use for our study. This part of the work is primarily creative, requiring problem-solving skills in applying psychological and methodological principles to real-life situations. Often an apparently simple problem will engender a complex research design because of the many environmental forces that one cannot control. Although meetings with managers might be involved in this phase, more often this time is spent alone or in consultation with small groups of team members.

The next phase is the data collection, which is usually a quiet time for us if the study has been well planned. This phase involves monitoring the people doing the actual interviews or data collection to ensure that the quality and quantity of the data are satisfactory. If data are being collected by interviewers, we must monitor them so that they maintain high standards. In addition, the number of respondents in each cell of the design must be monitored to ensure that sample sizes remain within specifications. The time here is spent in observing actual data collection, poring over daily data collection results, and meeting to resolve data collection problems.

After the data have been collected, we analyze them in the hopes of developing answers for our clients. Generally this stage consists of exploratory and planned analyses of the data to uncover answers. Typically, meetings will be held with data analysis experts to resolve problems, as the team begins to implement the analysis plan. More often than not, we will spend much of the time in this phase exploring the data and testing hypotheses about the evidence for different behaviors contained within the data, and the motivation for those behaviors.

Perhaps we need to know exactly which people are most loyal to a company and why. Let's say our survey is for Federal Express. Our survey data should quickly tell us which customers are loyal and use only FedEx for their mail. The next question is "Why are these customers loyal?" We pore through the questionnaire and divide "loyals" from "nonloyals" and look at whether there are any differences between the groups. We learn that nonloyals tend to live in the suburbs and loyals tend to live in more urban areas. We also find that the loyals have access to FedEx offices more readily than nonloyals do. After looking at each group's preferences we find that loyals have a strong preference for mail services that guarantee arrival times and that provide tracking of parcels, which are services that FedEx provides. In contrast, the nonloyals do not have strong preferences for arrival time guarantees and tracking. Nonloyals value inexpensive mail services and couldn't care less whether their parcels are tracked. From these data we conclude that the nonloyals do not exclusively use FedEx because this mail service does not meet all their needs. In addition, nonloyals do not have convenient access to Fed-Ex offices, so loyalty would be somewhat difficult even if they were so inclined. Although this example might be an oversimplification of the situation, it provides an idea of what analysis of the data could be like.

The final phase of the work is writing the report for executives and managers in the organization. At this stage, we must be able to translate the findings into business implications and communicate those implications to people who often have little interest in the underlying data. This phase is a demanding one that requires diligence and patience in boiling down the many findings so that one can tell a story that is clear and understandable. In addition, the report must be "user friendly" so it can be understood by numerous people over the next couple of years. Often we work closely with key individuals within the organization to determine the kind of report they would like to have and the information they most need. After submitting a draft report to key stakeholders, there may be several revisions to the report as points are clarified and ideas condensed to the required level. This step is especially important in giving the clients some ownership of the report and ensuring that key issues are discussed in the proper perspective. After the report is written, we may also present it orally to a select audience of executives and managers. This meeting may serve the dual purpose of presenting results to a larger audience and planning future research.

Where Do You Work?

Although consumer psychologists could work in business, government (such as tourism departments, and parks and recreation), and nonprofit (including academic) environments, they appear to be most prevalent in consulting and other for-profit companies. Some of the consulting companies employ consumer psychologists in divisions that specialize in research for nonprofit organizations. One of the authors worked for such a firm. For one of its clients, the firm determined which factors predicted whether alumni gave contributions to their undergraduate college. Other research that the firm conducted included work for a large metropolitan hospital that identified how patients felt about their experiences at the hospital and which factors were most predictive of a positive overall evaluation. This research allowed the hospital to identify and improve those factors most likely to make the patients' visits more pleasant.

Consumer psychologists generally work in the marketing research department of a company or in a consulting firm that specializes in conducting research. Usually, these environments will have additional resources and staff to assist in the collection and analysis of data. Because projects are often larger than one person could handle, these environments usually staff a team of people for every project. In smaller companies or with smaller projects, there may be fewer team members and fewer resources allocated for studies. Of course, the environment where the consumer psychologists work determines the types of projects they will typically conduct. Whereas a psychologist in academia might be free to pursue any area of interest, consumer psychologists in the corporate environment will usually research those areas where the company offers (or plans to offer) products and services.

What Kinds of Questions Do You Research?

The kinds of questions we answer depend on the nature of the organization and the kind of issues or problems it needs to address. Questions that we have attempted to answer have ranged from "What is the most effective design for a community police department?" to "How do one's values predict purchasing behavior in regard to certain products and services?" Perhaps more than other psychologists, consumer psychologists study a very broad variety of topics. One of our colleagues is well known for a very large national study he conducted about who watches public television and why (Frank & Greenberg, 1982). In addition, the questions change frequently as the products, strategies, and competitive environments change. For example, the face of the telecommunications industry has changed tremendously as a result of regulatory changes in the last several years. It may now be possible for companies that were legally unable to provide local and long-distance service to do so in the future. As a result, these companies will need to research the new markets opening to them. Local telephone companies will want to know whether it is feasible and profitable to provide long-distance service, and long-distance companies will want to determine whether they can and should offer local service. There is no doubt that researchers are going to be very busy in the upcoming years trying to answer these and many other questions.

What Do You Like Most About Your Career?

One of the greatest rewards of this profession is solving challenging problems. Because many business problems are so complex, neither of us has ever lacked for intellectual challenge. These challenges have included developing analytic modeling of consumer behavior and using complex multivariate techniques to understand the nature and motivation of consumer and business markets.

Another reward is the pleasure of conducting research that has an impact. We have investigated how companies can better serve customers, whether new products should be launched in the marketplace, and how companies can become more successful in gaining customer loyalty. As a result of our work, we have seen companies reorganize operations, modify old products, introduce new products, and create advertising and communications to entrench themselves in the hearts and minds of their customers. In short, we have been on the forefront of the changing face of American business.

Another aspect that we like about our careers is that the nature of our work is constantly changing. Unlike some psychologists who study the same problem for a lifetime, we will study numerous different problems throughout each year! Thus, our research is forever changing and rarely boring for long. In addition to the changes that we would normally see in a company over the years, we both have specialized in the area of telecommunications, where the entire industry is being changed by global, technological, and regulatory forces. We expect to participate in some very exciting research in this industry for years to come.

So, What Do You Like Least About Your Career?

Although we find our careers very rewarding, there are several pitfalls to becoming a consumer psychologist. Probably one of the most frustrating problems is the bureaucratic nature of organizations, because of which research results can sometimes be misunderstood or disregarded. There is nothing more frustrating than to work long and hard on a project and to see a report get shelved with little hope of ever resurfacing again. In addition, because we work in organizations where few people have as much formal research training as we do, it can be frustrating when people do not understand the research process or the function that research can play in answering important questions. Even more frustrating are colleagues who are somewhat distrustful of numbers and research findings. We have known only a few individuals who are like this, but they do exist and they can make our jobs very difficult.

In addition, these careers can often require long hours. Organizations have deadlines that they have to meet or competitors they have to beat into the market. For example, a recent project that one of us did with a telephone company required our team to have research results by a certain date because the company had to enter the market with a new service shortly after our deadline. If we had not provided it with the results within this time period, the company would not have been able to offer a highly valued service. As a result, the team spent many long nights to get data compiled and analyzed quickly.

A final problem that both of us have encountered is a great deal of travel. Although traveling can be a great opportunity to see new places, it can also be exhausting and disruptive of one's daily life. Typically, people who work in consulting firms tend to travel several times a month, whereas researchers who work within organizations travel depending on their rank within the company. Senior managers may travel more frequently than junior managers, but nevertheless they all have to oversee projects outside of their organization, and they have to meet with other executives, managers, and researchers within the field.

What Special Skills Are Required to Become a Consumer Psychologist?

There are numerous skills that are required of a consumer psychologist. One of the major skills is analytic acumen: the ability to analyze problems and think logically and rationally. This skill is required of all researchers, not just consumer psychologists, and it is probably the primary benefit of attending a graduate program in psychology. The other major skill is the ability to communicate well, including writing clearly and concisely and speaking in a clear and organized manner. Executives and managers have limited time to assimilate a great deal of information. In most cases, they do not want every small research finding categorized in a lengthy volume. Reports and presentations must be to the point, user friendly, and clear in their presentation of the results. If your findings are to be effectively implemented, you must be able to communicate them concisely.

Other skills that are helpful in this field include the ability to work in teams and get along with others. Research teams in the "real world" generally comprise numerous players who each form an integral part of the project. Typically, the team leader conceptualizes the project and the research design and guides the overall process of the research through communications with the team members. Other members include field specialists who oversee the data collection process and statistical analysts who specialize in analyzing the data with computer programs. The team leader generally interprets the results and helps the organization to understand the implications of these results. Because such research involves a high level of interaction and dependence on others, the ability to engage others as well as to get along with them is vitally important to every project's success. Of course, with smaller projects, sometimes the team leader also functions as the field specialist and statistical analyst all rolled together.

What Are the Salary Ranges for Consumer Psychologists?

Salary ranges vary depending on the level of education, work experience, and type of organization. The starting salaries for a person in market research vary from about $22,000 to $45,000 annually. The mean salary is $45,000 a year, including all organizations and levels. As you might expect, individuals with PhDs generally receive greater salaries than those with master's degrees, who usually are paid more than those with undergraduate degrees. Generally, for-profit companies pay larger salaries than nonprofit organizations, whereas consulting firms tend to have the highest salaries overall. These statements are only generalizations, and salary can vary significantly depending on the position.

Although the pay is reasonable, this field is not one that you enter for the money. Perhaps more important is the increased responsibilities that come with the higher salaries. Entry-level positions often involve grunt work that can vary from arranging meetings and facilities to assisting with data cleaning, transcript generation, and field monitoring. The fun of designing studies and managing project teams comes as one gains more experience and provides evidence of being able to handle those responsibilities. It is at this level that the non-monetary rewards become very fulfilling.

Why Did You Choose Consumer Psychology as a Profession?

We chose this profession primarily because it (a) allowed for the study of real-world problems, (b) provided an opportunity to work on a wide variety of problems, and (c) offered the opportunity to work with people rather than doing solitary work in an impersonal laboratory. Working on difficult research problems to improve the performance of organizations and the quality of life for consumers is both exciting and fulfilling. On the great days, you get the immediate satisfaction of seeing managers and executives implement your findings to change strategies, operations, products, services, and so forth. Best of all, the problems, research methods, consumers, and organizational environment are constantly changing, so there is a never-ending opportunity to have these great days. It all makes for a very challenging and rewarding work life.

References

Berrigan, J., & Finkbeiner, C. (1992). *Segmentation marketing.* New York: Harper Business.

Hiam, A., & Schewe, C. D. (1992). *The portable MBA in marketing.* New York: Wiley.

Frank, R. E., & Greenberg, M. G. (1982). *Audiences for public television.* California: Sage.

Suggested Readings

Coyne, R. K., & O' Neil, J. M. (1992). *Organizational consultation: A casebook.* Newbury Park, CA: Sage.

Egan, G. (1982). *The skilled helper: Models, skills, and methods for effective helping.* Monterey, CA: Brooks/Cole.

Englis, B. G. (Ed.). (1994). *Global and multinational advertising.* Hillsdale, NJ: Erlbaum.

Hakel, M. D. (1994). *The consulting academician in working with organizations and their people.* New York: Guilford Press.

Lagerspetz, K. M. J., & Niemi, P. (Eds.). (1984). *Psychology in the 1990's.* Amsterdam: Elsevier Science.

Poling, A., Methot, L. L., & LeSage, M. G. (1995). *Fundamentals of behavior analytic research.* New York: Plenum Press.

IV | CAREERS IN DIVERSE AREAS OF PSYCHOLOGY

Raymond S. Nickerson

Designing for Human Use: Human-Factors Psychologists

12

C hoosing a vocation is among the more important decisions one makes. An understanding of one's own interests, capabilities, values, and preferences is half of what is needed to make an informed career choice; the other half is an understanding of the demands and opportunities that different career options represent. My goal in this chapter is to convey an idea of human-factors psychology as a career that is sufficiently clear and complete to be useful to people who may wish to consider the possibility of entering the field and to people who have occasion to counsel others regarding career choices. This is not an easy task, because human-factors psychology does not fit snugly in a neat conceptual box. But this very fact—the hard-to-define nature of the field, which stems in part from the diversified character of the work that human-factors psychologists do and from the contexts in which they do it—makes the field an interesting one to consider and an exciting and rewarding one for people who are in it.

Raymond S. Nickerson is currently a research associate at Tufts University. He is the recipient of the Franklin Taylor award from APA's Division 21, past chair of the Committee on Human Factors of the National Research Council, and founding editor of the *Journal of Experimental Psychology: Applied.*

Human Factors as a Discipline

People who work in the field have called themselves by a variety of names, and still do—there is no universally accepted term. *Human engineer* was used quite a bit at one time, but I think it is used less frequently today. The term invites poor jokes—what other kinds of engineers are there?—and many members of the profession are not engineers in any case. *Human-factors engineer* addresses the first problem but not the second. *Engineering psychologist* and *human-factors psychologist* fail as general designations because not all members of the profession are psychologists. *Applied psychologist* fails for the same reason, and also, it is too broad. Each of these terms is appropriate for some subset of the people working in the field, but none of them is ideal for the field as a whole.

Human-factors specialist is often used and serves the purpose when one wants a designation that is broad enough to include engineers, psychologists, and people from other traditional disciplines but that also makes the focus of attention on human-factors problems explicit. *Ergonomist* has been used widely in Europe but less so in the United States. Some Americans may shy away from the term either because of its lack of familiarity or because it means, literally, the study of work, and this connotation is too narrow to represent much of what human-factors people do. Both of these objections may lessen if the term acquires a broader connotation through more extensive use, as appears to be happening. One sees the word being used with increasing frequency in advertisements of products that are claimed to have been well designed from a human-factors point of view.

People who make up the human-factors profession are likely to continue to refer to themselves in a variety of ways. Those whose training is primarily in engineering are likely to call themselves human-factors engineers or something else that makes the connection to engineering explicit: design engineers, systems engineers, and so forth. Those trained as psychologists are likely to refer to themselves in some way that emphasizes that fact, such as engineering psychologists, human-factors psychologists, or applied psychologists.

Because this book is addressed to people considering the possibility of pursuing a career in *psychology*, I will focus here mainly on human-factors professionals who are trained as psychologists, which is to say, people who have one or more degrees in psychology and think of themselves as psychologists first and foremost. I will use the term *human-factors psychologist* to refer generally to psychologists who spend a substantial portion of their time working on human-factors problems.

I want to note, however, that there are many people who might not identify themselves as (primarily) human-factors psychologists, but who function as human-factors psychologists part of the time and who contribute significantly to the field. In addition to human-factors work, they may, for example, do fundamental research, or they may do applied research not only on human-factors problems, but on problems in closely related areas as well, such as organizational psychology, personnel psychology, training, or military psychology. Some of the people in this category are managers who keep a hand in research or consulting.

What do human-factors psychologists do? Where do they work? (Who employs them?) How does one get to be a human-factors psychologist? What training should one who wants to be a member of this profession get? How should one decide whether one is cut out to be a human-factors psychologist? What are the future opportunities in this field? In what follows, I make some observations prompted by such questions. In some cases it may be possible to give something approaching an answer, because relevant data exist; in other cases, however, the best I can do is offer speculations or opinions based on my own experience.

What Human-Factors Psychologists Do

What do human-factors psychologists do on a day-to-day basis? At one level the answer is that they read, listen, think, talk, and write. They spend a large portion of a typical day attempting to absorb information (by reading, listening, studying plans, inspecting equipment or systems), thinking (planning, trying to figure out how to solve specific problems—or at least to make some progress on them), or trying to articulate ideas orally or in written reports.

Specific tasks that human-factors psychologists perform include designing and conducting experiments and interpreting their results, designing tests or evaluations of equipment for usability and safety, collecting or analyzing data for such evaluations, analyzing tasks by identifying the steps involved in performing them, helping to decide which functions of a person–machine system should be performed by a person and which should be performed by a machine, writing or critiquing technical reports, and a host of other tasks. For present purposes, it is helpful to partition the work that human-factors psychologists do into five categories: basic research, applied research, engineering, research interpretation, and teaching. The boundaries among these categories are not sharp, and many human-factors psychologists engage regularly in more than one of these categories of work.

BASIC RESEARCH

By basic research in this context, I mean research that addresses fundamental human capabilities and limitations, especially as they have relevance to how people can function in different work situations. It is the kind of research that, in the area of vision for example, would lead to a better understanding of visual processes (cone and rod vision, convergence, accommodation, eye movements) and their roles as determinants of visual phenomena and experiences (foveal and peripheral vision, color discrimination, dark adaptation, depth perception).

Much of what is learned from this type of research is incorporated into handbooks and design guidelines that serve as primary reference manuals for people actually engaged in design work. Such information is essential when one is designing a new display, say, and one needs to be sure that the information provided by it can be seen (or heard, or felt) by the users of the display in the conditions in which they are expected to use it.

APPLIED RESEARCH

By applied research here, I mean research that is aimed at solving fairly specific practical problems, often involving the design of systems that are intended to serve particular purposes. Staying with the example of vision, human-factors psychologists might do research aimed at developing displays that the pilot of a high-performance aircraft can see while continuing to look out the cockpit window. Some guidance for the development of such displays can be obtained from the handbooks that contain the results of basic research, but typically, what is in a handbook must be supplemented by additional information that is more specific to the situation of interest. The design of effective "helmet-mounted" or "head-up" displays requires the solution of problems that are relatively peculiar to such displays. More generally, display design involves a host of problems, the solutions to many of which are not deducible from the results of basic research.

RESEARCH INTERPRETATION
AND APPLICATION

There is a difference between doing research—basic or applied—and actually applying research findings to practical problems. Human-factors psychologists are often called on to apply the experimental findings contained in a voluminous psychological literature, insofar as they are relevant to the design of equipment and devices that people have to use and environments in which they have to live and work. This is a demanding job because it requires that one be very familiar with research methodology, with the substance of a field (so one will know how to find research results that are relevant to a specific problem, if they exist), and with the practical problem of interest. To do it well requires that one know a lot both about psychology as a science and about the area of design and engineering that has the practical problem. It requires, too, excellent skills of communication—the ability to speak the language of both psychology and engineering—and interpersonal interaction.

DESIGN AND ENGINEERING

Some human-factors psychologists do design and engineering. My sense is that a relatively small percentage of members of the profession function as engineers to this degree, but those who have the necessary engineering background can do so. The more common involvement of human-factors psychologists in design and engineering is as members of design or implementation teams where they have, or share, the responsibility of ensuring the adequacy of a design from usability and safety points of view.

I might have identified "evaluation" as a separate category of work, because human-factors psychologists often are called on to evaluate products or systems. I have chosen to consider this as part of the process of design and engineering, however, because evaluation is more and more being treated as a continuing aspect of system or product development. Complex systems are typically developed today by an iterative process in which successively more complete prototypes are implemented, each of which can be tested, and what is learned at each stage of development can be used to effect in the next stage.

TEACHING

Many human-factors psychologists teach at either the undergraduate or graduate level, or both. Many also combine teaching with research or with one of the other categories of activities.

A BRIDGING AND MULTIPLY CONNECTED FIELD

Some people see human factors as a subfield of psychology; others see it as a subfield of engineering. This is not surprising, because it has much to do both with psychology and with engineering. It is sometimes referred to as a bridging discipline, in part because it bridges these two domains and in part also because it bridges the worlds of research and applications.

The overlap in activity between human factors and several related fields is sufficiently great that the dividing line may be impossible to draw in some instances. Among the more obvious cases in point are experimental psychology, industrial and organizational psychology, military psychology, personnel psychology (selection and training), physiology (physical anthropology and biomechanics), mechanical and industrial engineering, architecture, and computer science.

The relationship of human-factors psychology to personnel psychology deserves special mention. Human-factors psychologists and personnel psychologists share the objective of seeing that individuals are able to function effectively in specific job situations, which means, among other things, trying to ensure that individuals' capabilities and limitations are well matched to the equipment they have to use and the tasks they have to perform. The personnel psychologist helps to determine how closely the capabilities and limitations of individuals match specific job requirements and how the match might be improved in particular cases through training. The human-factors psychologist is more likely to try to design jobs, and especially the equipment that is used on those jobs, so as to reduce the need for selection and training.

These are not mutually exclusive approaches to matching people to equipment and job requirements, but complementary ones. As a general rule, equipment that is well designed from a human-factors point of view should be usable by a more varied set of people than is equipment that is not well designed from a human-factors point of view, but there is still likely to be a need for selection and training, at least when the equipment that is to be used or the tasks that are to be performed are inherently complex.

Human-factors psychology is sometimes given a connotation that is sufficiently broad to include training, especially training that is intended to enhance the performance of person–machine systems. And, even with the narrower connotation of human-factors psychology, one can speak of the human factors *of* training, which has to do with the design and evaluation of training materials, methods, and systems. This is an especially important problem area with the increasing use of computer-based systems for purposes of training and education.

Design Improvement as a
Central Theme

A major objective of much of the work that human-factors psychologists do—some people consider this objective to be what defines the field—is to ensure that the design of the devices and systems that people use and with which they interact matches people's capabilities and limitations. Improvements in design are generally changes that make devices or systems easier to learn to use and safer or more comfortable to use without impairing their effectiveness.

There are many success stories that can be told of design improvements that have been implemented as a result of human-factors research. These include padded dashboards, collapsible steering columns, and other design innovations for automobiles motivated by safety considerations; the protective guards and kill switches that have been installed on much industrial equipment; conspicuous warning/ danger signs with understandable messages; "user-friendly" computer interfaces; internationally standardized symbols that are used to identify services and give directions in airports and on highways; and many other innovations.

Sometimes changes that are made as a consequence of human-factors research appear, after the fact, to be nothing more than common sense. But innovations that are recognized as commonsensical after they have been made typically are not easily recognized as such before the fact. The separation of automobile brake lights from the rear running lights and the placement of brake lights in a high (rear window) location may seem very commonsensical, but automobiles had been around for almost a century before this innovation was adopted, and adoption came only after many years of research demonstrated the effectiveness of this placement. Within a few years after the National Highway Traffic Safety Administration mandated that all new cars have center high-mounted brake lights (which became a requirement as of September 1985), the cost to consumers was estimated to be about $1 million a year, and the annual savings in property damages resulting from a 17% reduction in rear-end collisions to be about $910 million. The 20 years of research on rear lighting systems that preceded this mandated design change has been estimated to have cost the National Highway Traffic Safety Administration less than $5 million in total (Kahane, 1989).

Proposals to change the designs of things that have been in use for some time can meet very strong resistance from people who have become accustomed to the existing designs and who would be faced with new learning tasks if they were changed. Sometimes the resistance to change is overcome and new designs replace existing ones, perhaps because of the evidence that the benefits of change greatly outweigh the costs, but even then the opposition may persist and the change may take some time. The importance of human-factors considerations has long been recognized in aviation, and human-factors research has been responsible for many changes in the design of instrument displays, cockpit layouts, and operating procedures, but some of the more important changes have met stiff resistance from pilots when first proposed.

On occasion, resistance to change is sufficiently strong to preclude the implementation of changes that have been demonstrated to be effective, or at least to postpone them to the indefinite future. Numerous studies have shown the traditional "QWERTY" letter arrangement of the typewriter (now computer) keyboard to be less efficient than any of several alternative arrangements. Resistance to changing the layout has proved to be very strong, however, both among the many thousands of keyboard users who have mastered the conventional layout and have little interest in having to learn a new one and among manufacturers who are not keen on trying to convince consumers of the merits of an innovation they do not want.

The design of the coinage of most countries is far from optimal from a human-factors point of view. The U.S. system illustrates the point. There is no color coding: The penny is brown, and all of the other coins are silver gray. Neither size nor weight correlates perfectly with value: The nickel is larger than the penny, but the dime is smaller than both. Shape provides no clue to value, inasmuch as all coins (currently being minted) are circular. The absence or presence of serrations on the edge distinguishes the penny and the nickel from other coins but does not help distinguish the penny and nickel from each other or distinguish among the remaining coins. If one were to design a coin set with the goal of maximizing the ease of recognizing coins of different value, either visually or tactually, human-factors principles suggest that size should correlate perfectly with value and that each coin should have a set of easily perceived visual and tactile features that identify it uniquely. The problem of poor coin design probably does not cause most people much difficulty—if they have their sight, are selecting coins in the light, and are dealing with a system with which they are familiar. It can be a problem, however, for a blind person, a sighted person trying to identify coins in the dark, or a traveler using the coins of some country for the first time.

The resistance that adoption of the metric system is encountering in the United States also illustrates how difficult it can be to replace a deeply entrenched system with another, whatever the evidence of the relative merits of the systems involved. The point of these illustrations of resistance to change is that demonstrating the superiority of one design over another is only one step in the process of effecting change and often does not suffice to guarantee that the change will be made. Human-factors psychologists often find themselves playing the role of advocates, needing to try to persuade someone of the merits of applying an idea, say, a principle that has been established by human-factors research, to the design of something—a device, a display, a system, or a procedure. Sometimes this advocacy is successful, and sometimes it is not; change does not come easily when entrenched ways of doing things are involved.

Problem Areas

Although the roots of human-factors psychology extend back at least to the early part of the 20th century and perhaps to the later years of the 19th, interest in human-factors problems was greatly intensified by the extraordinary needs of the military during World War II (Carmichael, 1945; Grether, 1968; Stevens, 1946). The war effort produced a need for equipment that could be used effectively, and often in hostile environments, by people without extensive training. The design of such equipment required the careful application of what was known about human capabilities and limitations, and lack of the required knowledge stimulated research. The resulting research included studies of depth perception, dark adaptation, color coding, instrument illumination, camouflage, gun sighting and target tracking, sonar listening, gun battery operation, effects of fatigue on performance, clothing design and its effects on mobility and dexterity, map design, and runway markings, among many other topics.

Much of the research on human-factors problems beginning in the 1930s and extending through the World War II period focused on aviation—the effects of fatigue and altitude on pilot performance and the design of cockpit displays, the major contributors to pilot workload and causes of pilot error. The interest of human-factors researchers in problems of aviation has continued unabated over the years and remains strong (Wiener, 1990).

Today human-factors psychologists work on a wide variety of practical problems. Areas of interest include the design of instrument panels for aircraft cockpits, ships' bridges, and nuclear power plants; the handling quality of automotive vehicles; the safety of all-terrain and other recreational vehicles; the effectiveness of passenger restraint systems (seat belts, air bags, children's car seats); the safety of children's furniture and toys; the design of computer interfaces; the effects of various types of stress or stressors (heat, humidity, fatigue, noise, danger) on human performance; the lighting and layout of workplaces; the measurement of workload—especially cognitive workload—imposed by specific tasks; the design of household appliances, hand tools, and consumer products more generally; the design and evaluation of type fonts for legibility; the design of keyboards for typewriters, computer terminals, and music synthesizers; the configuration of spacecraft working and living capsules; the effectiveness of warning signals, product labels, and instructions; the effects of aging on skilled performance; and risk assessment, communication, and control.

The list could easily be extended—the diversity of problems on which human-factors psychologists work is really quite remarkable—but rather than extend it, I will discuss briefly a general problem that has received attention from human-factors psychologists since the earliest days of the profession, namely the problem of human error. The focus on this problem illustrates the practical concerns that motivate much human-factors work and the many opportunities the discipline presents for having an effect on the quality of people's lives.

The question of interest is what causes human error in various contexts and how the probability of error—especially error that can have dire consequences—can be reduced. Work in support of the World War II effort included the documentation of errors in the operation of gun batteries, and of the effects of fatigue on human performance (Grether, 1968). A better understanding of the errors that pilots made and of the causal factors involved—especially those that could be attributed to cockpit design—was also a research objective at this time (Fitts & Jones, 1947a, 1947b). Over time, the study of error in aviation extended beyond the cockpit and included the performance of airline crews, air traffic controllers, maintenance staff, and others whose work could have an effect on flight safety (Wiener, 1990).

According to a recent report from the Federal Aviation Administration, human error has been a causal factor in 66% of air carrier accidents and 79% and 88% of fatal commuter and general-aviation accidents, respectively. The Aviation Safety Reporting System, which collects confidential reports from aviation personnel regarding performance errors, mishaps, and "close calls" in the aviation industry, had, by 1990, recorded 180,000 reports since its establishment in the mid-1970s; approximately 70% of these reports involved problems of information transfer (Foushee, 1990).

Human error is also of great interest in areas of transportation other than aviation. It is believed, for example, to be the single most prevalent cause of motor vehicle accidents, accounting for over

60% of them (Perchonok, 1972). Automobile driving has been a focus of experimental investigation at least since 1928 (Lauer, 1960), and it continues to be a priority for study, especially in view of the fact that the annual number of fatalities from automobile accidents in the United States alone is around 45,000, despite improvements in per-passenger-mile statistics in recent years. When the number of fatalities is normalized to the number of registered vehicles, the number of licensed drivers, or the number of vehicle miles, a decrease in the death rate of nearly 50% is seen over a period of a couple of decades (Bureau of the Census, 1992; Transportation Research Board, 1990). This decrease is testimony to the effectiveness of several measures that have been taken to improve highway safety, but motor vehicle accidents still cause more deaths than do all other types of accident combined (not to mention the problems of 4 million injuries and a total estimated cost of automotive accidents of $70 billion per year in the United States), so their incidence still must be considered unacceptably high.

The following is an unsolved problem relating to automotive safety that has considerable practical importance and that illustrates the need for research in this area. Drivers engage in risky behavior; this is not in doubt. They drive too fast, drive while drinking, follow leading vehicles too closely, pass with insufficient forward vision, fail to use seat belts, drive unsafe vehicles, and so on. Why do they do this? In any particular case of risky driving, the driver either underestimates the magnitude of the risk that is being taken (skates on thin ice believed to be thick) or is fully aware of the risk that is being taken and takes it willingly (skates on ice recognized to be thin). Determining which of these possibilities holds in particular instances is important, because the two of them call for different approaches to modifying the risky behavior: The first calls for finding a way to make the driver aware of the risk that is being taken; the second requires something more than provision of this information, which the driver already has.

Railway accidents like the one that claimed the lives of 33 people and seriously injured 69 others near Clapham Junction Railway Station, England, in December 1988 have called attention to the need for more work on human error in rail transportation. An investigation by the British Department of Transport of the accident and the circumstances leading to it identified 16 types of human error that were considered to be instrumental in permitting this catastrophe (Secretary of State for Transport, 1989). Collisions of trains with motor vehicles at railroad crossings are more common than they should be and are often attributable to errors of judgment on the part of one or more of the parties involved.

Maritime transportation has its own set of challenges. Between 1970 and 1990 drowning was the third most common cause of accidental death in the United States (auto accidents and falls were first and second), averaging roughly 6,000 per year. Nearly every year shipwrecks are reported, some of which claim hundreds of lives. Among notable maritime disasters in recent years were the sinking of the Nile steamer *10th of Ramadan* in Lake Nassar in 1983 (357 lives lost), the collision of the Soviet passenger ship *Admiral Nakhimov* with the Soviet freighter *Pyotr Vasev* in the Black Sea in 1986 (398 lost), the collision in 1987 between the Philippine ferry *Dona Paz* and the oil tanker *Victor* in the Tablas Strait (more than 3,000 lives lost), and the capsizing of an Indian ferry on the Ganges in 1988 (over 400 lost).

Commercial fishing is considered one of the most hazardous occupations in the world (National Research Council, 1991). Reliable statistics on injury from shipboard accidents are not available, but the incidence is believed to be high relative to that of other occupations. In addition to physical injury and the loss of life and property, maritime accidents often have substantial deleterious effects on the environment. Oil spills of the magnitude of that of the *Exxon Valdez* make news, but the thousands of smaller spills that occur every year do not. According to U.S. Coast Guard data, the number of reported oil spills into water averaged a little under 3,000 per year between 1975 and 1989 (National Research Council, 1990, Fig. 2-11).

The cost of maritime accidents, in terms of injury, loss of life, loss of property, ship damage, and environmental impact, is very high. The desirability of reducing this cost is, by itself, a sufficient reason to apply human factors engineering to the design and operation of maritime systems. But there are other compelling reasons for doing so as well. Human factors research and engineering are focused not only on improving the safety of work situations, but on enhancing the productivity of workers and increasing the level of satisfaction of workers with their jobs. Productivity is an important issue in the maritime context as it is everywhere, and especially so in view of the fact that much of the maritime industry must compete in worldwide markets. Worker satisfaction poses some complex challenges because of the severe demands of many maritime jobs and the unusual circumstances in which they must be performed.

Issues of safety, productivity, and worker satisfaction tend to become especially complicated when work situations are undergoing rapid change. This appears to be the case in the maritime context at the present time. Automation of many ship functions has been accompanied with a significant downsizing of ships' crews over the last few decades. Modern U.S.-flag vessels carry crews of about half the size of comparable-tonnage vessels of about 30 years ago, and many foreign ships operate with much smaller crews than do U.S. ships of the same size (National Research Council, 1990).

Human error can, of course, have serious consequences in contexts other than transportation. Chernobyl, Bhopal, and Three-Mile Island are among the high-visibility catastrophes of recent years that have been attributed, in whole or in part, to human error. The problem is most likely to receive attention from the media and the general public when it appears to be implicated in spectacular incidents like these. But the aggregate effects of the countless incidents that are not newsworthy individually is much greater. During the first 2 years after the reporting of serious accidents caused by the misuse or malfunctioning of medical equipment became mandatory in the United States, an estimated 10,000 to 20,000 accidents were reported, the primary causes of which were equipment design flaws, maintenance or calibration problems, and user error (Bassen, 1986; Sind, 1990). Interest in error in medical contexts—in operating rooms, in nursing care, in the administration of drugs, and in the use of medical devices in the home—appears to be growing among human factors researchers (Bogner, 1994), and one expects to see more attention to this area in the future. It is easy to understand why human-factors psychologists are interested in human error and why the study of this problem has attained the status of a subarea of psychological research (Reason, 1990; Senders & Moray, 1991).

Many of the errors that people make can be attributed, at least in part, to the design of the equipment they use. Interest in a better understanding of the types of errors that are made in specific contexts is motivated to a large degree by the assumption that such an understanding can provide the basis for improvements in the design of equipment that will decrease the probability of occurrence of errors in its use (Weinberg, 1989–1990).

Closely associated with the subject of human error is that of accidents, inasmuch as many accidents are caused by human error. There are two basic directions that may be taken by efforts to reduce the number of deaths and the number and severity of injuries due to accidents. One is to attempt to decrease the incidence of accidents, and the other is to try to reduce the severity of the consequences of accidents when they occur. The first approach is illustrated by attempts to design equipment so as to make accident-causing errors in its use less likely. It is illustrated too by the taking of such simple measures as installing grab bars in showers and bathtubs in the interest of decreasing the likelihood of bathroom falls (very common among elderly people) and ensuring adequate lighting of stairwells (also a common location of falls by elderly people). The second approach is illustrated by the installation in automobiles of padded dashboards, seat belts, air bags, energy-absorbing steering columns, antilacerative laminated wind-shields, nonprojecting interior door handles, and head restraints; such devices may not decrease the likelihood of accidents, but they can reduce the severity of injury in the case of one.

Where Human-Factors Psychologists Work

Most professionals who are not in private practice work either in academic, industrial, or governmental organizations. Human-factors psychologists will be found in all three settings. According to Super and Super (1988), about one third of all psychologists were employed by colleges and universities as of the mid-1980s. At the same time, about 23% were employed by hospitals and clinics, 18% were in private clinical practice, 15% worked in public school systems, 4% were in business and industry, and 4% were in government positions. Human-factors psychologists make up a relatively small percentage of all psychologists (the Human Factors and Ergonomics Society is less than 1/13th as large as the American Psychological Association with its membership of about 75,000), and their interests, although broad, are considerably more focused than those of psychology in general. The employment pattern for human-factors psychologists would be expected to reflect this fact.

Among the human-factors specialists surveyed by the National Research Council (NRC), about 74% worked for private business, about 15% worked for government agencies, and about 10% for educational institutions (Van Cott & Huey, 1992). Considering only the subset of the sample who identified themselves as psychologists (who engaged in human-factors work) rather than as human-factors specialists or as members of some other profession (e.g., engineering, computer science), 47% worked in private business and 41% in a government agency. The important point for present purposes is that there are opportunities for people to do human-factors work in industry, in government, and in academia.

Six major areas, each of which individually accounted for at least 5% of human-factors work, accounted for about 83% of it in the aggregate at the time of the NRC survey. These areas were computers (22.3%), aerospace (21.6%), industrial processes (16.5%), health and safety (8.9%), communications (8.2%), and transportation (5.3%). The next three most mentioned areas were energy (2.2%), consumer products (1.4%), and office products (0.7%). The fact that no other area accounted for as much as 1.0% and that about 13% of the sample was classified as "something else" is a reflection of the diversity of contexts in which human-factors specialists work.

Among the major employers of human-factors psychologists, besides universities and government entities (such as the Department of Defense and the various branches of the military, the Department of Transportation, and the U.S. Post Office), have been large corporations that design, build, and market systems or consumer products or that provide consumer services. Examples include AT&T, IBM, Xerox, Eastman Kodak, and Exxon Corporation. Given the long-term focus of human-factors research on aviation, it is not surprising to find many human-factors psychologists employed by major aircraft manufacturers, such as Hughes Aircraft, McDonnell-Douglas, Boeing, and Lockheed. Human-factors psychologists are also employed by research organizations like Dunlap and Associates, American Institutes of Research, Bolt Beranek and Newman, Incorporated (now BBN Corporation), and the MITRE Corporation.

Compensation

Salary figures must be interpreted with care because salaries vary considerably not only within occupational categories but across them, and, especially in industry, higher salaries often reflect compensation for managerial responsibilities. Also, as noted above, human-factors psychologists work in several organizational contexts—industry, government, and academia—and we should not be surprised to find salaries to vary with these factors as well.

According to the National Research Council's survey mentioned above, which was conducted in 1989, the median annual salary for human-factors specialists in 1988 was $46,000 for those in nonsupervisory positions and $57,000 for those with supervisory responsibility; about 7% of nonsupervisors and about 14% of supervisors made more than $80,000 per year at the time.

According to a 1985 survey conducted by the American Psychological Association (APA), PhD-level applied psychologists working in industrial/organizational contexts were paid at a somewhat higher rate than psychologists with comparable years of experience working in other contexts (e.g., academia, human service organizations, research organizations) (Pion & Bramblett, 1985). The difference, on average, was somewhat over 20% (of the lower salary) at entry levels and as high as 45% at the most senior levels. At the time of the APA survey, the average salary of an applied psychologist working in industry ranged from about $37,000 for an individual with 4 years of experience or less to about $71,000 for one who had been working in the field for 20 years or more.

The "bottom-line" message for anyone considering the possibility of a career as a human-factors psychologist is that it is probably not the career one should pick if one's primary goal in life is to get rich. There are other lines of work for which the chances of spectacular financial rewards are much higher. On the other hand, salaries are very respectable—comparable to those of researchers and engineers in other fields. In short, one should not choose a career in human-factors psychology just for the sake of the money one can expect to make, but if moneymaking is not one's top priority, what the field offers in this regard is likely to be more than adequate.

How One Gets To Be a Human-Factors Psychologist

Many colleges and universities offer undergraduate and graduate training in human-factors psychology. The Human Factors and Ergonomics Society publishes a *Directory of Human Factors Graduate Programs in the United States and Canada,* which is updated every three years. The 1994 issue of the directory gives general information regarding how to apply to a graduate program and provides details (admission requirements, tuition, financial assistance available, course requirements, research/teaching opportunities, faculty, etc.) about graduate programs offered by some 65 universities.

USEFUL KNOWLEDGE AND SKILLS

What do human-factors psychologists need to know? What skills are they likely to find useful, if not essential, in their jobs? Given the wide variety of tasks one may perform, it should not be surprising that the knowledge and skills required to function effectively as a human-factors psychologist are substantial. One needs a strong foundation in basic psychology (perception, cognition, learning, motor performance, etc.), mathematics (especially probability theory and statistics), and experimental design. A broad familiarity with science, technology, and engineering is desirable, and deep domain knowledge (avionics, medicine, manufacturing, computers, power plant operation, etc.) in the area in which one expects to specialize is especially valuable.

Approaches to research typically involve the use of controlled experimentation, field observations, surveys, and analyses of various types—for example, analyses aimed at identifying critical incidents causing or contributing to a system malfunction or failure. Human-factors psychologists use a variety of tools in their work, including computer-based techniques for identifying and representing the various functional components of a complex system or process, showing the connections among the components that have implications for the flow of material or information through a system, and revealing delay-inducing bottlenecks. Some of the computer-based systems-analysis tools provide the capability to experiment with models or simulations of a system to determine the effects of design modifications on variables of interest, such as the throughput, or productivity, of the system as a whole. As is true of many fields these days, therefore, general facility with computers and experience in the use of specific computer-based tools are very useful.

Human-factors psychology does not generally lend itself to a monastic lifestyle. Most human-factors psychologists find themselves interacting with other people much of the time; often they work on large-system design problems as members of teams. For this reason, social skills are very important. To be an effective team member, one must be good at communicating—at listening and comprehending other people's ideas as well as articulating one's own. One must have a good sense of priorities and an understanding of the need for trade-offs. It seldom is possible to optimize the design of a complex system from all points of view, so compromises and trade-offs are necessary; one needs to be able to distinguish between those that are likely to make a significant difference in terms of design objectives that matter and those that are not likely to do so. A knowledge of group dynamics is useful, and it helps to know something of the art of negotiation.

It is difficult to overstate the importance of attitudes and character traits: respect for other people's views, the ability to see a situation from a variety of perspectives, an understanding of the limitations of one's own knowledge and capabilities, and a realistic grasp of what one does and does not bring to the table. Credibility and goodwill are musts if one is to function effectively in group situations. Credibility can vanish in a hurry if one pretends to know more than one does, and goodwill can do likewise if one fails to show respect for other people's knowledge and ideas. Being technically competent is good, but competence that is unaccompanied by diplomacy can come across as arrogance, and this does not make for good team performance.

FORMAL TRAINING REQUIRED

The specific courses, or types of courses, one should take by way of preparation for a career in human-factors psychology depend on the level of formal education one intends to attain. The individual who intends to seek a PhD will not want the same undergraduate education as the one who intends to enter the workforce as a human-factors specialist immediately after obtaining an undergraduate degree. My opinion—and I do not claim this to be the prevailing opinion in the field—is that the higher the degree one intends to obtain, the less emphasis one should put on human-factors, or even psychology, courses at the undergraduate level.

If one plans on pursuing a PhD in psychology, my advice is to go easy on vocation-oriented courses during the undergraduate years; there will be plenty of time to load up on these during graduate school. What one should aim to get in undergraduate school is a solid foundation in the sciences (including psychology as a science), mathematics (especially probability theory and mathematical statistics), English, and the humanities.

The advice regarding undergraduate courses would be quite different for one who plans to seek a job in human-factors psychology immediately upon receiving an undergraduate degree. In this case taking some more specialized, vocation-specific courses in undergraduate school is essential.

In graduate school, one should get a cross section of courses in psychology and engineering and the specialized training that is dictated by one's specific career aspirations. If one wishes, for example, to do human-factors work in information technology, one needs to take courses in computer science and communication; if one wants to do human-factors work in the area of health care, one needs to take courses relating to health care delivery, perhaps especially focusing on medical devices and instrumentation; and so on. Of course, one also needs to take the graduate-level courses in psychology and human factors that typically are part of a PhD curriculum.

Serving as an apprentice to an established researcher can be an invaluable part of graduate training if one is targeting a career in research. This type of experience can also be obtained with a postdoctoral appointment; however, postdoctoral appointments are used as a vehicle for facilitating the transition from student status to a professional position much less frequently in the behavioral sciences than in some other fields, such as, say, biomedicine (National Research Council, 1994).

How much education should one attempt to get in preparation for a career in human-factors psychology? I think the answer to this question is a little more involved than it might appear to be. One might assume that the answer is "the more, the better," and in a sense, I think this is correct. In general, I believe that more formal education is better than less, not only—or perhaps even primarily—because it generally means more employment options as well as opportunities for higher level jobs, but because learning has intrinsic value and enriches one's life in intangible, but very real, ways.

I think this general notion that more education is better than less needs to be qualified, however, by recognition of the fact that not everyone is suited by temperament or circumstances to go after a PhD. And, as it happens, although a PhD is important to anyone intending to pursue a career in research as an independent or lead researcher, there are many opportunities for work in human-factors psychology for people with a master's, or even a bachelor's, degree. According to a National Research Council survey, only about 37% of the human-factors specialists surveyed had doctorates, and about 34% had master's degrees (Van Cott & Huey, 1992). An earlier survey found a preference within government, industrial, and consulting organizations for human-factors specialists at the master's level (Kraft, 1970); this may reflect a need within these organizations for human-factors people to serve as resource people and as members of project teams rather than, say, as independent researchers or project leaders. Opportunities for people with only a bachelor's degree are undoubtedly more limited than are those for people with a higher degree, but they exist. Generally, at least for people with a bachelor's degree and no work experience, the opportunities would be limited to research assistant positions and to junior status on engineering teams.

This said, I want to stress, however, that a degree is an entrance ticket to the world of work, but only an entrance ticket. What one has learned in school is what is important. The knowledge, skills, and attitudes that one acquires—during school and after—and one's performance on the job are what will determine how far one will go once one is in the workplace. Whatever the level of degree one targets, one should take demanding, substantive courses. Most importantly, one should commit to lifelong learning—especially to learning in the workplace, from colleagues and associates and from continuing study. This undoubtedly seems like gratuitous advice, but I believe it to be sound and, although too obvious to require saying, all too easily ignored. Having the mind-set of a lifelong learner is extremely important, in my view, not only in human-factors psychology, but in any field, especially given the rapidity with which the world—and in particular the world of work—is changing.

Uncertainty about the future and what it holds for job opportunities makes the case for the importance of versatility. Versatility is an invaluable asset for any professional, especially in times of rapid and unpredictable change. If there were no other reasons for getting a strong general educational foundation—and there are other reasons—this fact alone would suffice to establish its importance. By a strong general educational foundation, I mean a solid grounding in science, mathematics, language, and the humanities.

Future Opportunities

Job opportunities in any profession are likely to fluctuate with general economic conditions. For human-factors psychologists, other factors that will help determine what the opportunities will be include changes in demands for college and graduate education and in government priorities for research funding. This is because many people in the field are engaged either in teaching or in research, and much of the research they do has been sponsored by one or another government agency in the past.

Since World War II, the military has been a major sponsor of human-factors research and applications. In the United States, research has been supported by numerous military and Department of Defense (DOD) organizations, notably the Air Force Office of Scientific Research, the Office of Naval Research, the Army Research Institute, and the Defense Advanced Research Projects Agency (now the Advanced Research Projects Agency). Similar military/defense establishments have supported human-factors research in many other countries. The application of human-factors knowledge and approaches in the design of military systems has been mandated by the U.S. government in the publication of Military Standards (MIL-STDs) and complementary DOD documents (e.g., United States Department of Defense, 1979, 1981, 1989).

Assuming a continuation of relative peace and no resurgence of the cold war, it seems unlikely that the military will provide the level of support for human-factors work in the future that it has in the past. On the other hand, the maintenance of a smaller military force that must be able to respond effectively on short notice to a variety of situations the details of which cannot be anticipated, and to do so using more complex equipment than has been used in any preceding conflicts, poses many human-factors challenges that can be met only with research.

In the private sector, human-factors work has been driven by two considerations: (a) Some of it has been mandated by the government, as noted above, and (b) industry has used it because of the belief that its use adds value (and hence marketability) to products. In a world of shrinking government budgets, it will be increasingly important for the discipline to be able to give evidence of the value its involvement in system and product development adds to the systems and products developed. Evidence that industry believes that attention to human-factors concerns makes products more marketable is seen in the care that producers take to highlight attention to such concerns in the promotion of their products

Reduction of human error in a variety of contexts and the development of error-tolerant designs are likely to continue to be a major focus of attention in the field. The search for ways to increase automotive safety will continue, and perhaps become even more intense in view of the anticipated continuing increase in the number of vehicles on the highways and the fact that the percentage of elderly drivers (drivers over 75 are about twice as likely as middle-age drivers to be involved in a crash) is expected to increase faster than the general population. According to projections of the Transportation Research Board (1988), there will be about 22 million people in the United States 75 years of age or older and still eligible for drivers' licenses by 2020.

About 20 years ago, Kulp (1976) listed the following as new directions for engineering psychology/human factors specialists: (a) health/medical care, (b) safety, (c) computer systems, (d) aerospace systems, (e) prosthetics, (f) environmental design, (g) oceanography, (h) architectural design, (i) recreation, (j) urban planning/problems, (k) systems design (personnel substystems design), (l) work design/job design, (m) training, (n) communication, (o) consumer products, (p) maintenance, (q) transportation, (r) manufacturing and quality control, (s) biomechanics and work physiology, (t) issues relating to handicapped people, (u) legal/law enforcement, (v) gerontology, and (w) welfare. Human-factors psychologists are, in fact, working on problems in all of these essential areas, and many of the areas represent major challenges and opportunities for work in the future.

In the same volume in which Kulp gave this list, Fox (1976) expressed the opinion "that the field of data processing, specifically information systems, has the greatest need and offers the greatest challenge for engineering psychology of any field since the early efforts on defense-related systems that began around 1940" (p. 172). Human-factors psychologists responded enthusiastically to the challenge posed by the rapid-fire series of innovations—still occurring—in information technology. I doubt that there is any other topic that has received more attention from human-factors researchers in the last couple of decades than has person–computer interaction. One evidence of the explosion of interest was the establishment of several new journals, including

Behavior and Information Technology, Human–Computer Interaction, and *Interacting with Computers,*during the 1980s; numerous handbooks, compilations of readings, edited volumes, and monographs appeared on the topic during the same period.

Human–computer interaction is likely to remain a major focus of human-factors research for the foreseeable future. The progress that information technology (computer and communication technology) has made in the last few decades is nothing short of phenomenal, and the rapid pace of change shows no signs of decelerating significantly soon. The implications of past and expected advances in this technology for our lives are only partially clear at this point, but they are certain to be profound; human-factors psychology, among other professions, has a significant role to play in helping to ensure that those implications are to our liking (Nickerson, 1986, 1995).

The National Research Council's Committee on Human Factors (1983, 1995) has published two reports describing needs and opportunities for human factors research, as well as a series of reports focused on specific research topics. The 1995 report emphasized needs and opportunities for research that are emerging from recent and ongoing technological developments. The problem areas discussed were (a) productivity in organizations, (b) training and education, (c) employment and disabilities, (d) health care, (e) environmental change, (f) communications technology and telenetworking, (g) information access and usability, (h) emerging technologies in work design, (i) transportation, (j) cognitive performance under stress, and (k) aiding intellectual work.

I believe that the problem of detrimental environmental change represents a challenge to human-factors psychology for the future, as it does to applied psychology more generally and to other fields as well (Nickerson, 1992; Nickerson & Moray, 1995). The problem itself is not new, although general awareness of it has undoubtedly increased in recent years. It has not been a major focus of research or activity by human-factors psychologists in the past. "Environmental psychology" has been recognized as a subfield within psychology at least since the late 1960s or early 1970s (Heimstra & McFarling, 1974; Stokols, 1978), but its major concern has been the question of how environmental variables—work and living spaces, extreme temperatures, humidity, oxygen deprivation, noise, industrial mishaps, crowding—affect human perception, behavior, or well-being. Relatively little attention has been given, by comparison, to the question of what can be done to decrease the detrimental effects on the natural environment that stem from human behavior. Whether human-factors psychologists will view this problem as one to which the field has some relevance and focus more on it in the future than they have in the past remains to be seen.

Societies, Journals, and Some Demographics

The largest professional organization in the field is the Human Factors and Ergonomics Society (HFES), which presently (1995) has a membership of about 5,500. The membership of the HFES is international, but the majority of its members are from the United States, and its annual meetings are held in this country. Several other countries have national societies. The International Ergonomics Association is an association of societies; as of 1993, it had 23 affiliated societies with an estimated combined membership from 40 countries of about 15,000 (Hendrick, 1993). There are several other professional organizations to which many human-factors psychologists belong, including the Society of Engineering Psychologists, which is Division 21 of the American Psychological Association.

The oldest journals in the field are *Ergonomics* and *Human Factors and Ergonomics* (formerly *Human Factors*); the first is published in Europe and the second in the United States. Both began publication in 1958, and both publish articles—mainly articles reporting research—on the full range of topics of interest to researchers in the field, although *Ergonomics* is somewhat more focused on physical work than is *Human Factors and Ergonomics*. Other English-language journals that publish human-factors articles include the *International Journal of Man–Machine Studies, Applied Ergonomics, Human Factors in Manufacturing*, and the *IEEE Transactions on Systems, Man and Cybernetics*. Articles on human factors may also be found, among those on other topics, in the *Journal of Applied Psychology*, the *Journal of Experimental Psychology: Applied*, the *Journal of Biomechanics, Accident Analysis and Prevention*, and many of the more theoretically or academically oriented journals reporting psychological research.

Human factors has been a male-dominated profession, as has engineering more generally, but the situation appears to be changing somewhat in that regard. Female representation in the HFES has increased more or less steadily from close to zero when the society was founded in 1957 to something in the neighborhood of 25% to 30% of the total membership today. I believe that if the membership were classified with respect to both age and sex, one would find the percentage of women within groups of different ages to vary inversely with age; in other words, the younger the group considered, the larger would be the percentage of women composing it. This conjecture reflects the opinion of the people with whom I talked about this subject. There seemed to be a consensus, too, that women in the field were generally finding it to be a congenial one in which to work and that the field offers many opportunities to women, as well as to men, for professional growth and advancement.

Sources of Additional Information

The reader interested in the early history of human-factors psychology will find accounts in Fitts (1947, 1952), Kappauf (1947), Mead (1948), Helson (1949), Kennedy (1951), and Mead and Wulfeck (1952). Somewhat later summary articles include those by Wissel and Hall (1957), Fitts (1958, 1963), Wood (1958), Chapanis (1960), Melton and Briggs (1960), Taylor (1963), and Poulton (1966).

A brief history of human factors as a discipline and of the HFES may be found in the *Directory and Yearbook* of the HFES. The directory, which is updated annually, also contains general information about the society and its officers (past and present), activities, award recipients, technical groups, local and student chapters, and members. The society publishes a brochure titled "Human Factors—Designing for Human Use," which describes the field and gives a brief account of its history, and one titled "Career Opportunities in Human Factors," which describes the requirements for working in the field and gives examples of what human-factors psychologists do. Both of these brochures are available from the society free of charge on request.

The HFES has 17 technical groups, each of which is composed of members who are especially interested in a specified area. The areas are aerospace systems, aging, communications, computer systems, consumer products, educators' professional, environmental design, forensic professional, industrial ergonomics, medical systems and functionally impaired populations, organizational design and management, personality and individual differences in human performance, safety, system development, test and evaluation, training, and visual performance. These group titles provide an idea of the range of interests within the human-factors profession.

An idea of the range of problems with which human-factors psychologists concern themselves also may be obtained by perusal of any of a number of handbooks, including Van Cott and Kinkade (1972), Woodson (1981), Boff, Kaufman, and Thomas (1986), Salvendy (1987), and Boff and Lincoln (1988). Collections of readings and review articles, such as those compiled by Sinaiko (1961), Howell and Goldstein (1971), and Hancock (1987), also provide a sense of the research activities of the field. As of 1993, there have been eight chapters on engineering psychology in the *Annual Review of Psychology*: Fitts (1958), Melton & Briggs (1960), Chapanis (1963), Poulton (1966), Alluisi and Morgan (1976), Wickens and Kramer (1985), Gopher and Kimchi (1989), and Howell (1993). The HFES has published a book of selected readings in human factors, edited by Venturino (1990), that contains a cross section of significant studies published in the field of human factors/ergonomics during the last 30 years.

Most of the references mentioned in the foregoing paragraphs are addressed to readers who already have a background in human-factors psychology, and might therefore be less informative to a reader considering whether to prepare for a career in the field. To get an idea of what human-factors psychology students study, one can consult any of a number of basic texts: Sheridan and Ferrell (1974), Bailey (1982), Kantowitz and Sorkin (1983), Sanders and McCormick (1987), Adams (1989), Cushman and Rosenberg (1991), and Wickens (1992). A specific undergraduate program in human factors is described by Gardner-Bonneau (1988). A brief description of the field aimed at a general audience is given by Parsons (1984).

Several books have been produced specifically for the benefit of people considering whether to enter this field. Super and Super (1988) contains general information regarding psychology as a profession and advice for those considering the possibility of pursuing a career in one or another subfield of psychology, including human-factors psychology. The American Psychological Association has published several books addressed to the same audience (Woods, 1976, 1987, 1988). Notable within these books, for present purposes, are chapters by Parsons (1976, 1987, 1988) dealing specifically with human factors as a profession. Parsons's 1976 chapter provides an excellent overview of how human-factors professionals bring psychology to bear on the problem of making effective use of technological devices and systems. The National Research Council report (Van Cott & Huey, 1992), mentioned several times in this chapter, contains much information about human-factors psychology and how people in this field spend their time that should be of interest to anyone considering the possibility of entering the profession.

Concluding Comment

Human-factors psychology provides members of the profession with many opportunities to do creative and consequential work. If you enjoy a challenge, and if you get satisfaction from effecting changes that sometimes can benefit many people in significant ways, it is a profession worth considering. What the future holds for the profession is not clear; a lot probably depends on the capabilities and energy of the people who enter it. Many of the challenges that have motivated the profession in the past are not likely to go away any time soon, and as technology continues to produce new devices and systems that people have to use and with which they have to interact, there will be many new challenges and opportunities for work on human-factors psychology in the future. The struggle that society is currently having in learning how to make effective use of computer networking while limiting the painful effects of potential misuses of this powerful technology illustrates the need for continuing attention to the general problem of ensuring that the products of technology serve legitimate human needs and socially acceptable ends.

I have the following simple view of jobs that involve problem solving. There are problems that are fun to work on because of the intellectual challenge they represent. There are problems that one can feel good about working on because solving them, or even making headway on them, can benefit people in tangible ways. And there are problems that one can get paid for working on. It is obvious that the sets defined by these types of problem are not identical, but they do overlap; there are problems that have all three properties. I believe that human factors psychology provides many opportunities to work on just such problems.

References

Adams, J. A. (1989). *Human factors engineering.* New York: MacMillan.

Alluisi, E. A., & Morgan, B. B., Jr. (1976). Engineering psychology and human performance. *Annual Review of Psychology, 27,* 256–330.

Bailey, R. W. (1982). *Human performance engineering: A guide for system designers.* Englewood Cliffs, NJ: Prentice Hall.

Bassen, H. I. (1986). From problem reporting to technological solutions. *Medical Instrumentation, 20*(1), 17–26.

Boff, K. R., Kaufman, L., & Thomas, J. P. (1986). *Handbook of perception and human performance* (2 vols.). New York: Wiley.

Boff, K. R., & Lincoln, J. E. (Eds.). (1988). *Engineering data compendium: Human perception and performance* (4 vols.). Wright-Patterson Air Force Base, OH: Harry B. Armstrong Medical Research Laboratory.

Bogner, M. S. (1994). *Human error in medicine.* Hillsdale, NJ: Erlbaum.

Bureau of the Census. (1992). *Statistical abstract of the United States: 1992.* Washington, DC: U.S. Department of Commerce.

Carmichael, L. (1945). Psychological principles in the design and operation of military equipment. *Proceedings of the Joint Army–Navy–OSRD Conference on Psychological Problems in Military Training* (Pt. I, pp. 4–7). Washington, DC: Applied Psychology Panel, NDRC.

Chapanis, A. (1960). Human engineering. In C. D. Flagie, W. H. Huggins, & R. H. Roy (Eds.), *Operations research and systems engineering*. Baltimore, MD: Johns Hopkins University Press.

Chapanis, A. (1963). Engineering psychology. *Annual Review of Psychology, 14*, 285–318.

Committee on Human Factors, National Research Council. (1983). *Research needs in human factors*. Washington, DC: National Academy Press.

Committee on Human Factors, National Research Council. (1995). *Emerging needs and opportunities for human factors research*. Washington, DC: National Academy Press.

Cushman, W. J., & Rosenberg, D. J. (1991). *Human factors in product design*. Amsterdam: Elsevier.

Fitts, P. M. (Ed.). (1947). *Psychological research on equipment design* (Report No. 19 of the Aviation Psychology Research Program of the Army Air Forces). Washington, DC: Government Printing Office.

Fitts, P. M. (1952). Men and machines—the design of equipment for efficient human use. *Engineering Experimental Station News, 24*, 6–10.

Fitts, P. M. (1958). Engineering psychology. *Annual Review of Psychology, 9*, 267–294.

Fitts, P. M. (1963). Engineering psychology. In S. Koch (Ed.), *Psychology, a study of a science* (pp. 908–933). New York: McGraw-Hill.

Fitts, P. M., & Jones, R. E. (1947a). Analysis of factors contributing to 460 "pilot-error" experiences in operating aircraft controls. *USAF Air Material Command Memorandum Report No. TSEAA-694-12*, July 1.

Fitts, P. M., & Jones, R. E. (1947b). Psychological aspects of instrument display. I. Analysis of 270 "pilot-error" experiences in reading and interpreting aircraft instruments. *USAF Air Material Command Memorandum Report No. TSEAA-694-12A*, October 1.

Foushee, H. C. (1990). *The national plan for aviation human factors* (Vols. 1–2)[Draft]. Washington, DC: Federal Aviation Administration.

Fox, W. F. (1976). Future directions in engineering psychology: Business information systems. In P. J. Woods (Ed.), *Career opportunities for psychologists: Expanding and emerging areas* (pp. 171–179). Washington, DC: American Psychological Association.

Gardner-Bonneau, D. J. (1988). Undergraduate preparation for a career in human factors. In P. J. Woods (Ed.), *Is psychology for them? A guide to undergraduate advising* (pp. 135–139). Washington, DC: American Psychological Association.

Gopher, D., & Kimchi, R. (1989). Engineering psychology. *Annual Review of Psychology, 40,* 431–455.

Grether, W. F. (1968). Engineering psychology in the United States. *American Psychologist, 23,* 743–751.

Hancock, P. A. (Ed.). (1987). *Human factors psychology.* Amsterdam: North-Holland.

Heimstra, N. W., & McFarling, L. H. (1974). *Environmental psychology.* Monterey, CA: Brooks/Cole.

Helson, H. (1949). Design of equipment and optimal human operation. *American Journal of Psychology, 62,* 473–497.

Hendrick, H. (1993, March 5). Presentation on the International Ergonomics Association to the Committee on Human Factors, National Research Council, Houston, TX.

Howell, W. C. (1993). Engineering psychology in a changing world. *Annual Review of Psychology, 44,* 231–263.

Howell, W. C., & Goldstein, I. L. (Eds.). (1971). *Engineering psychology: Current perspectives in research.* New York: Appleton-Century-Crofts.

Kahane, C. J. (1989). *An evaluation of center high-mounted stop lamps based on 1987 data* (Report DOT-HS-807-442). Washington, DC: U.S. Department of Transportation.

Kantowitz, B. H., & Sorkin, R. D. (1983). *Human factors: Understanding people–system relationships.* New York: Wiley.

Kappauf, W. E. (1947). History of psychological studies of the design and operation of equipment. *American Psychologist, 2,* 83–86.

Kennedy, J. L. (1951). Handbooks of human engineering data. *Annals of the New York Academy of Science, 51,* 1135–1145.

Kraft, J. A. (1970). Status of human factors and biotechnology in 1968–1969. *Human Factors, 12,* 113–151.

Kulp, R. A. (1976). New directions in engineering psychology/human factors. In P. J. Woods, (Ed.), *Career opportunities for psychologists: Expanding and emerging areas* (pp. 163–173). Washington, DC: American Psychological Association.

Lauer, A. R. (1960). *The psychology of driving: Factors of traffic enforcement.* Springfield, IL: Charles C Thomas.

Mead, L. C. (1948). A program of human engineering. *Personnel Psychology, 1,* 303–317.

Mead, L. C., & Wulfeck, J. W. (1952). Human engineering: The study of the human factor in machine design. *Scientific Monthly, 75,* 372–379.

Melton, A. W., & Briggs, G. E. (1960). Engineering psychology. *Annual Review of Psychology, 11,* 71–98.

National Research Council. (1990). *Crew size and maritime safety.* Washington, DC: National Academy Press.

National Research Council (1991). *Fishing vessel safety: Blueprint for a national program.* Washington, DC: National Academy Press.

National Research Council. (1994). *Meeting the nation's needs for biomedical and behavioral scientists* (Report of the Committee on National Needs for Biomedical and Behavioral Research Personnel). Washington, DC: National Academy Press.

Nickerson, R. S. (1986). *Using computers: Human factors in information technology.* Cambridge, MA: MIT Press.

Nickerson, R. S. (1992). *Looking ahead: Human factors challenges in a changing world.* Hillsdale, NJ: Erlbaum.

Nickerson, R. S. (1995). Human interaction with computers and robots. *International Journal of Human Factors in Manufacturing, 5,* 5–27.

Nickerson, R. S., & Moray, N. (1995). Environmental change. In R. S. Nickerson (Ed.), *Emerging needs and opportunities for human factors research* (pp. 158–176). Washington, DC: National Academy Press.

Parsons, H. M. (1976). Psychology for engineering and technology. In P. J. Woods (Ed.), *Career opportunities for psychologists: Expanding and emerging areas* (pp. 180–193). Washington, DC: American Psychological Association.

Parsons, H. M. (1984). Engineering psychology. In R. J. Corsini (Ed.), *Encyclopedia of psychology* (pp. 436–440). New York: Wiley.

Parsons, H. M. (1987). Human factors careers in high tech. In P. J. Woods (Ed.), *Is psychology the major for you? Planning for your undergraduate years* (pp. 51–53). Washington, DC: American Psychological Association.

Parsons, H. M. (1988). Psychology and modern technology. In P. J. Woods (Ed.), *Is psychology for them? A guide to undergraduate advising* (pp. 140–144). Washington, DC: American Psychological Association.

Perchonok, K. (1972). *Accident cause analysis.* Ithaca, NY: Cornell Aeronautical Laboratory.

Pion, G., & Bramblett, P. (1985). *Salaries in psychology.* Washington, DC: American Psychological Association.

Poulton, E. C. (1966). Engineering psychology. *Annual Review of Psychology, 17,* 177–200.

Reason, J. (1990). *Human error.* New York: Cambridge University Press.

Salvendy, G. (1987). *Handbook of human factors.* New York: Wiley.

Sanders, M. S., & McCormick, E. J. (1987). *Human factors in engineering and design* (6th ed.). New York: McGraw-Hill.

Secretary of State for Transport. (1989, November). *Investigation into the Clapham Junction railway accident.* London: Her Majesty's Stationary Office.

Senders, J., & Moray, N. (Eds.). (1991). *Human error: Cause, prediction, and reduction.* Hillsdale, NJ: Erlbaum.

Sheridan, T. B., & Ferrell, W. R. (1974). *Man–machine systems.* Cambridge, MA: MIT Press.

Sinaiko, H. W. (1961). *Selected papers on human factors in the design and use of control systems.* New York: Dover.

Sind, P.M. (1990). Human factors in medical equipment design: An emerging and expanding frontier. *Human Factors Society Bulletin, 33*(6), 1–4.

Stevens, S. S. (1946). Machines cannot fight alone. *American Scientist, 34,* 389–400.

Stokols, D. (1978). Environmental psychology. *Annual Review of Psychology, 29,* 253–295.

Super, C., & Super, D. (1988). *Opportunities in psychology careers.* Lincolnwood, IL: VGM Career Horizons.

Taylor, F. V. (1963). Human engineering and psychology. In S. Koch (Ed.), *Psychology: A study of a science* (pp. 831–907). New York: McGraw-Hill.

Transportation Research Board. (1988). *Transportation in an aging society: Improving mobility and safety for older persons* (Vol. 1, Special Report 218, Committee for the Study on Improving Mobility and Safety for Older Persons). Washington, DC: Transportation Research Board, National Research Council.

Transportation Research Board. (1990). *Airport system capacity: Strategic choices* (Special Report 226, Committee for the Study of Long-Term Airport Capacity Needs). Washington, DC: Transportation Research Board.

United States Department of Defense. (1979). *Human engineering requirements for military systems equipment and facilities* (Military Handbook MIL-H-46855B). Washington, DC: U.S. Department of Defense.

United States Department of Defense. (1981). *Human factors engineering design for army material* (Military Handbook MIL-HDBK 759A). Philadelphia, PA: Naval Forms and Publications Center.

United States Department of Defense. (1989). *Human factors design criteria for military systems, equipment and facilities* (Military Standard MIL-STD 1472D). Philadelphia: Naval Forms and Publications Center.

Van Cott, H. P., & Huey, B. M. (1992). *Human factors specialists' education and utilization: Results of a survey.* Washington, DC: National Academy Press.

Van Cott, H. P., & Kinkade, R. G. (Eds.). (1972). *Human engineering guide to equipment design* (Rev. ed.). Washington, DC: U.S. Government Printing Office.

Venturino, M. (Ed.). (1990). *Selected readings in human factors*. Santa Monica, CA: Human Factors and Ergonomics Society.

Weinberg, A. M. (1989–1990). Engineering in an age of anxiety. *Issues in Science and Technology, 6*(2), 37–43.

Wickens, C. D. (1992). *Engineering psychology and human performance* (2nd ed.). New York: Harper Collins.

Wickens, C. D., & Kramer, A. (1985). Engineering psychology. *Annual Review of Psychology, 36*, 307–348.

Wiener, E. L. (1990). The golden era of human factors in commercial aviation. *Human Factors Bulletin, 33*(8), 1–2.

Wissel, J. W., & Hall, S. A. (1957). Human engineering research—who should do it and why. *American Psychologist, 12*, 92–94.

Wood, C. C. (1958). Human factors engineering. *Ergonomics, 1*, 294–300.

Woods, P. J. (Ed.). (1976). *Career opportunities for psychologists: Expanding and emerging areas*. Washington, DC: American Psychological Association.

Woods, P. J. (Ed.). (1987). *Is psychology the major for you? Planning for your undergraduate years*. Washington, DC: American Psychological Association.

Woods, P. J. (Ed.). (1988). *Is psychology for them? A guide to undergraduate advising*. Washington, DC: American Psychological Association.

Woodson, W. E. (1981). *Human factors design handbook*. New York: McGraw-Hill.

Martin F. Wiskoff

Defense of the Nation: Military Psychologists | 13

What Is Military Psychology?

Most students never encounter a course in military psychology. Many may not even be aware that there is a discipline of military psychology. In fact, the Division of Military Psychology was one of the original 19 divisions created within the American Psychological Association in 1946.

The *Handbook of Military Psychology* (Gal & Mangelsdorff, 1991) defines military psychology as the "application of psychological principles, theories and methods, within a military environment" (p. xxvi). Driskell and Olmstead (1989), in their review of psychology and the military, stated that "the field of military psychology is defined neither by a common set of techniques (as is experimental psychology) nor by a common set of problems (as is developmental psychology) but rather by the area or context of application—the military" (p. 43).

Martin F Wiskoff is currently a director/senior scientist for BDM International, Inc., in Monterey, CA. He was previously a senior scientist for the Defense Personnel Security Research Center in Monterey, CA, and director of the Manpower and Personnel Laboratory at the Navy Personnel Research and Development Center, San Diego, CA. Dr. Wiskoff is a fellow and past president of the Division of Military Psychology of the APA. He is also the founder and editor of *Military Psychology*, a journal published by the Division of Military Psychology.

Why consider a career in military psychology? As I will describe in this chapter, military psychology is a microcosm of psychology and consequently offers opportunities to psychologists of all persuasions, including those who wish to spend their career or a portion of it in a military uniform. It is also a discipline that crosses international boundaries, with military psychologists found in many countries. Although my discussion is focused on U.S. military psychology, the problems addressed by the research are of concern to the militaries of all nations, and there is the potential for cross-national research efforts, technical exchanges, and even assignments to serve jointly with military forces of other nations.

Perhaps of greatest importance, military psychology offers the opportunity to make a significant difference in the lives of individuals and in the stability of our nation. A small sample of the types of contributions that can be made by military psychologists include (a) working in mental health or family counseling clinics to improve the lives of service personnel and their families, (b) performing research on the effects of battlefield environmental factors on soldiers in order to prevent or reduce battlefield casualties, and (c) analyses of humanitarian and peacekeeping missions to determine procedures that could save military and civilian lives.

I will first briefly review the proud history of U.S. military psychology. This provides a foundation for examining the nature of the career and the range of jobs and settings in which civilian and uniformed military psychologists are found. Subsequent sections cover academic preparation, professional linkages, and employment opportunities. I conclude the chapter by presenting my view of the advantages and disadvantages of a career in military psychology, as well as a personal perspective from my long association with the profession.

History of Military Psychology

The psychology of war has been studied by military tacticians for as long as human beings have waged battles. Success on the battlefront is dependent on behavioral issues, such as assessment of troop readiness and knowledge of an opponent's vulnerabilities, as often as on the actual size of the opposing forces. Prior to World War I, however, the practice of psychology in the military was strictly in the hands of the commanders and not influenced by the application of scientific principles by psychology professionals.

In the years leading up to the war, psychology had begun to emerge as a field of scientific study and application. American psychologists had become intrigued with the mental measurement work of Dr. Binet in France and with the scientific management movement to enhance worker productivity. However, it was the problems of assimilating millions of U. S. civilians into the armed services that brought the tools of psychologists to the military environment and created the discipline of military psychology in the United States.

At the start of the war, a group of psychologists headed by the president of the American Psychological Association, Dr. Robert M. Yerkes, met to discuss how psychology could assist in the war effort. The successful program of mental testing of recruits with the Army Alpha and Beta examinations, which resulted in the appropriate placement of new soldiers into military jobs and officer training, is indelibly identified as the genesis of military psychology. It also served as the subsequent model for group intelligence testing for both military and civilian applications.

In addition, during the short time frame from U.S. entry in 1917 until shortly after the war in 1918, psychologists addressed many other issues: measurement of troop morale and assimilation into the military; development of special trade tests to assess skills, such as combat leadership or flying aptitude; assessment of emotional instability; and measurement of human performance. Immediately after the war, psychologists conducted surveys to assess the attitudes of soldiers, including their opinions about their own military service. Psychologists who contributed during World War I—truly the first military psychologists—included such notables as Edwin G. Boring, James McKeen Cattell, G. Stanley Hall, Walter Dill Scott, Carl E. Seashore, Edward K. Strong, Lewis M. Terman, Edward L. Thorndike, John B. Watson, and Robert S. Woodworth.

There was a hiatus in the study and practice of military psychology during the 1920s and 1930s, but at the start of World War II the military reestablished a psychological research program during which more than 2,000 psychologists, civilian and uniformed, would address military problems. Military psychology, born in the first world war, matured in World War II. Former areas of inquiry were revisited, and many new ones were added: military leadership; the effects of environmental factors on human performance; military intelligence; psychological operations and warfare; selection for special duties; and the influences of personal background, attitudes, and the work group on soldier motivation and morale.

Military psychology was the dominant theme in psychology during World War II. As reported by Driskell and Olmstead (1989), "in 1943, fully half of the pages of the *Psychological Bulletin* were devoted to topics of military psychology, and from 1943 to 1945, one in every four psychologists in the country was engaged in military psychology"

(p. 45). After the war, much of what had been learned found ready application in other public and private sector settings.

In the more than 50 years since World War II, military psychological research has continued its tradition of innovation and has provided leadership to the civilian sector. Military service research laboratories were created, and extensive programs were established to fund research at universities and by private contractors. In addition, military psychologists have participated in large social policy programs conducted in the military that were designed to increase diversity and equal opportunity. These programs include integrating racial and ethnic groups, eliminating sexual discrimination and harassment, employing women in combat and in work settings designed for men, utilizing low-capability recruits and rehabilitating juvenile delinquents, drug testing, psychological treatment for personal lifestyle problems, and smoking abatement in the workplace. Military psychologists had the opportunity to research, evaluate, and make national policy recommendations concerning such programs.

The Department of Defense (DOD) employs more psychologists than any other organization or company in the world. The downsizing of the military in the 1990s has been accompanied by a corresponding reduction in research and psychological support to the operating forces. The future of military psychology is assured, however, as long as there is a need for troops to defend our country and perform peacekeeping missions around the world.

Types of Work Pursued in Military Psychology

The *Handbook of Military Psychology* (Gal & Mangelsdorff, 1991) is the most comprehensive single source of information concerning the types of work performed by military psychologists. To assist the reader in relating this discussion to the *Handbook,* I will use its seven major categories of military psychology (slightly modified) and add two areas (training and education, and manpower management decision-making support) that the *Handbook* covers only minimally. Because these nine application areas all have the same goal of improving the performance and adjustment of personnel within the military environment, the actual work conducted across the areas overlaps somewhat.

There is another "type-of-work" dimension that readers should keep in mind in reviewing the nine areas. Military research is funded within discrete categories on a dimension that ranges from *basic* to *applied*. The goal of basic research is to develop new knowledge or technologies with potential application to military problems. The more applied types of research seek to explore and evaluate the utility of new technologies in operational military environments. This often includes developing prototype systems (e.g., computerized performance measurement) and conducting feasibility testing with service personnel. An additional class of applied work involves conducting studies (e.g., surveys, database analyses) that provide management and policymakers with information on which to base policy decisions (e.g., whether to revise enlistment incentive programs).

Table 1 lists the nine areas of military psychology, along with the most closely related psychological disciplines. Each of the nine areas is described below.

SELECTION, CLASSIFICATION, AND ASSIGNMENT

This area focuses on (a) the cognitive and noncognitive assessment of military applicants and in-service personnel and (b) the prediction of performance in military jobs. Critical applications within the military are the screening and selection of entry-level enlisted and officer per-

TABLE 1

Types of Work Within Military Psychology

Military Application Area	Most Closely Related Psychological Disciplines
Selection, classification, and assignment	Evaluation and measurement, cognitive, industrial/organizational
Training and education	Experimental, cognitive, educational
Human-factors engineering	Human factors, ergonomics, experimental
Environmental stressors and military performance	Physiological, psychopharmacological, psychobiology, experimental
Military leadership and team effectiveness	Social, industrial/organizational
Individual and group behavior	Personality, social, adult development
Clinical and consulting	Clinical, counseling, consulting, family and health, community
Manpower management and decision-making support	Advertising, evaluation and measurement, social, industrial/organizational
Special subjects and situations	Psychology of women, study of social issues, peace, personality, health, clinical

sonnel; the appropriate classification and career placement of personnel; and selection for special-skill jobs as pilots, air traffic controllers, underwater demolition personnel, Marine embassy guards, and special intelligence operations personnel. Current research emphasis is on expanding the measurement domain to include (a) more comprehensive assessment of ability and skills using microcomputers and simulators and (b) evaluating the potential of new noncognitive constructs such as social intelligence and the contributions of motivation and values. In the wake of geopolitical changes, an interesting newer concern is the development of instruments to select, from among the soldiers who have been trained to fight, those who can best serve within peacekeeping forces.

TRAINING AND EDUCATION

This research domain seeks to develop the most effective and efficient means to train military enlisted and officer personnel and to increase operational readiness. Major applications for research are training for basic skills (e.g., reading, mathematics), military skills (e.g., infantry, seamanship), technical skills (e.g., electronics, foreign languages), and special areas (e.g., flight training, underwater demolition). Additionally, as military systems become more technologically complex, there is increasing focus on techniques for team training and for training in special skills. Research emphasis is on (a) developing models of cognitive and information processing; (b) understanding the nature of training task requirements and the design of instructional systems; (c) measurement of training performance through criterion-referenced procedures; and (d) wide-scale use of training devices, simulators, and computer-based training to enhance skill acquisition. A significant emerging area in technical training research is the use of computer-simulated operational scenarios, including technologies such as virtual reality.

HUMAN-FACTORS ENGINEERING

The goal of this area is to design the human–machine interface to improve the functioning of military systems and equipment. Early research concentrated on taxonomies of human performance and changing equipment design to enhance human performance. As systems have become more complex, emphasis has shifted toward improving human performance by reducing operator workload, reducing the impact of acute stress (as in battlefield conditions), and making greater use of job aids. A major current focus is on enhancing human decision making through the use of artificial intelligence and expert systems. This area is covered more fully in chapter 12 of this book.

ENVIRONMENTAL STRESSORS AND MILITARY PERFORMANCE

Military personnel often have to work under adverse operational conditions such as sustained operations without sleep; environmental extremes (noise, heat, cold, or high altitude); vehicles that induce high acceleration, vibration, stress, or motion sickness; and hazardous atmospheric conditions (toxic fumes; radiological, biological, or chemical warfare). This area addresses both the maintenance of health and the enhancement of performance during stressful military missions. Research is conducted on the interface of equipment, environments, and personnel through a combination of laboratory studies and field experiments in extreme environments.

MILITARY LEADERSHIP AND TEAM EFFECTIVENESS

Psychologists study the efficient operation of military leadership and units (including reserves) in wartime and the requirements for maintaining the capability in peacetime. One branch of this research concerns effective leaders, including their selection, training, and evaluation; performance at face-to-face troop levels; and executive-level policymaking. A subset of this work concerns political–psychological issues such as the study of the behavior of world leaders. A second branch of research involves the study of team processes such as team structure, communication, subordinate–supervisor relations, team cohesion, the functioning of small groups, and tactical decision making. Of current concern is the assessment and improvement of communication among multinational forces.

INDIVIDUAL AND GROUP BEHAVIOR

Research in this area studies the relationship of people to the variety of settings within the unique military environment, starting with acculturation to military life and spanning an individual's life course decisions (of which the military is only one portion). Specific research topics include organizational commitment; development of careers; quality of life and satisfaction; military families; morale and cohesion; epidemiology; maladjustive behaviors, including substance abuse; attrition from military service because of unsuitability; willingness to remain in military service; and the stress of military life, including the serious psychological reactions in the aftermath of combat. Potential problems with service personnel may be ameliorated using techniques from the other research areas, such as training for situations involving high stress and trauma.

CLINICAL AND CONSULTING

Included in this area are clinical practice and research. Military clinical psychologists are commissioned officers who provide mental health services and counseling to active-duty personnel and their families within the unique military environment. They conduct psychological testing and assess applicants for general fitness for duty and for highly sensitive jobs requiring security clearances. They also manage programs addressing specific issues such as substance abuse; family-related problems, including child abuse; stress reduction; and the promotion of health and wellness. Their jobs may involve providing consultation to military commanders on improving both the performance and mental health of individuals and the organizational effectiveness and readiness of units. Civilian psychologists are found in many of the same locations and also work in Veterans Administration hospitals and with the reserve forces.

MANPOWER MANAGEMENT DECISION-MAKING SUPPORT

To support decision makers within the individual military services or within DOD, psychologists often collect data through applied research and studies, as well as analyzing existing databases. Some examples of research include (a) conducting surveys to determine the propensity to enlist in the military, (b) developing and applying occupational analysis techniques to create military job structures, (c) designing methods for establishing training requirements, (d) creating procedures for conducting evaluations of enlisted-personnel and officer performance, and (e) managing the retention of military personnel. In addition, analyses of large military databases are conducted to address specific questions raised by congressional offices, the executive branch, and military policymakers. Recent efforts include evaluation of health problems of returning veterans of the 1991 Gulf War and assistance to military manpower planners dealing with force reductions.

SPECIAL SUBJECTS AND SITUATIONS

Because the military mission is unlike that of any other organization, it generates unique requirements for field and laboratory research and practice by uniformed and civilian psychologists. Only the military has to deal with issues concerning returning prisoners of war, hostage situations, specialized military forces, reserve readiness, military intelligence, personnel security and psychological operations, and the conduct of humanitarian missions. Since the end of the cold war, there has been increased emphasis on peacekeeping missions and seeking solutions to disagreements that do not involve armed conflict. Military psychologists study the performance of peacekeeping and multinational forces and also seek political solutions to reducing tension and maintaining peace.

Work Settings for Military Psychologists

Military psychologists often work in a broader range of settings than would be the case for most other psychological disciplines. We typically think of researchers as being employed in laboratories or in academia, and clinicians performing their services in hospitals or clinics. Because of the large number of bases, schools, offices, and other sites under military jurisdiction, however, there are opportunities for assignment at many different locations in the United States and abroad. For example, the Walter Reed Army Institute of Research, headquartered in Washington, DC, has field offices both in the United States and in Heidelberg, Germany. It is not unusual for civilian military psychologists to serve at several geographical locations during their careers; it is expected of uniformed psychologists. Temporary assignments to serve the troops in combat zones, develop studies, collect data, present research findings, and so forth are commonplace. Table 2 displays the six major types of settings in which military psychologists are located.

RESEARCH FACILITIES

By far the largest number of civilian military psychologists work at large government laboratories or smaller facilities, performing the wide range of research outlined earlier. Laboratories can employ from a handful to hundreds of individuals. In some settings, psychologists are the predominant professional group; in others, a few psychologists may be an integral part of multidisciplinary teams. Several laboratories are located on bases with operational military units, which facili-

---

TABLE 2

Descriptive Statistics for Variables Used in the Analysis

Major Settings	Examples of Locations
Research facilities	Military laboratories and field units; contractor offices
Educational facilities	Colleges and universities; military educational institutions
Medical centers, hospitals, and clinics	Military hospitals; outpatient clinics; mental health centers; drug treatment centers; prisons
Military schools and bases	Service training schools; military bases in the U. S.
Military deployments overseas	Military overseas bases and small missions; combat zones; military hospitals
Military organization offices	The Pentagon; service headquarters commands

tates interactions with military personnel, as well as data collection. Other organizations occupy leased commercial space.

A considerable number of other researchers are located at contractor offices across the United States, some of which may be co-located with government offices. A few contract organizations are similar to service laboratories in having a long history of military psychological research. Whereas in past years many contractors were solely devoted to DOD-supported research, recent reductions in defense spending have spurred contractors to seek a mix of clients, including DOD, other government agencies, and private sector organizations.

EDUCATIONAL FACILITIES

Psychologists at many universities perform research under contract to military organizations. In some instances, a faculty member and a small number of graduate students will work alone under a grant or contract. At the other extreme, some universities have set up institutes dedicated entirely to government-sponsored research. Many of these programs have existed for many years and support specific military needs for research and product development. Clinical research psychologists may find themselves at schools of medicine performing interdisciplinary medical research.

The military is also unique in having its own educational institutions such as military academies; command, staff, and war colleges; graduate education facilities (e.g., the Naval Postgraduate School, Monterey, CA); and special military colleges and schools (e.g., the Air Force Institute of Technology, Wright-Patterson AFB, OH). Psychologists as faculty members in these institutions teach classes, perform research, consult, and hold staff positions.

MEDICAL CENTERS, HOSPITALS, AND CLINICS

Clinical psychologists serve in the widest variety of settings, among which are military hospitals, outpatient clinics, mental health centers, day care centers, prisons, and ships. The military has major medical centers with modern facilities where the psychologist is a member of a team of medical professionals. Psychologists may also serve at smaller clinics and hospitals and at bases in isolated locations where they may have to function without much additional support. One of the characteristics of the uniformed psychologist's job is that there is generally a change of geographical location every 2 to 3 years.

MILITARY SCHOOLS AND BASES

The military operates a vast system for training enlisted and officer personnel. Military psychologists perform both research and educational support tasks at many entry-level and advanced training schools. Clinical psychologists serve as advisors to military base commanders concerning troop health and readiness. Psychologists also function as members of special forces and military intelligence units.

MILITARY DEPLOYMENTS OVERSEAS

Some military psychologists may spend significant time in overseas field settings, perhaps even in hostile environments such as Kuwait during the Gulf War. Clinical psychologists often go wherever there are concentrations of troops. They may be assigned to special operations units to assist in preparing troops for combat or to help evaluate soldier stress during humanitarian missions (e.g., Operation Restore Hope in Somalia). Researchers may be assigned to temporary duty overseas to collect data from U.S. operating forces.

MILITARY ORGANIZATION OFFICES

A final group of military psychologists holds positions within the operational and headquarters commands of each of the services and the Office of the Secretary of Defense. Some of these individuals are responsible for budgeting, planning, and monitoring the research programs of military laboratories and contractors. Still others are involved in developing policy by providing information and guidance to military decision makers.

Major Military Organizations That Support Psychological Research and Clinical Practice

Within each of the military services and the DOD, many organizations and offices employ or support the work of uniformed and civilian psychologists. Only the major organizations are shown in Table 3, along with a headquarters address. Areas of interest are indicated, specifically whether the organization primarily conducts research, supports research funding in academia and the private sector, or is responsible for uniformed clinical and research psychologists. Several organizations have field units, such as the U. S. Army Research Institute for the Behavioral and Social Sciences (ARI). The Navy Personnel Research and Development Center (NPRDC) is scheduled to be relocated in the late 1990s, with the manpower and personnel research function moving to the Bureau of Naval Personnel near Memphis, TN, and the training research function moving to the Chief of Naval Education and Training, Orlando, FL.

Table 3 also indicates which of the following four categories of research are conducted or supported by each organization: (a) manpower and personnel (e.g., selection, classification, and assignment; military leadership and team effectiveness; individual and group behavior; manpower management and decision making); (b) training systems (e.g., education and training, training devices and simulation); (c) human systems interface (e.g., human factors, man–machine relationships); and (d) biomedical, safety, and health (e.g., psychopharmacology, aviation systems, environmental and psychological stress).

Academic and Other Preparation

Military psychology is unique in that being a microcosm of psychology, it includes many entry paths. Only a few individuals enter graduate school with the idea of becoming a military psychologist, and those students most likely obtained their undergraduate degrees under some form of military sponsorship.

The level of education needed for a career depends on the particular area of specialization and the employment setting. At a minimum, a master's degree is required for conducting research at a laboratory and working in support roles at military schools, bases, and government headquarters. A PhD is more likely to be needed for academic positions and clinical practice at hospitals or clinics. For all jobs, the PhD opens up a wider range of opportunities for advancement and independence in choosing a career direction. The PhD also confers a certain level of status that is often valuable in dealing with military personnel.

The most appropriate type of education also depends on the particular area of specialization. Most students entering graduate training immediately after obtaining a bachelor's degree have not yet set their career sights on becoming a military psychologist. Some graduate students serve as research assistants to a professor who is conducting research under military sponsorship. Often military psychology becomes an attractive option for an individual seeking employment after obtaining an advanced degree, because a particular military institution is interested in the student's area of specialization.

Preparation for a research career in military psychology may be obtained at most universities that have accredited graduate-level psychology programs. Those interested in working in a particular military research laboratory should review available descriptions of work conducted at the laboratory and tailor their research specialization to coincide with emerging areas of interest. It may be possible to develop a doctoral dissertation using existing data from a military laboratory or by collecting data on military subjects.

The path for entry into the field can also involve joining the military. The Army, Navy, and Air Force offer research and clinical opportunities for uniformed psychologists. Students may enter one of the service academies with the goal of a research subspecialty in psychology. They may also join the military through other officer-commissioning programs such as the Reserve Officer Training Corps (during college), Officer Candidate School (after college graduation), or direct commission as an officer (on receipt of a PhD).

For more than 50 years, commissioned officers trained as clinical or counseling psychologists have served in the military. As a means of obtaining uniformed clinical psychologists, the military offers internships in basic clinical skills, the provision of acute care and short-term treatment, and the handling of combat crises. Some psychologists provide their required educational support payback service to the military

TABLE 3

Major Military Organizations That Support Psychological Research and Clinical Practice

Organization	Headquarters Address	Areas of Interest		
		Research and Studies	Research Funding	Uniformed Psychologists
Department of Defense				
Defense Manpower Data Center	1600 Wilson Boulevard, Rosslyn, VA 22209	Manpower and personnel Training systems		
U.S. Air Force				
Armstrong Laboratory Human Resources Directorate	7909 Lindbergh Drive, Brooks AFB, TX 78235-5352	Manpower and personnel Training systems		
Armstrong Laboratory Crew Systems Directorate	2601 7th Street, Wright-Patterson AFB, OH, 45433-7901	Human systems interface		
Armstrong Laboratory Aerospace Medicine Directorate	2510 Kennedy Circle, Brooks AFB, TX 78235-5301	Human systems interface Biomedical, safety, and health		
Air Force Occupational Measurements Squadron	Randolph AFB, TX 78150	Manpower and personnel		
Air Force Office of Scientific Research	Bolling AFB, Washington, DC 20332-6448		Manpower and personnel Training systems	
Directorate of Life Sciences				
Biomedical Sciences Corps Headquarters AFMPC	Randolph AFB, TX 78150			Clinical and research assignments
U.S. Army				
U. S. Army Research Institute for the Behavioral and Social Sciences	5001 Eisenhower Avenue, Alexandria, VA 22333-5600	Manpower and personnel Training systems	Manpower and personnel Training systems	
U. S. Army Research Laboratory Human Resources and Engineering Directorate	Aberdeen Proving Ground, MD 21005-2425	Human systems interface		
U. S. Army Research Institute of Environmental Medicine	U. S. Army Natick RD&E Center Natick, MA 01760-5007	Biomedical, safety, and health (environmental stress)		
Walter Reed Army Institute of Research	Information Office, Washington, DC 20307-5100	Biomedical, safety, and health (psychological stress)		Manager for research assignments

Organization	Address	Functions/Assignments
U.S. Army (continued)		
U. S. Army Aeromedical Research Laboratory	P. O. Box 577, Fort Rucker, AL 36362-5000	Human systems interface Biomedical, safety, and health
U. S. Army Soldier Support Center	Fort Benjamin Harrison, IN 46216-5000	Manpower and personnel (policy determination)
Army Medical Department and School	Fort Sam Houston, TX 78234	Biomedical, safety, and health (policy determination) Manager for clinical assignments
Army Special Operations Center	Ft. Bragg, NC 28307	Manpower and personnel (psychological warfare)
Army Medical Department Psychology	Office of the Surgeon General, The Pentagon, Washington, DC 20310	Clinical and research assignments
U.S. Navy		
Naval Aerospace Medical Research Laboratory	Naval Air Station, Pensacola, FL 32508-5700	Manpower and personnel Human systems interface Biomedical, safety, and health
Naval Air Warfare Center Aircraft Division	Warminster, PA 18974-5000	Human systems interface
Naval Air Warfare Center Weapons Division	China Lake, CA 93555	Human systems interface
Naval Air Warfare Center Training Systems Division	12350 Research Parkway, Orlando, FL 32826-3224	Training systems Human systems interface
Navy Command, Control and Ocean Surveillance Center RDT&E Division	53560 Hull Street, San Diego, CA 92152-5001	Human systems interface
Naval Health Research Center	P.O. Box 85122, San Diego, CA 92138-9174	Biomedical, safety, and health
Naval Personnel Research and Development Center	53335 Ryne Road, San Diego, CA 92152-7250	Manpower and personnel Training systems
Naval Submarine Medical Research Laboratory	Naval Submarine Base, New London, Groton, CT 06349	Human systems interface Biomedical, safety, and health
Office of Naval Research	800 North Quincy Street, Arlington, VA 22217-5660	Manpower and personnel Training systems Human systems interface Biomedical, safety, and health
Medical Services Corps	Bureau of Medicine and Surgery, Washington, DC 20372	Clinical and research assignments

and then return to civilian life; others choose to complete a 15-year or longer career in the military. Rath and Norton (1991) have provided an excellent description of the education and training of uniformed military clinical psychologists.

The attributes contributing to success in military psychology, although somewhat dependent on the particular area of work, are shaped by the nature of military organizations. A critical skill is the ability to communicate well both orally and in writing. Given that a military tradition of presenting information is the "briefing" using visual aids, most researchers will need to communicate technical details of their project, as well as its applicability to military problems, in nontechnical terms understandable to a lay audience. Also, because most research laboratories publish their findings in technical reports, good writing skills are helpful for advancement.

One additional requirement for most military psychologists is the need to interact with operating forces. Typical peacetime interactions involve test instrument administration, training evaluation, and clinical support to troops and their families on military bases. Studies addressing combat or its aftermath could involve on-site assessment of battlefield performance or evaluation of combat stress. Other psychologists may be assigned to operational, highly classified special forces units.

Professional Linkages

One of the most advantageous features of a career in military psychology is the opportunity to establish linkages with professionals performing similar work in other countries. In addition to interactions through professional societies, there are unique military-sponsored organizations for information exchange. For example, some researchers have had the opportunity to participate in NATO and other cross-national working groups on technical subjects of interest to a wide range of nations. An annual open meeting of interest to many is the International Military Testing Association that occasionally assembles outside of the continental United States. The U.S. Air Force sponsors a biannual Psychology in Defense Symposium at the Air Force Academy, which is attended by an international audience of psychologists.

Military psychologists have the opportunity to join national and local professional organizations that reflect their specific research interests. They can also publish the results of their research in a host of journals that cover the diverse areas of interest within the field.

The primary identification for many military clinicians and researchers is Division 19—the Division of Military Psychology—of the American Psychological Association (APA). Division 19 offers an affiliate membership status for students and for psychologists who are not APA members. It is common for military psychologists to belong to other APA divisions, such as Experimental Psychology (Division 3); Evaluation, Measurement, and Statistics (Division 5); Clinical (Division 12); the Society for Industrial and Organizational Psychologists (Division 14); Applied Experimental and Engineering (Division 21); Health (Division 38); and Family (Division 43). Many are members of other professional organizations such as the American Psychological Society, the Human Factors Society, the Inter-University Seminar, and the Academy of Management.

The Division of Military Psychology publishes its own quarterly journal, *Military Psychology*, which features original behavioral science research and scholarly integration of research findings performed in a military setting. *Military Psychology* has published contributions from a number of countries and has featured special issues on topics of particular interest to the military research community: team processes, training, and performance; women in the navy; stimulants to ameliorate sleep loss during sustained operations; military service and the life-course perspective; and military occupational analysis. Other special-issues topics scheduled for publication in 1997 and 1998 include the Enhanced Computer-Administered Test Battery, the impact of chemical protective clothing on performance, and equal opportunity research in the U.S. military.

Range of Opportunities and Typical Careers

The possibilities for a rewarding career are great because military psychology encompasses so many different types of job opportunities. It is possible to work in a relatively narrow area of specialization throughout a career, to move across various research areas, or to pursue research management opportunities. It is not unusual for researchers to remain in civil service for their entire career, either within one laboratory or in a mix of military laboratory and headquarters jobs. Others select a combination of environments, including academia, government employment, and working for a government contractor. Military researchers may function as members of a multidisciplinary team of scientists, either within the same laboratory or across organizational settings.

Uniformed psychologists can devote a sizable portion of their career in uniform or spend just a few years in military service. Some maintain a military connection after a short period of active duty by serving in the reserve forces. Many retire from the military in their 40s and pursue a rewarding second career.

A career as a military psychologist is perhaps best understood through examples. Following are two examples of possible careers within the field.

LABORATORY RESEARCH PSYCHOLOGIST

A typical psychologist working at a government research laboratory would begin a civil service career immediately after obtaining a master's or doctoral degree. The first assignment would probably find the researcher working within his or her graduate area of specialization as a member of a research team. Early in the career, the researcher would be given increasingly greater independence, including the freedom to develop research designs and plan new projects. Project responsibilities might include interaction with other service laboratories and monitoring contractual programs performed by researchers within academia and private contractor organizations. Other responsibilities would be added over time, such as justifying the relevance of the work to military problems and obtaining support from military sponsors.

The researcher would be expected to publish findings in laboratory technical reports or in refereed journals. Other significant opportunities for professional growth include presentations at professional meetings and interactions with colleagues in the United States and other countries. Some researchers might become adjunct professors at local universities, with responsibilities that could include part-time teaching and overseeing student thesis preparation.

Continued career growth would be reflected by promotions to head teams and larger organizational segments within the laboratory. Although increased managerial responsibility is an expected progression, some laboratories offer a limited number of dual career paths to accommodate personnel who wish to remain scientists. Tours of duty at other laboratories and at headquarters sites are a distinct possibility.

On retirement from the civil service, researchers might continue to pursue professional interests by maintaining contact with their laboratories in an emeritus status. Or, using their accumulated expertise and experience, they might pursue a second career in academia or with a research contractor organization.

UNIFORMED PSYCHOLOGIST

Uniformed psychologists typically fall into either a research or a clinical track. I will focus on the latter because the career of the uniformed research psychologist is very much like that of the government civil servant described above. The following 20-year career description is adapted from Rath and Norton (1991).

A uniformed clinical psychologist would serve a 1-year internship at one of several U.S. military sites after completing 4 years of graduate school. With receipt of the doctoral degree, the clinician would be assigned for 3 years to a hospital on a military base in the continental United States. This would likely be followed by another 3-year assignment to a military hospital overseas. At this point the officer might attend a 6-month officer development course and then assume a 1-year fellowship. This could be followed by an assignment as a director of a small residential alcohol rehabilitation center or as the staff psychologist for a large military unit. The next assignment might be as a faculty member at a service academy or other military school.

At this point, the officer would probably attend a 9-month command and staff course. The remainder of the career could be spent in a combination of certain nontraditional assignments (such as in survival schools or medical intelligence) or in a hospital setting as a chief psychologist. In addition to the training mentioned above, the officer would be expected to attain other professional leadership and specialized military education in order to advance in rank and responsibility.

On retirement from the military at a young age (mid-40s), the clinical psychologist would be likely to open a private practice, work in a clinic or hospital setting, or serve as a consultant to government and industry. Many clinicians maintain their association with the military in some capacity during fruitful second careers.

Employment Outlook and Financial Compensation

Even before the cold war era officially ended in the late 1980s, the military started downsizing. This trend continued through the mid-1990s. Military research facilities suffered a corresponding reduction in funding during this time, accompanied by hiring freezes, reductions in the number of research and support personnel, and reductions in funding for university and private research contracts.

It is unlikely in the near future that the military psychological research field will reach the high level of funding and personnel staffing it attained by the early 1980s. A changing world situation, however, would definitely influence the level and type of support required from military psychologists. Research with clear application to solving military problems stands the best chance of being funded in the future—for example, research from which the findings or products can directly improve the performance of personnel in combat by providing immediate feedback to field commanders and information for policymakers. Given government emphasis on cost reduction, research that promises to reduce the costs of military operations will also be looked upon favorably.

The opportunities for uniformed clinical internships have also decreased and will probably decline another 15% to 20% as military downsizing continues. In contrast, there may be future opportunities for postdoctoral fellowship training. The uniformed research community will also face employment reductions and restrictions in assignment opportunities. One potential growth area is that of special forces operations.

In general, the salary scale for military psychologists is aligned with government pay scales. Those entering civil service employment with a master's degree, but without prior experience, can generally expect to receive a salary at the GS-9 level. In 1997 that annual starting salary was a minimum of $29,579. The GS-11 level (starting at $35,786 in 1997) is generally given to entering researchers with a PhD. Individuals with an exceptional work history could be hired at a higher level, such as GS-12 for a new PhD (starting at $42,890 in 1997). At the high end of the government salary scale, GS-15s could earn more than $92,000 in 1997, and a few psychologists in the Senior Executive Service make more than $120,000.

Salaries at research contractor organizations heavily involved in government research tend to approximate the civil service scale, although there is greater flexibility in setting actual dollar amounts. Other entry-level salaries, such as at universities and with contractors primarily engaged in industrial/organizational research, are defined by the particular institutions and organizations.

Uniformed psychologists receive a package of pay and benefits that depends on the particular service program and rank at which an officer is commissioned. Psychologists going through a military academy start at the lowest entry level, whereas clinical psychologists entering to serve an internship start at a slightly higher rank.

Advantages and Disadvantages of a Career in Military Psychology

A compelling reason to enter the field for many military psychologists is the security of government employment and the unique benefits of the civil service and military retirement systems. Although reductions in force and changes in the government retirement system have diminished these advantages somewhat, government service still promises reasonable stability and the opportunity to make the types of contributions indicated earlier. There are additional reasons why employment in military psychology is attractive.

Given the military's need and penchant for the most current battlefield and management technologies, much military research is at the cutting edge of science. Military laboratories offer a psychologist the unique opportunity to conduct research without collateral requirements to teach or consult. Laboratory personnel can establish a career path to include increasing research management responsibilities and possible service in decision-making roles within government. Uniformed psychologists have unusual opportunities to perform research, to provide clinical services in a unique environment, or to consult on matters of international importance.

There are also advantages to employment as a military contractor or as an academic doing research for the military on a contractual basis. Military contractors enjoy a wider range of research opportunities and the likelihood of mixing military research with other public- and private-sector work. Academic psychologists have the opportunity for independence in their research focus and can tailor the direction to fit military needs and interests. In their research, they often have access to a pool of research subjects that is not easily available elsewhere. A Science Directorate article in the April 1995 *APA Monitor* stated, "Each year, 50 scientists at the Air Force's Armstrong Laboratory Lackland Test Facility in San Antonio, Texas, and 10 to 15 university researchers working on grants from the Air Force, have access to more than 35,000 Air Force recruits for four hours of their basic training" (Azar, 1995, p. 20). Whether the task is to evaluate training methodologies, conduct field experiments, collect survey data, or administer experimental test instruments, the opportunities for performing research on significant samples of relevant subjects are unparalled. The military also maintains large-scale computer databases on its population, going back more than 30 years, that are available for cross-sectional and longitudinal analyses.

Most military research has important applications in the private sector as well. Joint government–industry undertakings are becoming commonplace. Military issues and technologies cross national boundaries, and the international community of military researchers shares information at military and professional conferences and during exchange visits.

The major disadvantage of a career focus on military psychology is the uncertainty of government funding in the future. Opportunities may be more limited for laboratory researchers, uniformed psychologists, and contractors. Although salary levels are generally competitive with the private sector, civil service and military pay scales have more clearly defined upper limits than those for psychologists performing research or consulting in the private sector.

Why I Chose Military Psychology

The field of military psychology has provided me with support, friendships, and a full and rewarding professional career. While I was completing my PhD at the University of Maryland, I started working for the Army Research Institute (ARI) in Washington, DC. I had the opportunity to conduct interesting research in areas of testing and recruit assignment, and I also received invaluable assistance from my fellow psychologists and the ARI in completing my dissertation. After 4 years I moved to the Navy and spent 24 years in research, first in the Washington, DC, area, at the Bureau of Naval Personnel, and then in San Diego, CA, at the NPRDC. During my Washington, DC, employment I accepted an invitation to be a visiting professor for 1 year at the Naval Postgraduate School in Monterey, CA. This started a long-term love affair with Monterey that eventually led to my spending the last 3 years of my civil service career there as a senior scientist with a newly formed DOD organization, the Defense Personnel Security Research Center.

During my career I was given increasing responsibility that culminated in my assignment as the director of the Manpower and Personnel Laboratory at the NPRDC. I am proudest of the applications of our research, such as the selection system for the U.S. Naval Academy, that have made a difference to the Navy and the lives of military personnel. I was able to help initiate a major new DOD program in the emerging technology of computerized adaptive testing, and I served as the officer in charge of the program. Since my retirement from civil service at age 55, I have been heading a small contractor research group in Monterey, CA, conducting fascinating research into aspects of personnel security, counterintelligence, and espionage.

Military psychology has allowed me the opportunity to present and publish papers and to participate actively in my profession. A major career highlight was helping to create the APA journal *Military Psychology* that was first published in 1989. I have served as editor since that time.

My work and associations have crossed international boundaries. Several research programs have involved travel to different countries and joint projects with psychologists in these countries. Many of the manuscripts that I review for *Military Psychology* are submitted by authors residing outside of the United States.

Readings in Military Psychology

The *Handbook of Military Psychology* (Gal & Mangelsdorff, 1991) is the single best source of detailed information. Other recent descriptions of military psychology are by Taylor and Alluisi (1994) and Driskell and Olmstead (1989). The APA Division of Military Psychology publishes a newsletter, *The Military Psychologist*, which provides information on current happenings in the field. The DOD maintains a directory of individuals and organizations that perform and manage current people-related research and development for the DOD (Defense Technical Information Center, 1995). This directory can be accessed on the Internet through the MATRIS home page: http://dticam.dtic.mil/.

Articles and special issues in *Military Psychology* reflect some of the current research emphases. A good source of information on research programs within the service laboratories can be obtained from their documents, such as annual reports. The laboratories also publish technical reports on the results of their research, as well as bibliographies of these reports. The references and suggested readings below contain selected recent publications that cover in greater depth various aspects of work in military psychology.

References

Azar, B. (1995, April). Goal: Computer model that predicts behavior. *APA Monitor*, p. 20.

Defense Technical Information Center. (1995). *Directory of researchers*. MATRIS Office, DTIC-AM, San Diego, CA.

Driskell, J. E., & Olmstead, B. (1989). Psychology and the military: Research applications and trends. *American Psychologist, 44*, 43–54.

Gal, R., & Mangelsdorff, A. D. (Eds). (1991). *Handbook of military psychology*. New York: Wiley.

Rath, F. H., Jr., & Norton, F. E., Jr. (1991). Education and training: Professional and paraprofessional. In R. Gal & A. D. Mangelsdorff, (Eds.), *Handbook of military psychology* (pp. 593–606). New York: Praeger.

Taylor, H. L., & Alluisi, E. A. (1994). Military psychology. In V. S. Ramachandran (Ed.), *Encyclopedia of human behavior* (Vol. 3, pp. 191–201). New York: Academic Press.

Suggested Readings

Dillon, R. F., & Pellegrino, J. W. (Eds.). (1989). *Testing: Theoretical and applied perspectives*. New York: Praeger.

Ellis, H. A. (Ed). (1986). *Military contributions to instructional technology*. New York: Praeger.

Hunt, J. G., & Blair, H. D. (Eds.). (1985). *Leadership on the future battlefield*. New York: Pergamon-Brassey.

McGuire, F. (1990). *Psychology aweigh! A history of clinical psychology in the United States Navy*. Washington, DC: American Psychological Association.

O'Brien, T. G., & Charlton, S. G. (Eds.). (1995). *Handbook of human factors testing and evaluation*. Hillsdale, NJ: Erlbaum.

Rumsey, M. G., Walker, C. B., & Harris, J. H. (Eds.). (1994). *Personnel selection and classification*. Hillsdale, NJ: Erlbaum.

Sands, W. A., Waters, B. K., & McBride, J. R. (Eds.). (in press). *CAT-BOOK—Computerized adaptive testing: Inquiry to Operation*. Washington, DC: American Psychological Association.

Solomon, Z. (1993). *Combat stress reaction: The enduring toll of war*. New York: Plenum Press.

Wigdor, A. K., & Green, B. F., Jr. (Eds.). (1991). *Performance assessment for the workplace*. Washington, DC: National Academy Press.

Wiskoff, M. F., & Rampton, G. L. (Eds.). (1989). *Military personnel measurement: Testing, assignment, evaluation*. New York: Praeger.

Zeidner, J. (Ed.). (1986). *Human productivity and enhancement: Volume 1: Training and human factors in systems design*. New York: Praeger.

Zeidner, J. (Ed.). (1987). *Human productivity and enhancement: Volume 2: Organization, personnel, and decision making*. New York: Praeger.

Zeidner, J., & Drucker, A. (1983). *Behavioral science in the Army: A corporate history of the Army Research Institute*. Alexandria, VA: U.S. Army Research Institute for the Behavioral and Social Sciences.

Kelly D. Brownell and Peter Salovey

Health Psychology: Where Psychology, Biology, and Social Factors Intersect

14

Powerful Links Between Psychology and Health

Health psychology, although relatively new compared with specialities such as clinical, developmental, and social psychology, is an established, vital, and growing field of central importance to the nation's health. The primary aims of the field are to identify the links between the way people think, feel, and behave and their physical well-being, and to improve health with psychosocial interventions. To do so promises to have an impact on the major diseases of modern life (Taylor, 1990).

Kelly D. Brownell is professor of psychology at Yale University, where he also serves as professor of epidemiology and public health, director of the Yale Center for Eating and Weight Disorders, and master of Silliman College. He received his PhD in clinical psychology from Rutgers University and has served as president of the Society of Behavioral Medicine, the Association for the Advancement of Behavior Therapy, and the Division of Health Psychology of the American Psychological Association. His work is on eating disorders and obesity, exercise, and the origin and change of health behaviors.

Peter Salovey received his PhD in clinical psychology from Yale University in 1986. He completed his internship in clinical health psychology at the West Haven VA Medical Center. Dr. Salovey now serves as a professor of psychology and of epidemiology and public health at Yale and as director of graduate studies in psychology, and contributes primarily to the social/personality and health psychology training programs. Professor Salovey is just completing a 6-year term as associate editor of *Psychological Bulletin* and has been named the first editor of the *Review of General Psychology*.

In 1991, the United States Department of Health and Human Services released *Healthy People 2000*. This report contained specific health objectives for the United States to be reached by the year 2000. To attain the objectives set out in the report, the nation must "depend heavily on changes in human behavior" (p. 8). The central role of behavior in health is clear when one examines the leading causes of death (Table 1). The role of individual behaviors such as diet, exercise, smoking, alcohol consumption, breast self-examination, and PAP testing, the use of sunscreens and seat belts, and psychological processes such as stress and coping contribute in significant ways to each of the top 10 causes of death.

The magnitude of benefit from behavior change is staggering. If every smoker in the United States quit, there would be a 25% reduction in cancer deaths and 350,000 fewer fatal heart attacks each year. A 10% weight loss in middle-aged men would lead to a 20% decrease in coronary heart disease and would have a significant impact on diabetes, stroke, and some cancers.

An abundant literature shows that human behavior is associated with the etiology of disease and recovery from disease. This itself is not novel or surprising, but consider the following research findings as examples of the strength of this association:

1. To test whether inhibiting thoughts, feelings, and behaviors is associated with disease, Pennebaker, Kiecolt-Glaser, and Glaser (1988) had 50 healthy subjects write for 4 consecutive days about either traumatic or superficial topics. Compared with subjects who wrote about superficial topics, subjects who wrote about traumatic events had improved cellular immune system function and fewer health center visits.

2. Whether a person is depressed after having a heart attack is as strong a predictor of mortality 6 months later as is a history of previous heart attacks and the extent of physical damage from the heart attack itself (Frasure-Smith, Lesperance, & Talajic, 1993).

3. Ornish et al. (1990) randomly assigned men with severe coronary artery disease to receive their usual medical care or an intensive lifestyle intervention program involving a low-fat vegetarian diet, moderate aerobic exercise, smoking cessation, and stress management. The men in the lifestyle intervention group showed greater drops in overall cholesterol and low density lipoprotein cholesterol and had a 91% reduction in the frequency of angina (compared with a 165%

Ten Leading Causes of Death in the United States Population

1.	Heart disease
2.	Cancer
3.	Injuries
4.	Stroke
5.	Chronic lung disease
6.	Pneumonia/influenza
7.	Suicide
8.	Diabetes
9.	Liver disease
10.	Atherosclerosis

Note: From the U.S. Department of Health and Human Services (1991).

increase in a control group). Most impressive, however, are data on measures of blockage in the coronary arteries. The average diameter of blockages decreased in the lifestyle subjects and increased in the controls.

4. Friedman et al. (1986) reported a significant reduction in the recurrence of heart attacks in men who received a program designed to reduce Type A behavior.

5. Phillips, Ruth, and Wagner (1993) documented a profound effect of beliefs on health. They examined deaths in 28,169 Chinese-Americans compared with 412,632 randomly selected controls listed as "White" on death certificates. Chinese-Americans, but not Whites, died significantly earlier than usual when their disease and birth year combined in a way that Chinese astrology and medicine consider ill fated. The effect was particularly strong among individuals most strongly attached to Chinese traditions.

Definition of Health Psychology

A number of terms have been used over the years to connote the association of psychology with health. One of the first was *psychosomatic medicine*. This term and the field with the same name were born from the supposition that people could make themselves sick, or more consistent with popular understanding of the term "psychosomatic," people could suffer from a number of maladies for which there are not always discernable physical causes. Examples are headache, irritable bowel syndrome, and chronic pain.

Health psychology is a more recent term. Various definitions have been proposed, the core features of which are nearly identical. Two prominent definitions are those of Matarazzo and Taylor:

> Health psychology is the aggregate of the specific educational, scientific, and professional contributions of the discipline of psychology to the promotion and maintenance of health, the prevention and treatment of illness, the identification of etiological and diagnostic correlates of health, illness, and related dysfunction, and the improvement of the health care system and health policy formation. (Matarazzo, 1980, p. 815)

> Health psychology is the field within psychology devoted to understanding psychological influences on how people stay healthy, why they become ill, and how they respond when they do get ill. (Taylor, 1995, p. 3)

Another term used to describe the study of health and behavior is *behavioral medicine*. As described below in our discussion of the history of the field, behavioral medicine predates health psychology:

> Behavioral medicine is the interdisciplinary field concerned with the development and integration of behavioral and biomedical science knowledge and techniques relevant to health and illness and the application of this knowledge and these techniques to prevention, diagnosis, treatment, and rehabilitation. (Schwartz & Weiss, 1978)

For most purposes, the various definitions of health psychology, behavioral medicine, and psychosomatic medicine are indistinguishable. The same is true to some extent of professional organizations dedicated to the issue of health and behavior. These include the Division of Health Psychology of the American Psychological Association, the Society of Behavioral Medicine, and the American Psychosomatic Society. Each has a slightly different emphasis, but many professionals, including us, belong to more than one association. Although the potential for fragmentation exists because of different definitions and professional organizations, we interpret the growing number of groups and journals (e.g., *Health Psychology, Psychology and Health, Journal of Behavioral Medicine, Annals of Behavioral Medicine, Psychosomatic Medicine*) as signs of a field with considerable social importance and strong potential for career opportunities (Chesney, 1993; Stone, 1990). These opportunities will be discussed after a brief section on the history of the field.

The History of
Health Psychology

Although formal training in health psychology is an invention of the last two decades, the recognition that psychological factors play a role in physical health is not. In ancient Greece, Hippocrates believed that imbalances in bodily fluids (what he called *humors*) caused both psychological and physical problems. Too much blood might make a person feel sanguine but could cause epilepsy; too much yellow bile would lead to angry feelings and the risk of malaria or genital rot. The particulars in this theory are certainly incorrect, but its importance lies in the idea that psychological states like anger and physical illnesses such as malaria might share common underlying mechanisms. Hippocrates is often thought of as the first physician; we would consider him the first health psychologist.

If we move ahead more than 2,000 years to the 19th century, we encounter significant writings about *psychosomatic medicine* (a term coined in 1818), based on the notion that internal mental conflicts might express themselves as physical diseases. These ideas were compatible with Freudian theory, and so their popularity increased in the early part of this century, particularly through the writings of Franz Alexander and Florence Dunbar in the 1930s.

Modern health psychology places much less emphasis on conflict as the root of all health problems but still emphasizes the role of attitudes, beliefs, emotions, and behavior in the development, course, and cure of physical illness. The first clear delineation of health psychology as a field—in this case, actually as a subfield of clinical psychology—was a paper by Schofield (1969) that motivated the American Psychological Association 4 years later to appoint a task force on health research chaired by Schofield. Schofield pointed out the many ways in which psychological variables could influence health but also noted that psychology as a field was preoccupied with mental illness and had largely ignored physical health. The task force noted that in the late 1960s and early 1970s, only 2% of the articles listed in *Psychological Abstracts* addressed physical health and illness. By 1976, the task force issued a report calling for greater attention to the problems of health and illness and noted the strong potential for important psychological work on improving the maintenance of health, the prevention of illness, and the delivery of health care (APA Task Force on Health Research, 1976). The report called for the development of graduate training programs in this emerging area. At about the same time, the faculty in psychology at the University of California, San Francisco, established the first such program explicitly designed to train health psychologists.

Later in the 1970s, Gary Schwartz and Judith Rodin established the first significant graduate training program in health psychology on the east coast at Yale. A conference was held at Yale in 1977 concerning behavioral medicine, defined as the interdisciplinary field concerned with the integration of behavioral and biomedical sciences (Schwartz & Weiss, 1978). The Yale conference galvanized the field of behavioral medicine but also marked the beginning of a formal health psychology/behavioral medicine training program at Yale.

By 1978, the American Psychological Association became convinced that there was sufficient interest to justify the formation of a Division of Health Psychology. After intense discussions and negotiations, the founders of health psychology agreed that the new division should represent both basic research on psychological factors in physical health and the application of principles based on research to the prevention and treatment of disease itself. The division's journal, *Health Psychology*, appeared in 1982. By the next year, 2,000 psychologists had joined the division, and a formal conference concerning the education and training of health psychologists attempted to establish a set of guidelines that could be adopted by the growing number of departments of psychology that wished to establish formal training programs in health psychology.

In the ensuing dozen years, training programs in health psychology emerged at approximately 65 universities, numerous books further delineated the field, predoctoral internships for clinical students specializing in health psychology were developed, and membership in the Division of Health Psychology of the American Psychological Association grew to 3,161 individuals. Not surprisingly, training programs in health psychology have begun to emerge worldwide, especially in Sweden, Finland, Germany, the United Kingdom, Italy, and Spain (Richards, 1992). Health psychology has also been nurtured by our current political environment: Medical care costs have sky-rocketed, so there is a strong motivation to develop less expensive alternatives to traditional treatment (e.g., behavioral interventions) and to emphasize the prevention of disease.

A tension in the training of health psychologists is that although the field has developed as an enterprise concerned with basic research and the application of basic research, current training is being driven by the large numbers of clinical psychologists and clinical graduate students moving into health care settings (Richards, 1992; Stone, 1990). As a result, although there are programs in health psychology that do not emphasize clinical training—for example, the social psychology major/health minor at UCLA and the social psychology and health behavior group at Iowa State University—most now do. We say more about these issues in the section on training that follows.

Training in Health Psychology

UNDERGRADUATE PREPARATION

Psychology is one of the few fields in the arts and sciences in which increasing numbers of individuals are applying for graduate training. Not surprisingly, then, competition for admission to some doctoral programs in psychology is intense, and so adequate undergraduate preparation is important. Our experience at Yale is an extreme case of this competition. Students wishing to specialize in health psychology are admitted through the clinical or social psychology program. In a typical year, we can select three or four clinical students from a pool of about 350 applicants and three or four social students from a pool of about 100 applicants. It is safe to assume that the number and quality of applicants will increase with the stature and quality of the graduate program (and the host institution).

Successful applicants to most doctoral programs have majored in psychology or, if majoring in a different field, have taken psychology courses from across the discipline (e.g., abnormal, social, psychobiology). Courses in statistics and research methods are especially important. It is wise, of course, to take classes in health psychology or behavioral medicine if offered. Courses of study outside of psychology may include exposure to human biology, on the one hand, and the study of illness in other social sciences—such as medical sociology and medical anthropology—on the other.

At least as important as coursework, however, is gaining research experience as an undergraduate. This is one of the keys to success for admission to many graduate programs. Typically, research experience constitutes helping a professor or graduate student conduct an experiment. Some undergraduates also complete an independent "honors" thesis describing a study that they may have designed themselves. It is not necessary that research experience be in health psychology; it is more important simply to have some. Fretz and Stang (1980), in a very helpful guidebook for undergraduate psychology majors planning to apply to graduate school, suggested that one begin some kind of research collaboration no later than the junior year. Volunteer work with patients in hospitals or other medical settings can be helpful, as it shows commitment to the helping professions. It cannot, however, substitute for research experience for admission to most programs.

Even doctoral programs in clinical psychology rank undergraduate research experience as the most important component of undergraduate preparation (Eddy, Lloyd, & Lubin, 1987).

Many graduate programs emphasize research in collaboration with faculty more so than coursework, so the match between an applicant's interests and those of the faculty at potential graduate schools is critical. Students should examine carefully the rosters of faculty members to find the best fit.

GRADUATE TRAINING IN HEALTH PSYCHOLOGY

During the last 2 decades, individuals who identified themselves as health psychologists generally received their graduate training in clinical or social psychology and then applied their knowledge to problems in the health area (Taylor, 1987). In recent years, however, there has been a growing enthusiasm for more specialized training in health psychology at the graduate level. The reality is that doctoral training in health psychology can be found within traditional clinical psychology and social psychology programs, occasionally within other specialized programs such as psychobiology, and at times as a major field of specialization in its own right. More so than before, an applicant can look to the specific research.

Perhaps the most important decision that a prospective graduate student in health psychology needs to consider is whether he or she desires training that will lead to licensure as a clinical psychologist. Such a license permits the delivery of psychological services to clients. Many health psychologists do not desire such training; they are involved in university-based research and teaching, for example. But if a career that combines research and actual clinical practice is desired, it is best to consider health psychology programs embedded within doctoral programs in clinical psychology. Also, if you imagine a career as a professor in a medical school or as a researcher in a hospital setting, clinical training can be advantageous.

There is no standard doctoral program in health psychology. Rather, programs vary in their emphasis on coursework versus research and practical experiences, mentoring by a single faculty member versus opportunities to work with multiple faculty members, and an explicit structure versus a more self-designed format. There are excellent programs represented at both ends of these dimensions (e.g., our program at Yale emphasizes research, generally with multiple faculty members, in a self-designed sequence with few departmental requirements; other excellent programs can be much more structured). It is important to identify the learning environment that fits an individual's strengths. These differences may be clear from a department's application packet or can be learned through discussions with faculty or graduate students.

A central criterion in choosing a program is the availability of faculty members who can provide mentoring in an applicant's areas of interest. It is important to identify programs where, for instance, there is more than one professor engaging in research relevant to health psychology. This signals a commitment by the program to the area of health psychology, but also leaves a student with guidance when a faculty member moves, retires, or is otherwise not available. Moreover, if a student wishes to work with particular patient populations (e.g., women with breast cancer, people with AIDS, children with birth defects), it is important that treatment facilities for such individuals be located in the community. It is easier for a student to be engaged with such programs if a faculty member has already established collaborative ties.

Doctoral training in health psychology lasts from 4 to 6 years. Whether a student desires a career in academic research, research and practice combined, or practice only, it is advantageous to develop more than one area of specialization. As mentioned below in the section on career opportunities, either health psychologists specialize in particular psychological processes—social comparison, control, emotion—and then investigate how they are related to physical diseases, or they specialize in a particular disease or disease process—eating disorders, cancer, heart disease, chronic pain—and study the psychological variables that seem important to it. The first approach to specialization is more likely to characterize social psychologists working in health psychology, and the second approach is more typical of clinical psychologists.

A comprehensive listing of graduate programs in psychology is available in the book titled *Graduate Study in Psychology* published by the American Psychological Association (APA). Information on obtaining this book can be obtained by writing to the APA Order Department, 750 First Street NE, Washington, DC 20002-4242, or by calling 800-374-2721. This book describes all graduate programs in psychology, not just health psychology programs, but it does provide a great deal of information on applying to graduate schools, admissions criteria, and so forth.

An excellent guide titled *Doctoral Programs in Health Psychology* has been published by the Division of Health Psychology (Division 38) of the APA and can be obtained by contacting the Division Services Office at the APA address provided in the previous paragraph. This guide lists the program directors, the program title, and the areas of specialty within each program. This is a valuable resource for students interested in graduate training in health psychology.

SPECIALTY TRAINING

Internship

Individuals who desire licensure as clinical psychologists need to complete an internship prior to obtaining the degree. Clinical internships have developed special tracks for trainees in clinical health psychology. There are about 50 such specialized clinical internship sites in the United States and Canada. A list of these internship programs, complete with information on settings; addresses to send applications; the percent of time interns devote to child, adolescent, adult, and aging populations; and clinical orientations is available from the Division of Health Psychology of the APA (Division 38) (see address provided above). This is the most valuable resource available to potential interns.

Most internships in clinical health psychology emphasize the treatment of individuals whose primary reason for seeking care is a physical health problem. They may also have psychological disorders such as depression, sexual dysfunction, or anxiety problems. Not surprisingly, clinical health psychology interns often work as part of a medical team organized around patients' physical health problems (e.g., cardiac rehabilitation, chronic pain management, psychosocial adjustment to cancer). They are likely to devote less time than traditional clinical interns to placements in psychiatric inpatient wards or mental health centers. Interns in the health area may be involved in consultation–liaison work in which they are called on by physicians or other health care professional to provide assistance in understanding and treating psychological problems in a medical patient (e.g., adherence to a prescribed treatment regimen, substance abuse, coping with a disability). This often involves work with the family of the designated patient in order to deal with issues caused by the patient's illness and to facilitate the creation of a home environment more conducive to recovery. Finally, healthy psychology interns may administer programs, often to groups, concerning the modification of health-relevant behaviors like smoking, weight control, physical exercise, and the like.

Postdoctoral Training

The technical knowledge required to conduct research in health psychology has increased exponentially. Often, individuals who have obtained a PhD in one area of psychology (or even in a specialized health psychology program) find that continued specialized training would be helpful. Such individuals may apply for a postdoctoral training grant from the National Institutes of Health in order to work for

2 to 3 years with a designated mentor, usually at an institution other than the one where the PhD was completed. Postdoctoral positions sponsored by institutional training grants or individual research grants are also advertised. Because the market for academic jobs is competitive, recent PhDs may seek out these positions prior to applying for professorships. Some institutionally sponsored postdoctoral positions are designed especially for individuals whose training has not been in health psychology but who now desire this specialization.

Postdoctoral experience varies widely from program to program. Under the supervision of a professor, postdocs will work on research projects of their own design or participate in a program of research funded by a grant to the professor. Because the funding typically comes from a grant to the senior scientist, the postdoc will specialize in a designated area. There may or may not be clinical opportunities. A postdoctoral fellowship provides a person with advanced training, contacts in the field, and the opportunity to publish the results of the research.

A few institutions offer "respecialization" programs that are generally oriented toward psychologists who completed the PhD in nonclinical fields but now desire some clinical training, often sufficient for licensure. Unlike most postdoctoral positions, respecialization programs do not generally pay a salary (quite the contrary—they may require tuition) and are often oriented toward individuals hoping to work as practitioners rather than as academic researchers.

Career Tracks in Health Psychology

Individuals trained in health psychology have many potential career paths. We have grouped these into three broad categories: research careers, clinical/research careers, and careers as practitioners. However, two people in the same category may differ widely in the nature of their work, colleagues, and specific specialty areas.

Our own careers serve as examples of this diversity. Although we both teach in the same department of psychology (at Yale), we pursue different activities. One of us (KDB) is in clinical psychology and does research on body image, obesity, and eating disorders. Part of this work involves directing the Yale Center for Eating and Weight Disorders, a place where both basic and applied research are conducted, including controlled clinical trials testing approaches to treatment. Colleagues outside the department and the university include clinical psychologists and experts in metabolism, endocrinology, cardiology, and epidemiology.

The other of us (PS) is in social psychology and conducts research on the relationship between emotions and health and on the framing of public service announcements and educational programs to encourage preventive health behaviors. Although there is no "clinical intervention" involved in this research, there is intervention at the level of the individual, workplace, and community. Studies include tests of messages to promote mammograms and sunscreen to reduce the risk of breast cancer and skin cancer, respectively. Colleagues include other psychologists, especially those interested in attitude change and persuasion, and experts in oncology, dermatology, communications, and public health.

We underscore, therefore, that careers vary widely. This is a positive feature of health psychology as a field, as there are many options for partitioning duties among research, teaching, training, and practice, even within an institution.

RESEARCH CAREERS

Health psychologists have a wide array of research opportunities. In some cases, these are specific to a disease, as with research on cancer, heart disease, diabetes, alcoholism, eating disorders, obesity, diabetes, AIDS, and arthritis. Others focus on a general area of psychosocial functioning that may span many areas (e.g., social support, coping). Yet others emphasize some aspect of lifestyle (e.g., diet, smoking, exercise) or a specific population (e.g., the study of women's health or health in minority populations). The opportunities are as vast as health itself.

There are research opportunities in both basic and applied areas. At the basic end, some researchers study behavior genetics and even molecular biology. Other basic research might include studies with laboratory animals on issues such as the effect of stress or diet on the development of cancer or heart disease. Controlled clinical trials to test different interventions would be an example of more applied work. Reseach testing different messages to promote health behavior would have both basic and applied implications.

Although many individuals in the field of health psychology are engaged in research, relatively few do research exclusively. In university settings, research is combined with teaching and the training of graduate students. In a medical school, research may be the exclusive task, especially if a person entering the field is hired by a more senior investigator to work on specific research projects. More often, individuals in a medical school setting combine research with teaching or clinical activity. Some research opportunities are available in the corporate world or with government (e.g., as a scientist working with the National Institutes of Health or National Center for Health Statistics).

CAREERS AS PRACTITIONERS

Practice in the field of health psychology, as with research, can take many forms. Some clinical psychologists work in private practice or in mental health settings, but specialize in the treatment of people with health-related problems. Working with alcoholism, eating disorders, or individuals with chronic pain are possibilities.

Psychologists in practice may work in conjunction with other health professionals to deliver clinical service. Psychologists work with physicians in screening people for surgical procedures such as plastic surgery, gastric bypass surgery for obesity, or organ transplant surgery. Populations may need counseling as a result of a medical crisis (e.g., mastectomy, being the primary caregiver for a chronically ill person).

There is the burgeoning area of health care delivery and preventive services, where psychologists provide services in the form of consulting. With the advent of managed care, psychologists can be quite involved in decisions on the delivery of both mental health and physical health services. With preventive services becoming more important, psychologists will be central to the delivery of preventive programs and management issues such as recruitment and retention in programs, adherence to prescribed treatment regimens, and relapse prevention (Brownell, Marlatt, Lichtenstein, & Wilson, 1986).

Corporate health settings provide additional opportunities. Many businesses, both large and small, encourage employees to make use of health promotion services. Weight loss, stress management, exercise, and smoking cessation programs are among those offered. Larger businesses may have an on-site facility. A psychologist, especially one with additional training in an area such as nutrition or exercise science, is an attractive candidate to direct a corporate health program.

COMBINED RESEARCH AND CLINICAL CAREERS

Clinical psychologists trained in health psychology may combine clinical work and research. The most obvious example is a person who does work with a clinical population in which some means of assessment or intervention is the focus of the research. Many others work with individuals with clinical problems in research, but are not involved in intervention. For example, research on Type A behavior has examined whether measures of hostility are related to angiographic evidence of blockage in the coronary arteries. A psychologist involved in this research may not be involved in the clinical management of heart disease, but is nonetheless working with a clinical population.

The variation in combined research and clinical careers is enormous. The nature of the clinical work varies greatly, depending on the target population and employment setting. The same is true for research. Adding even more to the flexibility in careers is that health psychologists vary in the proportion of time allotted to research and clinical work. As a result, the field of health psychology can accommodate many different interests and lifestyles.

COMPENSATION

Figures on salaries for health psychologists have not been assembled in a systematic way. The chapters in this book on clinical psychology and consulting psychology will be good guides for what an individual might earn with a background in one of these two areas. Salaries in university departments of psychology (or related areas) will not be affected by whether the person specializes in health psychology. Work in government settings is likely to pay about the same as in academic departments, and work in corporate settings might pay more. Salaries in medical schools are generally higher than in academic departments at the assistant professor and sometimes the associate professor levels, but at the level of professor, the gap closes considerably, and approximately equivalent pay is the rule. Compensation for private practice or consulting may be small or large, depending on the amount of work available, the reputation of the professional, and the amount of time devoted to work.

A Day in the Life of a Health Psychologist

What follows is a description of a typical day in the life of one of us (KDB), although the activities the two of us engage in are quite similar. As is clear from the preceding section, various combinations of research, clinical work, teaching, and administration are available to a person with a background in health psychology. Thus, it is difficult to define a "typical" day in the life of a health psychologist.

A day begins with a research meeting, known in our department as a "lab meeting." Attended by 12 to 18 graduate students, undergraduate students, postdoctoral fellows, research assistants, and faculty members, individuals or groups of individuals present their work. The work can range from studies in the earliest stages of planning to papers nearly ready for publication. This format provides valuable opportunities to prepare and deliver scientific presentations and to acquire feedback on ideas. New and controversial work in the field may be discussed, and emerging trends in the field are identified.

Following the research meeting is a class. Graduate classes with 8 to 20 students take the form of seminars with lively class discussions, presentations, and critical review of a particular field. Research papers from the literature form the reading list. Undergraduate classes in health psychology may draw 70 to 120 students and involve lecture and some discussion. Teaching is important to the work of health psychologists employed in college and university settings.

The next activity involves the supervision of graduate students, postdoctoral fellows, and undergraduate students involved in research. Individual meetings are held to discuss both conceptual and practical aspects of specific research projects. The aim is to generate new knowledge and to communicate this through publication to other professionals. The joy of being a research mentor lies in working with trainees to nurture their scientific skills, sharing the wonder of discovery and watching new careers take shape.

Clinical supervision takes place in both individual and group meetings. Trainees present case studies of the clients they are seeing and receive feedback from both the professor and fellow students. Once each week the clinical forum is held in a group setting called the "team meeting." Cases are presented, preceded by an analysis of existing literature on the clinical problem seen in the case, and followed by general discussion of the details of the case.

Another feature of a day's work usually involves professional activities at the national or international rather than the local level. This might involve writing scholarly papers, editing books, reviewing articles for journals, working as editor of a journal, preparing a lecture for a professional meeting, discussing issues by telephone or computer with collaborators or colleagues in different cities or countries, or planning a national meeting.

Such a day is characterized by a diversity of activities and interaction with individuals at much different stages of their careers. Health psychologists in academic settings are likely to engage in each of these activities to a certain extent, with the exception of the clinical work that would be done by psychologists with training in clinical psychology. Because the field is developing rapidly and important discoveries occur frequently, being in a setting involving teaching, research, and training can be both stimulating and rewarding.

Advantages of the Career and Attributes Needed for Success

There are many advantages of a career in health psychology. Some professionals most treasure the new and growing stature of the field, as well as the fact that the necessary expertise to understand problems such as cancer, heart disease, AIDS, stress, and addiction lies at the intersection of several disciplines and areas of study. Others value the opportunity to help people with something as important as health and well-being. Still others find the scientific challenges to be most interesting, as there are many important unanswered questions in the field (e.g., is there a cancer-prone personality, or is there a single best means of coping with stress, or by what means does social support lead to increased longevity?). The field is large enough, is growing in so many directions,and has such a bright future that professionals with diverse interests can be accommodated.

Little is known from a scientific perspective about attributes needed for success in a career in health psychology. Because so many different career paths are available (teaching, research, clinical work, and consultation, among others), different personal attributes will be necessary, depending on the specific job demands.

What is common across all career paths is exposure to a field in which new information becomes available at a striking pace and where not only the information itself, but the sources of the information, are difficult to foresee. As an example, a decade ago few would have predicted that molecular biology and genetics research would have such a profound impact on our understanding of both wellness and disease. The AIDS epidemic drew a number of researchers and clinicians into an entirely new field and exposed those professionals to new information on epidemiology, public health models of disease control, and immunology. Therefore, being both open to and excited by rapid developments in the field, and being open minded about the contributions of many disciplines, is a prerequisite for competence in health psychology.

Summary

We began this chapter by claiming that health psychology is a field with considerable vitality and opportunities for professional growth. These opportunities exist across many topic areas and with many combinations of professional activities. With changes in the health care system, growing recognition that behavior is central to the nation's health, and increased emphasis on prevention, the prominence of the field will only increase with time.

References

APA Task Force on Health Research. (1976). Contributions of psychology to health research: Patterns, problems, and potentials. *American Psychologist, 31*, 263–274.

Brownell, K. D., Marlatt, G. A., Lichtenstein, E., & Wilson, G. T. (1986). Understanding and preventing relapse. *American Psychologist, 41*, 765–782.

Chesney, M. A. (1993). Health psychology in the 21st century: Acquired immunodeficiency syndrome as a harbinger of things to come. *Health Psychology, 12*, 259–268.

Eddy, B., Lloyd, P. J., & Lubin, B. (1987). Enhancing the application to doctoral professional programs: Suggestions from a national survey. *Teaching of Psychology, 14*, 160–163.

Frasure-Smith, N., Lesperance, F., & Talajic, M. (1993). Depression following myocardial infarction. *Journal of the American Medical Association, 270*, 1819–1825.

Fretz, B. R., & Stang, D. J.(1980). *Preparing for graduate study in psychology: Not for seniors only.* Washington, DC: American Psychological Association.

Friedman, M., Thoresen, C. E., Gill, J. J., Ulmer, D., Powell, L. H., Price, V. A., Brown, B., Thompson, E., Rabin, D. D., Breall, W. S., Bourg, E., Levy, R., & Dixon, T.(1986). Alteration of Type A behavior and its effect on cardiac recurrences in post myocardial infarction patients: Summary of the results of the Recurrent Coronary Prevention Project. *American Heart Journal, 112*, 653–665.

Matarazzo, J. D. (1980). Behavioral health and behavioral medicine: Frontiers for a new health psychology. *American Psychologist, 35*, 807–817.

Ornish, D., Brown, S. E., Schernitz, L. W., Billings, J. H., Armstrong, W. T., Ports, T. A., McLanahan, S. M., Kirkeeide, R. L., Brand, R. J., & Gould, K. L. (1990). Can lifestyle changes reverse coronary heart disease? The Lifestyle Heart Trial. *Lancet, 336*, 129–133.

Pennebaker, J. W., Kiecolt-Glaser, J. K., & Glaser, R. (1988). Disclosure of traumas and immune function: Health implications of psychotherapy. *Journal of Consulting and Clinical Psychology, 56*, 239–245.

Phillips, D. P., Ruth, T. E., & Wagner, L. M. (1993). Psychology and survival. *Lancet, 342,* 1142–1145.

Richards, J. C. (1992). Training health psychologists: A model for the future. *Australian Psychologist, 27,* 87–90.

Schofield, W. (1969). The role of psychology in the delivery of health services. *American Psychologist, 24,* 565–584.

Schwartz, G. E., & Weiss, S. M. (1978). Behavioral medicine revisited: An amended definition. *Journal of Behavioral Medicine, 1,* 249–252.

Stone, G. (1990). An international review of the emergence and development of health psychology. *Psychology and Health, 4,* 3–17.

Taylor, S. E. (1987). The progress and prospects of health psychology: Tasks of a maturing discipline. *Health Psychology, 6,* 73–87.

Taylor, S. E. (1990). Health psychology: The science and the field. *American Psychologist, 45,* 40–50.

Taylor, S. E. (1995). Health psychology (3rd ed.). New York: McGraw-Hill.

U. S. Department of Health and Human Services. (1991). *Health people 2000: National health promotion and disease prevention objectives.* Washington, DC: U.S. Government Printing Office.

Robert J. Sternberg

Epilogue:
Preparing for a Career
in Psychology

Many of the readers of this book are college students contemplating a career in psychology, whereas others are people who are already employed who are considering switching fields, either from a field other than psychology or from one area of psychology to another. This chapter is addressed primarily to those who are not already in the field of psychology, but who are considering entering it.

As you have seen from the chapters of this book, different fields of specialization within psychology require slightly different preparation. But there is a common core of college coursework that will prepare you for just about any career in psychology.

Ideally, you will choose to major either in psychology or a closely related discipline, such as cognitive science, biology, or child development. The psychology major will generally give you the most flexibility for whatever type of career in psychology you might want to pursue. But for those who know the particular subfield in which they will want to specialize, other majors may work just fine. For example, someone who wants to be a behavioral neuroscientist would probably do quite well majoring in biology.

Whatever your major, a solid and broad background in psychology will be a definite plus if you want to go on to graduate school. Most graduate schools do not want their graduate students to have to take undergraduate psychology courses, nor do they want to repeat, at the graduate level, training that students will be presumed to have had as undergraduates. Moreover, some graduate programs require for admission the Graduate Record Examination (GRE) in psychology, an advanced test that is difficult to master without a solid background in psychology.

At the very least, potential candidates for graduate school should have taken the introductory psychology course, a course in statistics, and courses in most or all of the traditional basic areas of psychology, such as biological (or physiological) psychology, clinical (or abnormal) psychology, cognitive psychology, developmental psychology, social psychology, and personality. It is an excellent idea to take at least one laboratory-based course and perhaps a course on history and systems.

Most students also will have had some advanced courses, such as learning, experimental design, thinking, adult development, social cognition, or whatever. Success in advanced courses shows that you will be able to handle the more rigorous challenges of the graduate-school curriculum.

If you do not major in psychology, consider minoring in it. In this way, you will at least have the fundamentals of the field. And whether you major in psychology or not, getting a broad background outside psychology is considered important by many graduate schools. Courses in the natural sciences, mathematics, and computer science are often especially highly regarded. Courses in sociology, anthropology, linguistics, and other social sciences will help give you a broader perspective into the nature of human beings.

I strongly urge college students to get as much training and experience in writing and even effective speaking as they can. It is difficult to overstate the importance of communication in psychology. Psychologists frequently find themselves writing case reports, articles for publication, grant proposals, and even books. Strong writing skills are essential. Psychologists also frequently find themselves speaking in front of audiences to other psychologists, students, parents, educators, businesspeople, or whomever. Public speaking skills are thus a big plus for psychologists to learn.

Many professors at the graduate level strongly urge college students to get research experience beyond that provided in lab-based courses. Such research experience can be had by working in a professor's laboratory, working on an independent project supervised by a professor or advanced graduate student, or working for some nonuniversity organization that conducts psychological research. Many applicants to graduate school have good credentials. Research experience, perhaps more than any other single attribute, is what can separate out those who will potentially become the most successful applicants to graduate school.

Research experience has another advantage. When you apply to graduate school, you typically need three letters of recommendation, preferably from psychologists. Working with someone in a laboratory provides an excellent way to get to know one or more psychologists, who will then be in a better position to write for you. One of the saddest things I encounter as a professor is when a student reaches the senior year, has not gotten to know any psychology faculty members well, and then is scrounging at the last minute for people to write letters.

Research experience is not the only way to get to know faculty well, of course. Taking small seminars from them or working with them on student–faculty committees provides another kind of opportunity to get to know faculty. But courses and committees often do not give faculty members the same kinds of insights as does research experience about your research skills, and many graduate schools are particularly eager to attract students with such skills and experience.

Many graduate programs require applicants to take the GRE for admission. One session (the general test) assesses verbal, quantitative, and analytical skills, and another session (the subject test) tests for subject-matter knowledge. In some schools, the general test is required and the subject test is optional. It is best to prepare for this test over the long term by getting an excellent, broad education. The Educational Testing Service provides information about the test, and there are also books and courses that help in preparing for the examinations. The preparation materials may or may not raise scores, but they may give you the confidence you need to be able to do your best on the tests.

When students apply to college, they may want to consider that admissions offices seeking a diverse and interesting student body sometimes value extracurricular activities. Such activities typically count much less at the graduate level, unless they are related in some way to the graduate education for which you are preparing yourself, such as working in a psychological clinic or hospital, doing psychological research, being a member of a psychology club, and so on. Occasionally, though, other kinds of life experiences are valued for their contributions to student maturity. Many psychologists believe, for example, that successful work experience of almost any kind can bestow a kind of maturity that one cannot obtain merely from being a student. Some students take a year or two off in order to get such experience. This experience can be helpful, again, especially if it somehow relates to one's particular career orientation, for example, being a research assistant for a psychologist.

You should remember one other thing: When you fill out the application for graduate school, the essay you write will be considered very seriously. Graduate school admissions committees look for signs of understanding of, commitment to, and purpose in the field. Thus, merely saying you want to study psychology because you are interested in human nature is more likely to hurt you than to help you. Showing an understanding of what a particular program has to offer and of what the faculty members in a particular program do can help you gain admission to the program of your choice. No one expects you to know exactly what you want to do in graduate school. However, admissions committees do expect you to have formed at least some tentative interests.

Perhaps the single most important thing you can do is to get advice from faculty members, especially ones in the area of psychology you are interested in pursuing. College students are often shy about seeking advice. They shouldn't be: That's what faculty are there for. Seek out advice, and you will find that a lot of your preparations can go much more smoothly than you might have thought was possible.

When you consider going to graduate school, remember that graduate school is not a continuation of the same kinds of activities you engaged in as an undergraduate. Course work will generally be less emphasized, especially after the first year or two. At that point, research, teaching, and, in some cases, clinical experience typically will be emphasized more. In graduate school, you make the transition from being merely a consumer of psychological knowledge to being a producer or a user of psychological knowledge.

Some people who decide to enter careers in psychology will have, as undergraduates, majored in a field other than psychology and will have decided, whether immediately upon completing college or some years thereafter, that psychology is the field that truly interests them. Students can be and regularly are admitted to graduate programs whose main undergraduate concentration was in another field. The field need not even be a closely allied one, such as biology, sociology, or anthropology. In our program, from time to time, there are students who majored in English literature, French, or mathematics.

If you are switching fields, however, you will probably want to make sure that you pick up course work that gives you the equivalent of a college minor or, preferably, a college major in psychology. Graduate schools generally assume that enrolled students have undergraduate training in psychology, and their programs cannot repeat all the material of the undergraduate program. Many local colleges offer returning students opportunities to pick up the courses they need, through part-time, summer, or other special programs. You may even be able to achieve much of the training on your own through independent reading.

A high score on the GRE Advanced Test in Psychology may convince some programs that the individual has mastered the basic material of psychology, regardless of course preparation. Moreover, some graduate programs will admit students for a master's degree who majored in other fields, despite the students' minimal background in psychology, and decide later whether the students are qualified to pursue the doctorate. Gaining some research experience, such as by working as a research assistant, can also be invaluable.

Remember, though, that graduate schools differ widely in what they view as acceptable background for entrance into their programs. Some schools, for example, may view an undergraduate major in computer science or biology as being every bit as useful as an undergraduate major in psychology. Other schools may view relevant work experience as a decided advantage. You really need to discuss the issue of your background with the appropriate official (usually a director of graduate studies) in each program in order to ascertain the program's expectations for admission.

You can start preparing for a career in psychology at almost any time. I hope you do seek out a career in psychology and that you are as happy with such a career as I am. But whatever you decide to do, good luck!

Index

About the Editor

ROBERT J. STERNBERG is IBM Professor of Psychology and Education in the Department of Psychology at Yale University. Sternberg is a doctoral graduate of Stanford and has taught at Yale for more than 2 decades. His interest in careers in psychology has led him to teach a graduate-level course on psychology as a career. He has been president of two APA divisions (General Psychology and Educational Psychology) and has been the editor of *Psychological Bulletin*. Sternberg has won two awards from APA: the Early Career Award and the McCandless Award. He has also served on editorial boards of numerous APA journals. Sternberg maintains active programs of research in intelligence, creativity, styles of thinking, and love and is the author of over 500 books, articles, and book chapters.